EVERYDAY CONSUMPTION

Purdue Studies in Romance Literatures

Editorial Board

Íñigo Sánchez Llama, Series Editor
Elena Coda
Paul B. Dixon
Beth Gale

Patricia Hart
Laura Demaría
Allen G. Wood

Howard Mancing, Consulting Editor
Floyd Merrell, Consulting Editor
Joyce Detzner, Production Editor
R. Tyler Gabbard-Rocha, Production Editor

Associate Editors

French
Jeanette Beer
Paul Benhamou
Willard Bohn
Thomas Broden
Gerard J. Brault
Mary Ann Caws
Glyn P. Norton
Allan H. Pasco
Gerald Prince
Roseann Runte
Ursula Tidd

Italian
Fiora A. Bassanese
Peter Carravetta
Benjamin Lawton
Franco Masciandaro
Anthony Julian Tamburri

Luso-Brazilian
Fred M. Clark
Marta Peixoto
Ricardo da Silveira Lobo Sternberg

Spanish and Spanish American
Catherine Connor
Ivy A. Corfis
Frederick A. de Armas
Edward Friedman
Charles Ganelin
David T. Gies
Roberto González Echevarría
David K. Herzberger
Emily Hicks
Djelal Kadir
Amy Kaminsky
Lucille Kerr
Howard Mancing
Floyd Merrell
Alberto Moreiras
Randolph D. Pope
Elżbieta Skłodowska
Marcia Stephenson
Mario Valdés

 volume 85

EVERYDAY CONSUMPTION IN TWENTY-FIRST-CENTURY BRAZILIAN FICTION

Lígia Bezerra

Purdue University Press
West Lafayette, Indiana

Copyright ©2022 by Purdue University. All rights reserved.

♾ The paper used in this book meets the minimum requirements of American National Standard for Information Sciences—Permanence of Paper for Printed Library Materials, ANSI Z39.48-1992.

Printed in the United States of America
Template for interior design by Anita Noble;
template for cover by Heidi Branham.
Cover image:
0% de nós by Antonieta Carpenter-Cosand

Library of Congress Cataloging-in-Publication Data

Cataloging-in-Publication Data on file at the Library of Congress

978-1-61249-758-7 (harcover)
978-1-61249-759-4 (paperback)
978-1-61249-760-0 (epub)
978-1-61249-761-7 (epdf)

Contents

vii **Acknowledgments**
1 **Introduction**
    4 Theories of Consumption
    8 Historicizing Consumption in Latin America
    15 Consumption and Everyday Life
21 **Chapter One**
    A Consumer's Dystopia
    23 Bonassi's *Luxúria*: Brazil, Country of the Future! Are We There Yet?
    29 Everyday Violence
    35 Everyday Numbness
    38 The Factory and the Country: The Right Turn?
    46 Sant'Anna's *O Brasil é bom*: Federal Republic of Consumption
    49 The Growth of Neoconservatism
    54 Brazil, a Country of "Nice" People
    60 Brazil Isn't Too Bad. Or Is It?
    62 Policing Consumption
67 **Chapter Two**
    The Consuming Self
    70 Lísias's *O livro dos mandarins*: What Is in a Name?
    73 Of Great Leaders and Neoliberal Thought
    83 Failure: The Narrative Behind the Narrative
    88 Bernardo Carvalho's *Reprodução*: Information in the Era of Reproduction
    93 Talking to Oneself
    97 The (Dis)Information Era
    101 A Time of Crisis
    104 Language and Power
    108 Of Utopic Futures
111 **Chapter Three**
    Consumer Culture's "Collateral Damage"
    113 Invisible Lives
    118 Everyday Death
    122 Of Meat Consumption
131 **Conclusion**

Contents

135 Chapter Four
A Consumer's Dreams and Nightmares
137 Galera's *Mãos de cavalo*: A Mass-Mediated Sensibility
150 Laub's *A maçã envenenada*: Between Kurt Cobain and Imaculée Ilibagiza
165 Conclusion

167 Chapter Five
Working-Class Consumption
176 Consuming Together
180 Aesthetic Interruptions of the Mundane
184 Low and High
189 Tactical Consumption
193 Conclusion

195 Conclusion

201 Notes

211 Works Cited

225 Index

Acknowledgments

This book would not be possible without the support of so many people who directly or indirectly contributed to its writing. I am deeply indebted to Cris Lira and Cecília Rodrigues, who offered their invaluable feedback upon reading portions of this book. I am also extremely grateful for their friendship and sisterhood.

So many other colleagues, mentors, and friends were supportive of this project and I am extremely grateful to them, especially to Luciano Alencastro, Odirene Almeida, Karol Bastos, Sophia Beal, Lúcia Bettencourt, Kátia Bezerra, Regina Dalcastagnè, Patrick Dove, Paulo Dutra, Fernanda Guida, Jeremy Lehnen, Leila Lehnen, Anderson da Mata, Margo Milleret, Robert Moser, Luciana Namorato, Joana Oliveira, Emanuelle Oliveira-Monte, Pushpa Parekh, Rosana Pinheiro-Machado, Andrew Rajca, Bruno Sales, Vivaldo Santos, Marco Severo, Luciana Sousa, Ted Striphas, Ana Catarina Teixeira, Lucía Tennina, Manolisa Vasconcellos, Frans Weiser, and my esteemed colleagues at Arizona State University, Christiane Fontinha de Alcântara, Nina Berman, David William Foster (in memoriam), Glen Goodman, William Hedberg, Cézar Ponti Medeiros, Ana Hedberg Olenina, and Julia Sarreal. My sincere thank you to my students at Spelman College and Arizona State University, who inspired me and taught me so much. My special thanks to my student Antonieta Carpenter-Cosand, whose talented artwork is featured on the cover of this book. I also want to thank the anonymous readers of this book, whose rigorous and critical reading allowed me to make substantive improvements to the content of the manuscript, as well as Joyce Detzner and Tyler Gabbard-Rocha, whose patience, kindness, and good humor have made the publication process a pleasure. Thank you as well to the Institute for Humanities Research and the School of International Letters and Cultures at Arizona State University for their support.

I am deeply indebted to my parents: my mother Escolástica, the first inspiring educator I ever knew; my father Fernando (in memoriam), whose excitement for me completing more schooling than him when I was about to start fifth grade I will never forget; to my grandmother (Mãe) Maria (in memoriam), the first person to teach me the alphabet from an empty cardboard television box; and to my stepfather Alby, who so many times took me to school

Acknowledgments

and back when I first arrived in Fortaleza from the countryside at the age of fourteen. I am also indebted to my mother-in-law Janice and my father-in-law Steve, who welcomed me into their home for so many summers of hard work since the beginning of my PhD, particularly in 2017 and 2018, years when the majority of this manuscript was written. I'm additionally grateful to my brother Bruno and my sister-in-law Patricia, for their moral support.

Finally, I cannot express enough how grateful I am to my husband Michael, whose incredible love and support means everything to me. For the conversations about literature, media, and consumption, the walks when I needed time to breathe, the multiple conference arrangements he helped me make, including driving me to several of them when we were graduate students, the proofreading of the entire manuscript, for so much patience and love, my sincerest thank you to this menino véi, for everything. And to our daughter, Elena, minha Nena, thank you for teaching me every day about love. May your curiosity and your desire to learn guide you through a path of kindness and happiness, little one.

I dedicate this book to all of them, for everything they all have taught me.

Tempe, August 2021

Introduction

In the late 1980s and early 1990s, Brazil adopted a series of neoliberal reforms, including ample privatization and severe fiscal adjustment, in an attempt to overcome the deep economic crisis in which the country was steeped. The process began during the administration of President Fernando Collor de Mello (1990–92)—who would be impeached two years into his tenure—and continued through President Fernando Henrique Cardoso's government (1995–2003). Both Mello and Cardoso ran against Luís Inácio Lula da Silva, a union leader who founded the social democratic Partido dos Trabalhores (PT—Workers' Party) in the 1980s. It was not until the 2002 elections, when Lula ran a second time against Cardoso, on a more moderate, less anti-capitalist platform, that he managed to win Brazil's highest office. The social policies that he implemented through income distribution programs such as *Bolsa Família*, allowed many Brazilians to rise above the poverty line, granting them access to several consumer goods that had not been within their reach previously. Consumption, thus, became key during the Lula years, as it helped to strengthen the economy while alleviating socioeconomic disparities. In an address to the nation in December 2008, then-president Lula (2003–11) had a special request for Brazilians in the face of the looming 2008 economic crisis:

> E você, meu amigo e minha amiga, não tenha medo de consumir com responsabilidade. Se você está com dívidas, procure antes equilibrar seu orçamento. Mas se tem um dinheirinho no bolso, ou recebeu o décimo-terceiro e está querendo comprar uma geladeira ou um fogão, ou trocar de carro, não frustre seu sonho com medo do futuro. Porque se você não comprar, o comércio não vende, se a loja não vender, não fará novas encomendas à fábrica e aí a fábrica produzirá menos e a médio

Introduction

prazo o seu emprego poderá estar em risco. Assim, quando você e sua família compram um bem, não estão só realizando um sonho, estão também contribuindo para manter a roda da economia girando. E isso é bom para todos. ("Trecho" 00:00:45–00:01:30)

(And you, my friend, do not be afraid of consuming responsibly. If you have any debt, first of all, try to balance your budget. But if you have a little money in your pocket, or if you received your end-of-the-year bonus and you want to buy a fridge or a stove, or get a new car, do not give up on your dream because of fear of the future. Because if you do not buy, stores will not sell, and if the store does not sell, it will not place new orders to the factories and then the factory will produce less and in the medium term your job will be at risk. This way, when you and your family buy a good, you are not just making a dream come true, you are also contributing to keep the economic wheel spinning. And this is good for everyone.)[1]

A year later, in another presidential address, Lula thanked the Brazilian people for their faith in the nation's economy, demonstrated by their positive response to his request that the nation continue to consume. As evidence of the success of this strategy, he noted that Brazil was not only one of the last countries to be affected by the crisis, but also one of the first ones to overcome it ("Pronunciamento" 00:01:26–38). Consumption, thus, appears in his speech as an act of social solidarity: by participating in the economy, Brazilians helped to avoid, collectively, potentially catastrophic consequences for themselves as individuals and for the country as a whole.

Indeed, a renewed growth in consumption, after a brief period of slowdown, played a role in Brazil's quick recovery between 2009 and 2010, along with a series of measures that helped to shield the Brazilian economy from further damage (N. Barbosa; Sader "A construção" 141). On the other hand, the Lula administration's emphasis on inclusion via consumption faced serious challenges when the crisis deepened in 2014 (Biroli 22). These challenges revealed the fragility of a model that, albeit considered by some as postneoliberal for its prioritizing social policies (Sader, "A construção" 138), has proven to have structural limits that stem from its ties to the logic of capital (Pinheiro-Machado, "Imaginar" 235).

The importance of consumption during Lula's government, and in President Dilma Rousseff's subsequent tenure (2011–16), for daily life in Brazilian society, has been the theme of much cultural production in the country. Notable examples include Anna Muylaert's 2015 film *Que horas ela volta?* (*The Second Mother*), which addresses social mobility, and the development of a new subgenre of Brazilian funk, *funk ostentação* or ostentation funk, in which *funkeiros* sing about owning brand items, such as Nike shoes, and Citroën cars.

Literature has also represented consumption in the daily life of Brazilian citizens at the beginning of the twenty-first century, at times addressing the issue in question by directly mentioning the socioeconomic and political context referenced in Lula's speech quoted above. Arguing for a more balanced approach to consumer culture in Brazilian cultural studies, this book maps out representations of consumption in Brazilian literature in the twenty-first century. It considers ten works by eight different authors, all of which were published between 2006 and 2015, thus covering most of the Lula and Rousseff years. The book shows that the narratives in question make a critique of everyday consumption in twenty-first century Brazil, highlighting how our interactions with commodities connect seemingly disconnected areas of everyday life, such as eating habits, the growth of prosperity theology, ideas of success and failure, discourses on masculinity, one's online behavior, and one's relationships to and through commodities. All narratives analyzed here take a critical stance with respect to consumer culture, recognizing the challenges it poses to social equality and, more broadly, to human survival. Similarly, all narratives under study share a view of consumer culture as mundane practice, expressed by characters' everyday interactions with the world of goods in which they inhabit. Collectively, the narratives present a wide spectrum of more or less hopeful portrayals of existence in consumer culture, which I define in each chapter of this book as follows: *totalizing dystopia, utopic reinvention, radical temporary suspension, oscillatory awareness,* and *transformative hope.*

While not intended to be exhaustive, the types of portrayal above support the argument the book makes in favor of broadening the debate on consumption in twenty-first century Brazilian letters, so as to include a pluralistic perspective from which to approach what I call here *narratives of consumption.* Critics analyzing this fiction privilege narratives that depict a world of alienation and dystopia (Dealtry; Delgado; Dias; Lehnen, "O fruto"; V. Pereira) or caution readers about the dangers of the market-oriented nature of these writers' careers (Schøllhammer; Resende). Underlying these studies is a concern with aesthetic judgment of culture based on binaries such as good/bad or elevated/degraded that inform analyses of fiction written in the 1970s and 1980s such as Tânia Pellegrini (1999), Therezinha Barbieri (2003), and Malcom Silverman (2000).

As a result of reducing the act of consuming to aesthetic subjugation, literary criticism on Brazilian fiction in the twenty-first century inadvertently ignores the diversity of perspectives from which writers grapple with consumption. Identifying this variety is key to understanding how this literature can help us reflect on the (im)possibilities of achieving a more egalitarian society. I use the term narratives of consumption precisely to convey this variety in contrast to the world of alienation that critics have most frequently privileged. Ultimately, a broader reading of these narratives reveals literature's relevance to readers' acquisition of consumer literacy, understood as the ability to identify the complexity of power dynamics in everyday consumption.

Theories of Consumption

Brazilian cultural approaches to consumption have their origins in European cultural studies. The concern with aesthetic judgment described above echoes one of three general theoretical perspectives on consumer culture that can be summarized according to their focus on one of the following aspects: the production of consumption, modes of consumption, and the emotional pleasures of consumption (Featherstone 13).

The Frankfurt School, a neo-Marxist group founded in the early twentieth century, gathered scholars who developed some of the most influential work pertaining to theories on the production of consumption. One of the most important names in this endeavor was Theodor Adorno, who viewed the products of the culture industry as weapons of manipulation and domination of a homogeneous, usually economically disadvantaged class of subjects who have little or no individuality ("the masses"). A refugee from Nazi Germany living in the United States, Adorno was preoccupied with the dangers of homogenization and with what he considered a pseudo-individuality propagated by mass culture. He argues that mass culture is illusory because it provides entertainment predesigned to give individuals an only temporary escape from the exploitation that they experience in everyday life. Adorno and Max Horkheimer propose in their well-known essay "The Culture Industry: Enlightenment as Mass Deception" (1944) that the consumption of mass culture leads to degradation, alienation, and cultural homogenization. Combining Marxist theory with psychoanalysis, the leaders of the Frankfurt School "radicalized the critique of commodity reification" (Boucher 104). While Marx predicted that, in the process of its evolution towards stagnation, capitalism would be overthrown by the exploited class, through a socialist revolution that would lead to a new form of society (communism), research conducted by members of the Frankfurt School on German workers threw the possibility of transformation predicted by Marx away when it identified that most of the workers were conservative and resistant to sociocultural changes (107).

For the Frankfurt School, the culture industry also had a negative impact on the arts, which became trivialized, as it was directed towards distracting the masses from the oppression of everyday life and as it surrendered to clichés and repetition (Boucher 117). It followed then that society, in this context, turns into

> a reified object, a total system that can be calculated mathematically, which becomes a second nature for the modern individual, ruling over them like a capricious fate. Under the signs of ideas of "progress" and "community," the administered society turns its vision of complete control and its nostalgia for lost solidarity into a potent ideology that functions as the modern myth, under various designations. (120)

According to Adorno, the commodity could erase the memory of its original use-value, liberating it to take up a variety of cultural values, a process that post-structuralist Jean Baudrillard addresses in his work later in the twentieth century (Featherstone 14–15). For Baudrillard, the endless possibilities for a sign to take up other meanings leads to a culture of sheer reproduction, ultimately effacing the lines that separate reality from the world of images. Everyday life becomes so aestheticized that meaning loses stability and the masses "become fascinated by the endless flow of bizarre juxtapositions," the depthless culture that we find in Frederic Jameson (Featherstone 15).

Commonly viewed as more optimistic are theories of consumption that pay particular attention to questions of pleasure and dream in consumer society, the second perspective on consumption to which I referred above (Featherstone 13). The most emblematic work in this strand is that of Walter Benjamin, whose perspective has been repeatedly contrasted with Adorno's and Horkheimer's. Benjamin sees the possibilities of the copy and the consequent destruction of the aura of art inaugurated by commodity culture as potentially positive in the sense that "mechanical reproduction emancipates the work of art from its parasitical dependence on ritual" (Benjamin 1172). Seen through these lenses, mass culture has the potential to spike transgressiveness and playfulness. In this context, where the lines that separate high and commercial culture become blurred, there emerges a skepticism towards the effectiveness of advertisement on consumers and advertisement becomes celebrated as art (Featherstone 25).

A third strand of theories of consumer culture offers a sociological perspective, focusing on the "production of consumption." The main names of this strand are Pierre Bourdieu and Mary Douglas and Baron Isherwood, who address the use of goods and the bonds and distinctions that they create in society (Featherstone 13). This sociological view reveals the complexity of the world of goods, in which commodities are seen as part of a dynamic and intense flow of exchanges that alters their status in various ways depending on what social relations they mediate. Looking at what consumers actually do with commodities, and therefore dealing with the question of actual practice that a focus on production overlooks, these theories pave the way to envisioning possibilities of resistance and change.

Such a focus on practice is also espoused by one of the pioneers of Cultural Studies, Stuart Hall. In "The Culture Gap" (1984), an essay in which he considers the difficulties of the Left in keeping up with the profound impact that capitalism had on culture in the twentieth century, Hall argues that "[t]he Left was not incorrect in seeing the massive manipulation, the advertising hype, the ballyhoo, the loss of quality, the up- and down-market division, which are intrinsic to commercial consumerism. The difficulty was that this manipulative side was *all* that was seen" (19, emphasis in the original). For this reason, it is important, according to him, to not become disconnected from the diversity and complexity of our daily existence in consumer capitalism (22).

In the Brazilian context, Antônio Cândido ("Literatura e subdesenvolvimento" ["Literature and Underdevelopment"]) is an important precursor to Cultural Studies. His work highlighted Brazil's culture dependency on European paradigms, helping to shift the focus from structuralist analyses to interrogations about the relationship between literature and culture. While unquestionably important for Brazilian Cultural Studies, Cândido's "Literatura e subdesenvolvimento" reveals the predominance of a continuing preoccupation with aesthetic judgment and with the negative impact of mass culture on literary quality. He warns that, in the context of a society that went from "oral folklore" to mass culture, skipping the reading phase during its modernization process in the twentieth century, it was important to remain "extremely vigilant" in order to prevent Latin American literature from being influenced by "the instruments and the values of mass culture," which, according to him, seduced so many artists and theorists of the time that he was writing (41). The perception of the potential degrading effects of "low" culture on literature is also evident in Silviano Santiago's "Literatura e cultura de massas" ("Literature and Mass Culture") an essay published in *O cosmopolitismo do pobre: crítica literária e crítica cultural* (*The Cosmopolitanism of the Poor: Literary Criticism and Cultural Criticism*), but originally from 1993, more than twenty years after Cândido's. In this piece, Santiago reflects on the relationship between mass culture and literature, departing from Benjamin's considerations regarding cinema and its relationship to its consumers. Admitting that mass culture and literature can have "positive confluences" in the form of popular music lyrics, Santiago nevertheless emphasizes that what he calls "a grande literatura (ou literatura literária)" ("grand literature [or literary literature]") is characterized by an independence from the market, which separates it, then, from other types of literature corrupted by capitalist interests, such as the best-seller (121). Since the 1990s, a Cultural Studies approach to literary criticism has become more common in Brazilian letters, although, as I previously indicated, it has largely remained informed by a view of consumption that privileges its manipulative side.

The analysis carried out in the present book embraces Cultural Studies while intending to follow Hall's advice on not dismissing everyday consumption as manipulation and alienation exclusively. Rather than a preoccupation with aesthetic judgments of the works in question, I engage with a Cultural Studies approach to literature that was paved by Raymond Williams in *Marxism and Literature* (1979). In other words, *Everyday Consumption in Twenty-First-Century Brazilian Fiction* seeks to understand how twenty-first century Brazilian fiction that deals with consumer culture unveils social tensions around consumption in current everyday life in Brazilian society. Furthermore, the book identifies what type of possibilities of change, if any, these narratives envision for the future.

An essential aspect of this everyday life is neoliberalism, understood here as a "form of reason" that frames our existence in economic terms (Brown 17). In a strictly economic sense, neoliberalism in Brazil has its roots in the military regime of the second half of the twentieth century, becoming intensified in the 1990s during President Fernando Henrique Cardoso's tenure, an intensification that I will address in more detail in Chapter 2. As a "form of reason," it has become particularly entrenched since the stabilization of the Brazilian *real* in the 1990s and the subsequent booming of consumption that spread into the working-class during the Lula years. It is important to highlight, however, that, as I will show in the analysis, neoliberalism as a form of reason in Brazil also has its contradictions, for the neoliberal subjectivity that developed through consumption has also resulted in a certain level of politicization (Pinheiro-Machado "From Hope").

Historicizing Consumption in Latin America

The novels under study are part of a history of engagement with commodity culture that spans Latin American literature in general and that dates back to the last decades of the nineteenth century, when the arrival in Latin America of technologies such as those pertaining to cinema provoked a mixture of excitement and concern. These mixed reactions surfaced, for instance, in the contrast between Mexican poet Amado Nervo, who worried about the effects of cinema on literature, and his countryman Tablada, who expressed excitement about the possibilities of the cinematograph for art. The initial rejection of the blurring of the lines between high and low cultures shifted into the twentieth century, when writers began to open themselves up to the language of mass media, incorporating techniques from cinema, photography, and other commercial products. This dialogue became so widespread that it is hard to identify Spanish American writers from the twentieth century who have *not* been impacted by mass media to some

Introduction

degree: Vicente Huidobro, Roberto Arlt, Adolfo Bioy Casares, Julio Cortázar, Guillermo Cabrera Infante, Mario Vargas Llosa, Carlos Fuentes, José Agustín, Gustavo Sainz, Luiz Zapata ... the list goes on and on (Paz-Soldán and Castillo 6–8).

Brazilian letters had a similar experience. In the last decades of the nineteenth century, many writers welcomed new technologies with a mixture of suspicion and excitement:

> *Reshaping* in Lima Barreto; *mimesis* without qualms in João do Rio; *refusal* or embarrassed (but lucrative) assimilation in [Olavo] Bilac; and a pervasive *displacement* in [Godofredo] Rangel—these are no more than a few of the forms assumed by the dialogue between literary technique and the dissemination of new techniques in printing, reproduction, and broadcasting in turn-of-the-century Brazil. (Süssekind, *Cinematograph* 11, emphasis in the original)

In this way, many canonical and non-canonical Brazilian writers at the end of the nineteenth century engaged, to varying degrees, with the new world of technology and mass media of the time. Poetry and advertisement curiously blended to announce a variety of products, from cough syrup to candles (Süssekind, *Cinematograph* 41–42). On the other hand, similar to what happened in modernist poetry in Spanish-speaking Latin America (Paz-Soldán and Castillo 2–5), there was also an impulse to keep these realms separate by employing literary techniques such as the use of ornamental language, the emphasis on interior spaces as expressions of individuality in the face of the massification outside, and the attempt to slow down time by resorting to memory and digression (Süssekind, *Cinematograph* 21, 62).

Preoccupations with the degrading effects of capital can also be seen in the work of nineteenth century writers such as José de Alencar and Machado de Assis. Alencar's *Senhora* (1875), for instance, problematizes the commodification of love in a relationship mediated by money. The male protagonist, Seixas, corrupted by his desire to practice conspicuous consumption, goes bankrupt and finds himself accepting the novel's heroine, Aurélia, in marriage in exchange for a dowry. Nevertheless, through hard honest work and the rejection of luxury goods, Seixas is able to recover his dignity. True love wins in the end when it is no longer mediated by capital. In the case of Machado de Assis, romantic relationships

Introduction

also appear at times mediated by capital, such as expressed by Brás Cubas's famous sarcastic statement that Marcela loved him for "quinze meses e onze contos de réis" ("fifteen months and eleven *réis*"; *Memórias* 61). Machado also addressed capitalist greed, again with sarcasm, in his *crônica* "O sermão do Diabo" (1893), in which the devil lays out his commandments to his disciples, among which, the following: "14. Também foi dito aos homens: Não matareis a vosso irmão, nem a vosso inimigo, para que não sejais castigados. Eu digo-vos que não é preciso matar a vosso irmão para ganhardes o reino da terra; basta arrancar-lhe a última camisa" ("14. It has also been told to men: You shall not kill your brother, nor your enemy, so that you will not be condemned. I tell you that you need not kill your brother to win earth's kingdom; suffice it to rip off his last shred of clothing").

As new technologies became more banal, however, Brazilian writers began to embrace them. Indeed, in the 1920s, *modernismo* enthusiastically welcomed the dialogue with new technologies and mass media, in a search of a national identity against the blind acceptance of foreign influences. At the beginning of the twentieth century, a cultural movement against this Europeanization began to grow, finding in the indigenous figure used by nineteenth century writers, as well as in the Afro-Brazilian, inspiration for the creation of a "true" Brazilian identity.[2] It is in this context that writer Oswald de Andrade, one of the leaders of *modernismo*, postulated that, through cultural cannibalism (a metaphorical "eating" of foreign culture that would transcend the mere act of copying European cultural models, which was identified as an impediment to Brazil's cultural modernization), Brazilian writers would find the way to create "poetry for export," or *poesia de exportação*, and finally become players rather than followers in the arts. Through the concept of cultural cannibalism, de Andrade attempted to reconcile primitivism with modernization vis-à-vis the expansion of the urban masses. As Heitor Martins points out, de Andrade borrowed the idea of cultural cannibalism from the European avant-garde, albeit ironically, which mitigates its ability to subvert European views of indigenous populations as cannibals and liberate Brazilian art from European models (32). Like Spanish American *modernismo*, Brazilian modernist writers incorporated elements that they celebrated as representatives of the national character in order to promote a discourse of national integration. However, contrary to Spanish American *modernistas*,[3] they enthusiastically embraced the mixing of these elements with popular culture and the language of mass media. As Styliane Philippou puts it, "[t]he white cultural elite appropriated the local and marginalised, nationalised it and, thus, universalised it. At the same time, they also appropriated universalist Modernism, nationalised it and thus particularised and localised it" (251).

Nevertheless, while the modernist movements in Latin America attempted to integrate the nation through literature, it was mass media that managed to effect this integration in the 1920s and 1930s. As urban centers grew rapidly as a result of the intensification of migration from the countryside, media such as radio and cinema converted what Jesús Martín-Barbero terms "the political idea of the nationhood" into "the daily experience of nationhood" by representing the popular classes' way of life (164). These media provided popular classes with the necessary guidelines to navigate mass society.

By the 1960s, television had become the main medium through which economic and political ideals were propagated in Latin America, with radio playing a lesser but significant role. According to Martín-Barbero, the political role of the media in Latin America changed in this era becoming economic in focus and supporting the development of a consumer society. At a time when military regimes ruled a number of Latin American countries, mass media presented consumption as the path towards modernity. As Martín-Barbero shows, a television system largely based on a North American model of privatization of networks spread dreams of consumption throughout Latin America, while reducing cultural differences within each country to a minimum in the way it addressed audiences.

Latin American literature and art responded by seeking to blur the lines between high and low culture. Artists and writers sought to incorporate mass culture and kitsch into high art as "allegories for profound changes in the body of Latin American society" (Santos 16). Devising "an aesthetic of difficulty," Brazil's Tropicalist movement denounced the manipulation of the media by the government, incorporating mass culture into texts that borrow from avant-garde traditions from the beginning of the twentieth century (4). In this way, writers used mass culture to create hermetic texts, opposing the easily accessible language of

Introduction

the media. This contradiction pushed high and low cultures closer together, only to set them further apart, thus in practice continuing to draw the line between high and low culture. In Brazil's neighbor Argentina, for instance, Manuel Puig and the conceptual art movement Tucumán Arde utilized the language of mass culture, exploring its appropriations of popular culture, in order to respond critically to the introduction of consumer culture in Latin America (Santos 13). These appropriations of mass culture, thus, differed from the appropriations of the beginning of the twentieth century in that they did not seek to support a sense of national unification. In the 1960s, writers and artists were contesting the very notion of a single national identity by highlighting the cultural heterogeneity of the urban masses.

This dialogue with the European avant-garde movements continued to explore the tensions between high and low culture in Latin America well into the second half of the twentieth century, contrary to Andreas Huyssen's argument that the avant-garde died in the 1960s.[4] The fiction of writers such as Julio Cortázar, Manuel Puig, César Aira, Clarice Lispector, Haroldo de Campos, and Augusto de Campos all bear its mark (Speranza 27; Santos 162). In the 1980s, the dialogue between literature and mass culture became even more open in the work of Silviano Santiago, João Gilberto Noll, Sérgio Sant'Anna, Valêncio Xavier, and Rubem Fonseca, to name a few. Flora Süssekind characterizes Brazilian fiction in the 1980s as a fiction of "glasses and hinges," in which characters' contact with reality is always mediated by some product of mass culture, and their private lives are also exposed through glass windows ("Ficção 80" 243). An important theme for this generation is the professionalization of the writer and literature's commodity character. Fonseca, the most important name of Brazilian crime novel, and Sant'Anna, for example, address these issues in narratives such as *Bufo & Spallanzani* (1986) and the short story "O duelo," respectively (Barbieri 29–30).

An apprehension that Jameson's "depthless culture" is spreading in the Latin American literary expression of the 1990s surfaces particularly strongly when the publication of *McOndo* (1996) renovates the debate about high and low cultures in Latin American letters. The book, a collection of short stories organized by writers Alberto Fuguet and Sergio Gómez, was viewed by some critics as marketing strategy; a symptom of the damage that consumer culture can do to literature. Critic Diana Palaversich, for instance, states in her article "Rebeldes sin causa: Realismo mágico vs. Realismo virtual" that *McOndo* writers, "más que como hijos rebeldes y desencantados de García Márquez, deben ser vistos como hijos obedientes del neoliberalismo" ("more than as rebellious, disillusioned children of García Márquez, should be seen as obedient children of neoliberalism"; 70). Playing on Macondo, the name of the village where Gabriel García Márquez's *Cien años de soledad* (1967) takes place, Fuguet and Gómez propose the term "McOndo" to refer to an urban Latin America. In contrast to Márquez's portrayal of Latin America as "exotic" and "magical realist," the short stories of the collection portray this space as full of McDonald's restaurants and Macintosh computers.

A similar collection of short stories, *Geração de 90: Manuscritos de computador* (*Generation of 1990: Computer Manuscripts*), organized by Nelson de Oliveira and published in 2001, synthesized a movement in Brazil that was similar to that of the *McOndo* writers. Critics received the *Geração de 90* with suspicion as potentially commercial fiction masquerading as literary fiction (Schøllhammer 17). Like the McOndo authors, the *Geração de 90* focused on their nation's large urban centers and on the contradictions of a country that had not overcome chronic social problems such as poverty and social inequality, and yet embraced new technologies, primarily symbolized by the computer. In terms of themes and affiliations, this generation is characterized by the free and pacific coexistence of various ways of representing social reality and experimenting with different languages and genres, without any guilt (Carneiro 31). Fernando Bonassi, Marçal Aquino, Arnaldo Bloch, and André Sant'Anna are among some of the main names of this generation. The *Geração 00* (Generation 2000), a group of writers that emerge on the literary scene in the early 2000s, in turn, can be characterized by an intense eclecticism that is open to dialogue with previous generations and writers from other geographies (Schøllhammer 147). This group, which also addresses consumer culture in their work, includes writers such as Daniel Galera, Michel Laub, Santiago Nazarian, and Ana Paula Maia.

The fiction analyzed in this book is thus part of this history of intersections between literature and consumption; between "high" and "low" culture. In these narratives, the daily life of characters, who are ordinary and oftentimes anonymous people, reveals itself in the mundane details of their roles as (potential) consumers of a variety of commodities. These narratives portray Brazilian society primarily as a consumer society, unveiling and contesting the ways in which consumption influences everyday social dynamics. To a large extent, this literature has focused, as has historically been the case, on the experience of the middle classes (Dalcastagnè, "Uma voz" 35). The narratives selected for the present study include portrayals of both middle- and working-class characters. Middle-class consumers are the protagonists of Michel Laub's *A maçã envenenada* (*The Poison Apple;* 2013) and Daniel Galera's *Mãos de cavalo* (*Horse Hands;* 2006), with their young adult characters struggling with memories of their childhood, their adolescence, and their young adulthood. Similarly, the middle class is featured in Ricardo Lísias *O livro dos mandarins* (*The Book of Mandarins;* 2009), which explores the obsessive and rather naïve personality of a man willing to do anything to be successful in the corporate world. The middle class is also at the center of B. Carvalho's *Reprodução* (*Reproduction;* 2013), which tells the story of a nameless character, simply referred to as "o estudante de chinês" ("the student of Chinese"), whose prejudiced worldview is (mis)informed by what he reads online. The remaining narratives addressed in this book focus on working-class characters, with the exception of Sant'Anna's *O Brasil é bom* (*Brazil Is Good;* 2014), which portrays both segments of society in question. Ana Paula Maia turns her attention to slaughtermen in *De gados e homens* (*Of Cattle and Men;* 2013), firefighters and coalminers in *Carvão animal* (*Animal Charcoal;* 2011), and trash collectors in *O trabalho sujo dos outros* (*The Dirty Work of Others;* 2009). Fernando Bonassi, in turn, depicts the so-called "new middle class" of post-2003 Brazil in the novel *Luxúria* (*Lust;* 2015), as does Sant'Anna in some of the short stories of *O Brasil é bom*. Nevertheless, these narratives still offer, albeit from a critical standpoint, a middle-class perspective on working-class consumers. A different point of view can be found in Marcus Vinícius Faustini's *Guia afetivo da periferia* (*Affective Guide of the Periferia;* 2009). In this narrative, the consumer habits of the working class appear connected to affective memory, social relations, and everyday tactics to deal with economic hardship or to subvert social hierarchies. In other words, commodities and consumption here point, ultimately, to underlying socioeconomic and cultural dynamics (Douglas and Isherwood 152). The act of consuming often conveys a sense of victory over everyday hardship and a break from a grueling routine between a low-paying job and less than ideal living conditions. Although memories of consuming certain products are portrayed as affective, these memories are not simply romanticized. Much to the contrary, the narrator demonstrates that he is aware of the social injustices that stem from uneven consumer power and which he notices in the city where he grows up, Rio de Janeiro.

Consumption and Everyday Life
Two central concepts underlie the analysis carried out in this book: consumption and everyday life. Both concepts are elusive, widely debated and contested. It is not my intention to trace the history of these two concepts here—for that, I refer the reader to Mike Featherstone's *Postmodernism and Consumer Culture* and Michael E. Gardiner's *Critiques of Everyday Life*—however, it is important to briefly understand how the two inform each other.

In the case of the term *consumption*, it can be understood more broadly and from a sociological perspective as "a use of material possessions that is beyond commerce and free within the law" (Douglas and Isherwood 37). In theories of consumer society, specifically, consumption has been associated with excess, hedonism, and alienation, on one hand and with the delimitation of social boundaries, on the other hand (Featherstone 13). Considering the shifting and contextual nature of the term (Miller, "Consumption" 32), and in an attempt to define it in a way that is useful for understanding the novels addressed in this book, consumption will be taken here as a social activity that mediates several spheres of daily life in Brazil today in ways that take both global and local forms. The specificity of this mediation varies in the works analyzed here and goes hand in hand with their approach to everyday life.

Like consumption, the idea of everyday life has been described from opposing perspectives in cultural studies. One trend, conforming to the interpretation of philosophers such as Lukács and Heidegger, understands the everyday as an inauthentic, "aesthetically impoverished existence" (Felski 16). A second trend, following philosopher Henri Lefebvre, sees everyday life as the place of the authentic and the natural. Whereas the first trend associates

Introduction

degradation and alienation with everyday life, the second describes the everyday as full of possibilities for resistance and subversion. All the narratives analyzed in this book depict the everyday quality of the manifestations of the power of consumer capitalism, although their view of the extent of this power and of the space that there is for change varies. For Bonassi and Sant'Anna, consumption is the result of the manipulation of desires that leads to totalizing alienation and disengagement. There seems to be no space for change in everyday life. It is important to note, however, that this is especially the case in these writers' portrayal of working-class consumers, a problematic perspective, considering the writers' middle-class status in post-2003 Brazil, as I discuss in Chapter 1. In the case of Lísias and B. Carvalho, consumption is similarly portrayed as an alienating activity. Characters never seem to have a moment when they see beyond the neoliberal bubble that they inhabit. There is a limited, rather utopian space for change, however, which the writers suggest to be located in the realm of art, that is, outside of everyday life. In Maia's novels, there is a similar gesture towards a possibility of change, this time effected from within everyday life, albeit carried out either by nature in some sort of mythical way or by workers who are, somewhat like Bonassi's and some of Sant'Anna's characters, portrayed from a middle-class perspective that can at times be rather reductive. For Galera's and Laub's protagonists, everyday consumption takes place between both alienation and disalienation, a movement between the two that opens up possibilities of doing things differently. Finally, it is in the work of Faustini that we find the most hopeful view of everyday existence in consumer culture. Faustini's protagonist identifies ways of consuming that are communal, subversive, affective, and, therefore, concrete ways in which one can exist in consumer culture beyond an empty, selfish, and socially and politically disengaged expression of desires.

In this way, by both addressing the constraints that capitalism poses to everyday life in the twenty-first century and suggesting the existence of cracks through which change might flourish, the fiction mapped out here proposes a critique of Brazilian everyday life that connects consumption to multiple aspects of local and global everyday living. Overall, these narratives can help to envision a collective and solidary project of society, in which consumption can be practiced in more just and sustainable ways. Each chapter focuses on a group of narratives that shows the different positions listed above. Given the variety of perspectives, each chapter employs a set of theoretical references that best help us understand the representation(s) of everyday consumption that it addresses.

Chapter 1, "A Consumer's Dystopia," discusses images of Brazil as a dystopic space, where consumption has corroded social relations and where capitalism has completely conquered the everyday, leading to alienation, despair and, ultimately, to total destruction. The chapter focuses on Bonassi's 2015 novel *Luxúria* and Sant'Anna's 2014 collection of short stories titled *O Brasil é bom*. It demonstrates that these narratives represent a radically negative side of consumption in Brazilian everyday life in the twenty-first century. As such, these novels can be seen as what I call narratives of *totalizing dystopia*. Taking as a point of departure Wendy Brown's idea that the spread of a neoliberal rationality onto several spheres of everyday life erodes interpersonal relations, I discuss how the narratives represent consumers as subjects who blend into an alienated, prejudiced, and/or violent mass. Principally targeting the consumption incentives of the Workers' Party administration, Bonassi's and Sant'Anna's works in question suggest that Brazil is a country of no future. Utilizing sociological analysis of the context addressed by the narratives in question, I contend that Bonassi's and Sant'Anna's views of consumption, while insightful in many ways, are rendered problematic when considering their view of working-class consumers.

In Chapter 2, "The Consuming Self," I propose a reading of Lísias's *O livro dos mandarins* and B. Carvalho's *Reprodução* as novels of *utopic reinvention* with respect to their portrayal of life in and beyond consumer culture. Utilizing Bauman's theory of liquid modernity and Neil Postman's idea of the impact of technologies on human rationality, I discuss these novels' critique to a subjectivity fostered by consumer capitalism's narratives of success and by the commodification of information in the twenty-first century. I contend that while criticizing the never-ending quest for more that characterizes what Zygmunt Bauman calls the postmodern utopia, the novels take a utopian stance concerning their vision of a possible way out of consumer capitalism.

Introduction

Chapter 3, titled "Consumer Culture's 'Collateral Damage,'" addresses the representation of the invisible violence of consumer capitalism in three novels by Ana Paula Maia: *O trabalho sujo dos outros, Carvão animal,* and *De gados e homens* . Utilizing Bauman's notion of the collateral damages of capitalism and Rob Nixon's concept of slow violence, I discuss Maia's unveiling of violent practices that are obscured by the banal quality of our consumption. These practices have very concrete consequences for the environment and especially for those who bear the heaviest weight of consumer society, namely, low-income workers in professions such as coal mining, slaughtering, and trash collecting. I contend that these narratives by Maia take a step further in relation to the stories analyzed in the previous chapters with respect to their view of the potential for change in consumer society. I propose calling these works by Maia narratives of *temporary radical suspension*, for they envision drastic changes that, albeit temporary, destabilize everyday life in consumer capitalism in concrete ways within the scope of the fictional universes that she creates.

Chapter 4, "A Consumer's Dreams and Nightmares" focuses on the consumption of popular culture in Galera's *Mãos de cavalo* and Laub's *A maçã envenenada* . Based on Lefebvre's concept of the moment and his reflection about the dialectical relationship between alienation and disalienation, I propose that the novels in question be read as narratives of *ambivalent awareness*. I use the term to refer to the novels' representation of everyday consumption as marked by an oscillation between awareness and oblivion of the effects of consumer culture on one's subjectivity. These effects include not only negative but also potentially positive ones, in the sense that, at times, it is consumer culture itself that triggers the protagonists' critical reflection about social reality.

In Chapter 5, "Working-Class Consumption," I examine the representation of working-class consumption in Faustini's *Guia afetivo da periferia* (2009). I contend that Faustini's view of consumption as social practice both criticizes consumer society and identifies uses of commodities that go beyond notions of alienation and greed. His perspective complicates portrayals of working-class consumption such as the ones presented by Bonassi, Sant'Anna, and Maia, thus envisioning dialectical relations between subjects and commodities that, in the words of Daniel Miller, negate rather than affirm the economic system in which these relations take place by reassuring us of our subjectivity beyond mere products of the system in question (*Theory* 147). I call fiction such as Faustini's *Guia afetivo* narratives of *transformative hope*.

The selection of writers and narratives for this analysis intends to provide a relatively broad perspective on the representation of consumption in Brazilian fiction in the twenty-first century by including writers from diverse backgrounds who highlight different issues that pertain to consumption.[5] These issues, which are also pertinent to other regions of the globe, range from recent political life to the environment, increasing political polarization, escalating social inequality, and affective relationships to and through commodities. It is imperative to respond to the urgent need for better understanding (and ultimately solving) these and other issues involving consumption. The present analysis takes up this very task by examining how the narratives in question imagine ways in which we (can or cannot) exist in consumer culture.

Chapter One

A Consumer's Dystopia

"They are biting off more than they can chew." The "they" in question are Brazilian low-income consumers. The person who expressed this opinion was one of the middle-class participants of an ethnography on working-class consumption of luxury goods conducted by anthropologists Rosana Pinheiro-Machado and Lucia Mury Scalco in the city of Porto Alegre, Brazil. At Pinheiro-Machado's presentation during the 2016 Brazilian Studies Association Conference, when she provided the example above, the audience could not help but gasp at some of the opinions expressed by some of the research subjects about children's requests for Christmas gifts during the National Mail Service's Christmas charity action. For the middle-class participants of the ethnography in question, anything considered luxury goods (expensive branded items, primarily) was deemed inappropriate, whereas requests that evoked merit and humbleness were seen as adequate.

Branded items, cell phones, air travel, housing that reproduces certain comforts of luxury dwellings, bank accounts, and financing were some of the items that came within reach of the so-called "new middle class" in Brazil during the Lula administration (Oliven and Pinheiro-Machado 53). With the growth in consumption among what some would actually call "the new *working* class"[1] came much push back from those who saw (and likely still see) themselves as the "legitimate" middle class, adequate consumers of certain products, as the comments by Pinheiro-Machado and Scalco's subjects mentioned above indicate.

These socioeconomic shifts in Brazilian society are the focus of Bonassi's 2015 novel *Luxúria* and Sant'Anna's short story collection *O Brasil é bom* (2014), which I analyze in this chapter. Both authors harshly criticize Brazil's policies of social inclusion via consumption during the Worker's Party's tenure. Both of them depict a dystopic nation, where one can identify echoes of a familiar, long-standing discourse on development that masks the brutality of an everyday life mediated by consumer goods. As the authors in question peel the layers of Brazil's social reality, a country of violence, prejudice, instability, debt, and tense social relations emerges. This dystopia, the narratives under analysis suggest, stems from a culture of consumption, represented as highly problematic for its shaping of self-centered individuals and its pervasive presence in multiple spheres of social life, such as work, leisure, sex, and religion. The narratives link this presence to the spread of a neoliberal rationality. As theorized by Brown, this rationality advances onto every sphere of life, on a path toward the catastrophic obliteration of democracy, as relations of solidarity disintegrate, and society loses even its forms of speaking about them (17). It is this disintegration, and therefore the abyss of total destruction of democratic societies, that Bonassi and Sant'Anna contemplate in their narratives. Read together, these literary works paint a radically negative image of Brazil, leaving little hope for any kind of positive change. In this way, based on the view of consumption in everyday life conveyed by the works in question, I call them *narratives of totalizing dystopia*.

I will first discuss Bonassi's portrayal of his protagonist's downfall as an omen of Brazil's future demise due to a culture of voracious and conspicuous consumption, fueled by social policies that promote the inclusion of low-income sectors of society by increasing their consumer power. Second, I will look into Sant'Anna's representation of Brazil as a similarly dystopic nation. I will discuss Sant'Anna's criticism of President Lula's social policies, of middle- and upper-class prejudice manifested via consumption, and of the rise of neoconservatism in the 2010s.

As a product of the contradictions of the context in which they were written—that is, of the strengthening of a neoliberal mentality that curtails the freedom that it promises—Bonassi's and Sant'Anna's works under study highlight serious problems in Brazil's socioeconomic and political landscape in recent years, while reproducing some of the same neoliberal ideas at the heart of middle-class prejudice about working-class consumption. While Bonassi essentially blames working-class consumers' "irrational" consumption for Brazil's demise, Sant'Anna's stories, despite presenting a broader view of how consumer culture affects Brazilian society by pointing fingers at different sectors, also condemn the pleasures of working-class consumption without acknowledging the social dynamics and the contradictions of consumer capitalism that affect this segment of society. In Sant'Anna's case, the presence of an implicit narrator, who unifies the snapshots of various characters' daily lives presented as if objectively captured by a camera, underscores a point of view that does not merely reproduce but rather intervenes as a commentator of this reality, at times positioning him/herself rather conservatively. In this way, the narratives analyzed in this chapter portray the working class ambiguously as victims and perpetrators of their own downfall and of Brazil's ultimate demise, thus surrendering to an extent to neoliberal narratives of responsibilization, that is, of expecting individuals to be entrepreneurs of their selves (Brown 84).

Bonassi's *Luxúria*: Brazil, Country of the Future! Are We There Yet?

Luxúria tells the story of a working-class Brazilian family that indulges in the consumption of goods that they cannot afford. The family is comprised of three members who do not have names and are simply referred to as the man, the woman, and the boy. Their voracious consumption ends up destroying them once the man, overwhelmed by his accumulating debt and the loss of his job, kills his wife and child, subsequently committing suicide.

As the title suggests, *Luxúria* is about lust and desire. The Portuguese word, which refers to one of the seven deadly sins, comes from the Latin word *luxŭrĭa* /luksuria/, which means "extravagance, profusion, luxury, excess." In Portuguese, *luxúria* is connected to *luxo*, which derives from the Latin word *luxus*. The latter also means excess, indulgence, and luxury (Lewis and Short). The title, thus, suggests a particular view of the consumption it portrays as excessive and conspicuous, motivated by extreme and irrational desires. Ultimately, consumption appears in the novel as a sin that eventually causes the characters' downfall, which in turn stands for the country's inability to prosper.

The story, classified by the narrator as a *relato* (report), and filled with meta-references such as "conforme descrito no capítulo quatro" ("as described in chapter four"; Bonassi, *Luxúria* 335), presents itself as the real account of the life of a working-class family that, through consumption, has now supposedly ascended into the middle class. A sentence that prefaces the narrative frames the novel's mimicry of real life from the beginning as it alerts readers that what they are about to read is "[b]aseado em pessoas e acontecimentos reais, lamentavelmente" ("based on real people and real events, unfortunately"; 8). The opening scene stresses the dystopic tone of the narrative. Tropical heat, pollution, and heavy traffic trap the protagonist in an inferno; a concrete jungle of pointless routine and apathy, as the real owners of capital fly over in their helicopters, avoiding the miserable conditions experienced by those driving down below. While the government claims that "[é] um momento histórico" ("it's a historical moment"), the narrator translates this moment into "[n]unca tantos tiveram tão pouco" ("never before have so many had so little"; 9).

The reality to which the novel alludes is the period of about thirteen years of the Workers' Party's tenure in the presidency, roughly up until the novel's publication. One of the settings of *Luxúria* is a neighborhood called Bairro Novo (New Neighborhood), comprised of subsidized houses, in a reference to the program Minha Casa, Minha Vida (My House, My Life),[2] which offered subsidies not only for buying houses but also for remodeling them (Mattoso 115). It is through the government's credit program that the protagonist is able to start the project of building a pool in his backyard. *Luxúria* is, in a sense, the story of this pool, the protagonists' main object of lust. It is the story of what the pool represents: a family's blind desire to consume that ignores their financial inability to do so, which drives them into debt and, ultimately, self-destruction.

Failure is also embedded in Bairro Novo as a whole. While its name suggests that the neighborhood represents a new era of progress, it soon becomes clear that this progress is mere promise. As the narrator comments, Bairro Novo "[n]ão se encontra, nem nunca se encontrou no centro de algo importante, muito menos numa periferia em torno de qualquer coisa que valesse a pena orbitar" ("is not and never has been at the center of anything important, much less in a *periferia* around anything worth orbiting"; Bonassi, *Luxúria* 22). Bairro Novo's failure to be the thriving neighborhood that the government promised it would be becomes evident when a truck fails to deliver construction materials because it does not fit into the poorly designed or rather unplanned narrow streets (157). The scene suggests how unsuitable it seems, from a middle-class perspective at least, to build a "lavish" pool in a low-income neighborhood and, by extension, to expect a country to prosper when a good portion of its "progress" is based on the acquisition of material goods that are beyond one's actual means and that are prioritized over basic infrastructure.

The wider availability of credit mentioned above is at the center of *Luxúria*. The chapter "Crédito fácil" ("Easy credit"), as the title suggests, touches directly on this issue. At a place symbolically called "Paraíso das piscinas" ("Pool paradise"), the husband and his wife acquire the goods with which they hope to attract the attention of their neighbors and friends. Motivated by the salesman's pitch, they come to see the pool as compensation for working hard and as a matter of "public health"; mental health, to be more precise. Capitalizing on the unhappiness produced by mass society as a way to sell goods—the rationale that would have propelled mass consumption in the first place (Ewen 45)—the salesman states that the protagonist deserves the pool, for it will provide him with relaxation moments much needed in order to continue to be productive. However, instead of providing the protagonist and his family with the paradise promised by the store, the purchase of the pool only makes their lives more difficult, affecting their mental health in quite the opposite way. The negative aftermath of purchasing the pool, thus, confirms the manipulative force of the commodification of leisure in consumer society, in which "we work to get our leisure and leisure only has one meaning: to get away from work. A vicious circle" (Lefevbre, *Critique* 40).

If initially the husband feels powerful, experiencing the "sabor de senhor" ("taste of [being] a [slave] master"),[3] his power dwindles as the narrative progresses and infrastructural problems derail construction (Bonassi, *Luxúria* 181). The pool becomes a symbol of obliteration, which suggests that the ideology of consumption that sweeps the country will eventually be responsible for ending this moment of prosperity that is only liquid, fragile.

The pool embodies a sense of decay, fall, and dismantling from the very beginning of its construction. Work starts with two men digging themselves into a hole amidst buried trash made up of disposable containers and old credit card statements that seem to miraculously resist deterioration (Bonassi, *Luxúria* 223). This resistance is symbolic, for it represents not only previous critical moments of the country's economic life, such as the 1980s economic crisis, when foreign debt skyrocketed, but also a lasting economic stress that, the novel predicts, would be set in motion in the country once all those acquiring debt like the protagonist eventually failed to pay their dues.

The construction of the pool moves slowly, like the traffic in the city shown in the novel's opening scene, reinforcing the sense that the country is stuck, or at the very least, on the brink of stalling. Boxes of tiles, packs of cement, and cans of paint acquire everyday uses around the protagonist's house, serving as chairs, coffee tables, couches, and footrests, evoking a sense of precariousness, improvisation, and delay (Bonassi, *Luxúria* 255–56). Meanwhile, the dirt dug out by the construction workers, which makes up the foundation of the houses in the neighborhood, emits the smell of excrements. The narrator calls this dirt "o solo da pátria" ("the nation's soil"), thus suggesting that the economic growth that the country experiences at the time when the pool is constructed has its foundations on a dirty political and economic past that seems to be repeating itself. The pool continues to bring more burden than joy to the man and to his family, as the protagonist is forced to leave work in order to deal with an accident that damages part of the plumbing during construction. As a consequence of the damage, the hole where the pool is expected to be placed is filled with sewage, spreading a bad smell through the neighborhood (259–60). Later on, heavy rain causes the concrete box of the pool to detach from the ground, making it float in sewage, eventually damaging the man's house as well as his neighbors' houses. Further emphasizing the idea of decay, the narrator compares the pool to a wound in the neighborhood, suggesting that this so-called "progress" is an open sore on the body of a sick nation, infected by the virus of consumption (254).

Not only the pool, but virtually everything that the family "owns" is not really theirs, as the narrator notes several times throughout the novel. Everyday life initially blinds the family to the fact that their car, their appliances, and the pool itself, belong to the banks from which they borrowed money, for they are merely another one of the neighborhood's "famílias financiadas" ("financed families"; Bonassi, *Luxúria* 205). Toward the end of the novel, the narrator highlights the protagonist's deteriorating status by no longer referring to him as "o homem de que trata esse relato" ("the man whom this report is about"), but rather as "o devedor de que trata esse relato" ("the debtor whom this report is about"). At this moment, the narrative reaches a turning point, when the everyday life of spending money the family does not actually have is interrupted. The protagonist states "*Eu dormia muito bem antigamente, esquecia tudo no dia seguinte, mas agora tudo me carrega para um certo ponto, este ponto morto em que me encontro agora ...*"4 ("*I used to sleep well before, having forgotten everything by the following day, but now everything pushes me to a certain end, the dead end in which I find myself now*"; 316). This interruption, however, rather than the utopic idea of the Festival envisioned by Lefebvre (*Everyday Life* 191), that is, rather than the restoration of the human potential suppressed by modernity, will bring only doom to the protagonist.

Chapter 54, titled "No fundo do poço" ("Rock bottom"), further stresses the man's downfall. He questions whether he still is, as he believed initially, "o melhor do mundo" ("the best one in the world"), and realizes that credit cards and loans are not the same as actual physical money, that they are just "*promessa de plástico*" ("*a promise in plastic*"; Bonassi, *Luxúria* 302). A deeper sense of awareness comes soon after this moment, when the man, depressed and abandoned to his own luck, concludes:

> *Meu dinheiro não dá para o que eu desejo. Meu desejo não dá para a oferta do mundo. Eu nem sei o que eu desejo. Este é o meu motor contínuo. Eu sei, eu creio que este é "o" momento histórico de oportunidades, que elas são novas, fáceis, disponíveis, mas em meio a tudo isso o meu fôlego está decaindo, falindo, parando, e eu estou afundando como um tubarão que quer morrer afogado.* (343)

> *I don't have money to fulfill my desires. My desires are not compatible with what the world offers me. I don't even know what I desire. This is my continuous drive. I know, I believe that this is "the" historical moment of opportunities, that they are new, easy, available, but amidst all this my breath is weakening, fading, stopping, and I am sinking like a shark that wants to drown.*

The protagonist's thoughts capture his realization of the incompatibility between what consumer capitalism demands from him and what his socioeconomic condition allows him to achieve. The protagonist's psychological state, as well as that of the society around him, unveils the failure of the early twentieth-century project of controlling the psyche of the "irrational masses" in order to secure the future of democracy. As shown in Adam Curtis' 2002 documentary *The Century of the Self*, between the 1920s and the 1950s, public relations and advertising executive Edward Bernays, together with psychologist Ernest Dichter, applied Freud's theory of the unconscious to advertising. Their goal was to manage consumers' emotions, manipulating their desires by rationalizing associations between products and people's innermost wants. The justification for said manipulation of the unconscious, which was also used in politics, was that, in their view, the irrational masses had to be controlled in order to guarantee a democratic future, which depended on the existence of a stable society. It was believed that, left to their own devices, the masses would be led by primitive irrational forces (*Century* 01:50:48–01:54, 01:37:29–01:38:36). Bonassi's *Luxúria* shows this project turned onto its head: the control of consumer desires here is what actually leads to irrationality. Anger and other strong emotions lie just beneath the surface, ready to erupt any minute in a society sickened by brutal competition and individualism manifested through consumption. Melting into a mass of indistinguishable consumers, characters without names are "seduced" by the possibilities of Brazil's new socioeconomic conditions. All spheres of the characters' everyday lives have been colonized by capital, as they have been sucked into the modernity that Lefebvre cautions against, in which individuality and leisure have been erased. They carry out lives "deprived of reality, of links with the world—a life for which everything human is alien" (Lefebvre, *Critique* 149).

The loss of control that the novel represents is exacerbated by the fact that the protagonist is fired from his job due to his many absences to deal with the aforementioned construction problems. This event pushes the protagonist over the edge, culminating later on with him killing his whole family and committing suicide at the end of the novel. The cycle of destruction is then complete: the desired pool, as a symbol of ascension into middle-class status, only brings spiraling debt, emotional distress, job loss, and ultimately, death. In this way, the novel suggests that the level of consumption that it portrays can only be sustained for so long. It is an illusion that only leads to destruction. The utopia of a democratic society of individuals with managed emotions is radically negated, as is the possibility of overcoming the constraints of everyday life under capitalism.

Everyday Violence

One of the main ways in which Bonassi expresses the fallacy of the idea of a society of controlled emotions through consumption is by portraying violence, which abounds in the novel. Underlying this violence is greed, competition, and the consequent stress of living in a world that seduces individuals with consumer goods while making it ever more challenging for the majority of the population to acquire them. Violence contaminates social relations through microaggressions in several spheres of life, including spaces such as the home, the school, work, and the medical office.

At the very beginning of the novel, the protagonist points out this everyday violence in Brazilian society, which ranges from mumbled insults to murder, by characterizing the traffic in which he is stuck as "*Guerra com 'g' maiúsculo!*" ("*War with a capital 'w!'*"; Bonassi, *Luxúria* 10). To emphasize the everyday nature of these aggressions, the narrator places several of them in the background of the main actions of the plot, often when highlighting the protagonist's behavior as a consumer. This strategy creates a connection between consumption and violence, suggesting that the quest for the first often leads to or is backed by the latter.

One example of this connection between consumption and violence lies in the novel's representation of sex, which functions as an index of the protagonist's consumer power or lack thereof. The title of the novel itself, in its reference to lust, implies this index, which appears for the first time when the protagonist uses the word "luxúria" as an adjective to describe the materials that had been delivered for the construction of the pool (Bonassi, *Luxúria* 183).

The very decision to purchase the pool is born out of the protagonist's envy when he meets his wife's dentist at the latter's office and feels intimidated by all the diplomas displayed on the wall. To the dentist's display of his education, the factory worker responds with a comment that he has bought a pool. The narrator notes that the man "sente que dá o troco, e que suplanta o outro de alguma maneira, já que agora pode até mesmo realizar seus sonhos" ("feels that he retaliates, and defeats the other man in some way, since now he can even make his dreams come true"; Bonassi, *Luxúria* 18). For the protagonist, his purchasing power, albeit stemming from loans, has leveled the playing field. This battle for goods is also a battle for sexual prowess in a chauvinistic environment. As

Chapter One

suggested by the narrator, the protagonist's behavior is motivated by feeling threatened by the dentist as a male, when the latter talks to the woman as if she were his wife (15). The protagonist, thus, utilizes goods to mark his territory, so to speak. His resentment comes across in a dialog in which he insults the dentist only to take it back when asked to repeat:

> *Filho da puta.*
> *Como disse?*
> *Bom dia, doutor* (14)
>
> Son of a bitch.
> Pardon me?
> Good morning, Doctor

    Dialogues such as the one above abound in the novel. We also encounter these exchanges, for instance, at the factory where the protagonist works, between the man and his boss; or at home, between the housekeeper and the man's wife. These exchanges highlight the underlying tensions in daily interactions in current Brazil, when one finds cordiality only at the surface, beneath which lies the violence of a profoundly hierarchical society of evermore deteriorating relations. The protagonist is constantly "put in his place" by those socially above him. From this perspective, consumer power is not enough to provide him with the prestige that comes with belonging to certain social echelons. The contrast between the dentist, with his diploma on display, and the factory worker, holding little formal education, also emphasizes the devaluing of manual labor in relation to intellectual activities of "higher" realms (Gardiner 75).

    In addition to using goods as a way to mark his territory as a male, the protagonist sees his wife as an object that he owns. Specifically, he expresses this ownership through an aggressiveness toward her as a sexual object. This relation of possession is evidenced, for example, after they leave the dentist's office and are stuck in traffic. In this instance, the couple discusses the idea of purchasing the pool. The woman questions her husband about whether they can afford it. Upon arguing that they have credit, he grabs her genitals. According to the narrator, he does so as if saying "*você sabe de quem é, não sabe?*" ("*you know who you belong [it belongs]*[5] *to, don't you?*"; Bonassi, *Luxúria* 21). In this context, grabbing the woman represents the man's affirmation of his masculinity as the breadwinner, both sexually and financially capable and strong, the real owner of their assets, his wife included.

The novel connects sex with consumption and violence again in two other moments, which indicate the protagonist's ascension and his decline, respectively. In the former instance, the man, in a kind of delirium, first imagines his backyard as larger and his pool as more lavish than what they are in reality. Following this moment, he begins to act violently, kicking the family's dog and aggressively having sex with his wife, after opening a bottle of (cheap) champagne, a symbol of his new found "opulence" (Bonassi, *Luxúria* 92–95). His reaction suggests both his sense of superiority for being able to consume and his underlying despair to prove his (male) power in an attempt to negate his economic decline.

In the second instance when sex, consumption, and power intertwine, there is a symbolic confrontation between the protagonist and another man, as they run into each other walking their respective dogs. This confrontation, which is also about social status, is signaled by the contrast between the protagonist's dog, a "vira-lata" ("street dog"), and the stranger's dog, a Doberman pinscher. The protagonist feels diminished by the other man's dog breed due to the high social status that "owning" such a dog conveys in Brazilian society. Distracted, he stumbles on his dog's leash and falls as he fails to control the animal. His lack of control contrasts with the attitude of the other man, who commands his dog with confidence. The encounter, in addition to conveying social competition, functions as a foreshadowing of the man's downfall, as indicated by the protagonist's realization that "… o outro cachorro, o dobermann, e o homem, o rapaz, … ao contrário dele próprio e do vira-lata, eles estão plenamente aptos e capazes, cheios de perspectivas e possibilidades de vitória sobre a caça e a perpetuação das espécies" ("the other dog, the Doberman pinscher, the man, the young man, … in contrast with himself and his street dog, are fully apt and capable, they have plenty of chances to win the hunt and to perpetuate the species"; Bonassi, *Luxúria* 267). The strength that the stranger and his dog exude, as beings capable of perpetuating their lineage, stands for the perpetuation of middle- and upper-class privilege. The contrast between the protagonist and the stranger highlights the socioeconomic differences between

Chapter One

the two, which are masked by the protagonist's mere illusion of wealth. His stumbling wakes him up, albeit only for a moment, from his consumer's dream, as he is forced to confront what real wealth looks like in Brazilian society.

In the Darwinian battle between the two, it is the wealthy stranger who is likely to survive after the period of only apparent economic growth is over. The protagonist's defeat also suggests his defeated masculinity, for the intersection between being male and being poor does not grant one with the same privileges as being male and rich. The protagonist's defeat, and that of the social class that he represents, is communicated by his dog's reaction, as the animal, intimidated by the Doberman pinscher,

> põe o rabo entre as pernas e, se arrastando, deita de costas no asfalto, abrindo as pernas para o dobermann, exibindo-lhe a barriga rosa-pálido com um princípio de sarna, e os órgãos genitais, murchos—num gesto de total submissão na linguagem dos cães e dos homens. (Bonassi, *Luxúria* 268)

> puts his tail between his legs and, dragging himself, lies on his back on the asphalt, opening his legs to the Doberman pinscher, exposing his pale-pink belly that shows signs of scabies, the genitalia wilted—in a gesture of total submission in the language of dogs and men.

In other words, the dog's emasculation mirrors that of his human's, whose (consumer) power is in reality inferior to that of the stranger with his pedigree dog.

As foreshadowed by this encounter, the protagonist's sexual prowess deteriorates as the construction of the pool faces several obstacles. One particular instance of the narrative represents this deterioration. One night, faced with sexual impotence, the man behaves violently toward his wife, in an ambiguous scene that suggests rape. However, he ends up "vencido, castrado" ("defeated, castrated"; Bonassi, *Luxúria* 294). He lies in bed feeling the "enorme vazio, o permanente sentimento de desconfiança e a frustração generalizada, envenenando progressivamente as demais áreas da vida" ("the enormous emptiness, the permanent feeling of mistrust and the generalized frustration that progressively poisons the other areas of [his] life"; 294). These feelings stem from the failure to perform not just sexually, but also as a consumer, given that his plans to build the pool are not coming to fruition in the way that he imagined.

A Consumer's Dystopia

Violence also manifests itself in everyday micro aggressions that permeate racial relations in Brazilian society, conveyed in the novel through consumption, as interactions between the wife and the housekeeper illustrate. As the narrator points out, the housekeeper is expected to do far more than what she is paid to do, her labor thus consisting of a cheap commodity. The following passage conveys this exploitation, as it shows the woman's multiple requests to the housekeeper for doing tasks beyond her duties:

> *Traga um copo de água, tenho sede. Fez comida? Tenho fome de qualquer coisa, fora de hora. Já limpou o quarto do menino? Não encontrou nada? Faça direito que embaixo da cama dele tem coisa ... Não está fazendo nada, põe o pano de prato no sol, por favor ... Dar banho no cachorro, sim.* (Bonassi, *Luxúria* 75-76)

> *Bring me a glass of water, I'm thirsty. Did you cook? I'm hungry for something, anything, between meals. Have you cleaned the boy's room? Haven't you found anything? Pay close attention because there has to be something under his bed ... If you've run out of things to do, hang the kitchen towel to dry, please ... Yes, give the dog a bath.*

Interactions such as these are common in Brazilian middle-class households, in which the boss "administrando, constrangendo, e cobrando e premiando às vezes, faz valer cada centavo daquilo que paga à diarista" ("managing, embarassing, demanding, and sometimes awarding, gets every penny's worth of the money she pays the housekeeper"; Bonassi, *Luxúria* 76).[6] The woman not only exploits the housekeeper, but also makes sure to segregate her, for example, prohibiting her from showering in their bathroom or by watching her every move so as to avoid potential theft.[7] As Maria Helena Machado, professor at the Department of History at Universidade de São Paulo and specialist in slavery and post-abolitionism social movements in Brazil, points out in an interview to the Brazilian newspaper *Zero Hora*, the dynamic between today's housekeepers and their bosses dates back to a time when enslaved women were charged with taking care of their masters' white babies. These women were, according to Machado, often separated from their own children while forced to breastfeed and raise their masters' offspring. As pointed out by Lourdes García Navarro in a National Public Radio (NPR) piece titled "Brazil Enslaved," the link between this past and today can be seen in statistics that reveal that at least 600,000 people, 96% of which are women, more than half of which are Afro-Brazilians, work in the service sector.

Victims of exploitation exploiting others is a common theme in Bonassi's *Luxúria*. While the woman bosses the housekeeper around in a similar way to the man's bossing around the construction workers, the housekeeper is a victim of sexual abuse and domestic violence just like her boss is (129). Bonassi thus highlights the compounded oppression on individuals who are oppressed for their race, gender, and socioeconomic status all at once. The housekeeper stands as an example of one of the most oppressed segments of Brazilian society: working-class black women.

Violence is also present in schools, where bars on windows and high walls with barbed wire and pieces of sharp glass on top isolate children who are told to "shut the fuck up" (Bonassi, *Luxúria* 295). They learn the ABCs according to an exercise in which, instead of the usual positive words with which children associate letters of the alphabet in school activities, has an alphabet of violence that includes words like knife, grenade, lynching, Nazi, and gun (96). The lesson is presented by the narrator as an ordinary one, so as to suggest the banality of violence, as it is normalized for citizens from a young age.

It is also with violence that debts are collected in a country where a kind of private justice system prevails, guaranteeing that those with capital continue to stay in power. The novel suggests this status quo when heavily armed debt collectors without uniforms, wearing black attire that covers their whole body, including their faces and hands, arrive at the protagonist's house and force him to sign papers that will roll his debt to another company, accruing even more interest. This scene equates financial capitalism with organized crime, which may count on extra-official forces, such as the "oficiais de justiça terceirizados" ("private justice officials"), to make sure it remains hegemonic. The novel further highlights the prevalence of this system in chapter 53, which transcribes, in a parodic tone, a letter that the protagonist would have received communicating that his application for more credit has been declined. The letter is signed by "o seu Poder Judiciário" ("Your Judicial Power"), sarcastically reminding its addressee that nothing in the country is really his, including structures meant in principle to protect his interests as a citizen (Bonassi, *Luxúria* 270).

Violence is thus everywhere you turn in the Brazil that Bonassi portrays in *Luxúria*. It is present even in the subtler form of long lines in public and private establishments, which subject citizens/customers to unpleasant waits and cause much frustration. Furthermore, it is embedded in the city's architecture, characterized by the presence of enclosed spaces where walls and windows can only keep the aggressive smells and sounds of the city away for so long (87).

Everyday Numbness

In *Luxúria*, the power of consumer society's alienating forces also results in the characters becoming numb to the violence that surrounds them. Television reports road accidents ignored by the "indiferentes que têm pressa" ("indifferent ones in a hurry"; Bonassi, *Luxúria* 174). People's indifference, the narrator suggests, stems from the rhythm of capitalist life, in which one is always in a hurry, for "time is money," as the saying goes. The swelling of cities that lack adequate public transportation and where owning a car is a status symbol aggravates this sense of hurry and indifference toward others.

In this environment, characters operate like automatons, as in the case of the protagonist, who lives in a "sistema estruturado: na repetição mecânica, mas estudada e detalhada, ele ocupa a mente o dia inteiro, a semana inteira, o ano inteiro. Encontra um porto seguro para aqueles pensamentos desesperados que todos temos, e não enlouquece" ("structured system: in the mechanical, however calculated and detailed, repetition, he keeps his mind busy all day long, all week long, all year long. He finds a safe haven in those desperate thoughts that we all have, and [in this way] does not lose his mind"; Bonassi, *Luxúria* 57). Everyday repetition appears as an alienating but necessary condition for the man's existence. In their despair, characters end up resorting to antidepressants, which further numb them, reducing their conscience to practically nothing, as they become zombie-like. The protagonist's wife, in particular, becomes addicted to these drugs, needing ever-higher doses in order to be able to deal with the emptiness of her daily routine of sitting around the house all day, and the uncertainties regarding their financial situation. The medication is offered at public health centers, creating a rumor that the government wants to manipulate citizens by medically numbing them (363). The state thus appears as a totalizing power, capable of controlling citizens not only through propaganda, but even through subtle chemical intervention.

These rumors of government manipulation and this heightened sense of an impending catastrophe associated, ultimately, with the result of social policies implemented by left-wing administrations, create a parallel between the narrator's stance and the problematic way in which Brazilian mainstream media has historically treated counter-hegemonic efforts. The monopoly of a handful of corporations, run by a small number of rich families, over Brazilian telecommunications is a well-documented fact (Lima 103), as well as the influence of giant Rede Globo on the result of elections and, more recently, on the success of the 2016 ousting of President Rousseff. Taking a close look at Globo's political influence since the 1980s, Luis Felipe Miguel (2016) documents the network's strategies in support for right-wing candidates. According to Miguel, Globo was part of a fraudulent scheme in the 1982 election for Rio de Janeiro's governor. In the 1989 presidential election, the television network, after rather openly campaigning for the right-wing candidate, edited the last debate between candidates Fernando Collor de Melo and Luís Inácio Lula da Silva so as to make Melo appear stronger, significantly impacting public opinion. In the 1998 electoral campaign, Globo strategically aired news that favored the election of Fernando Henrique Cardoso—again over Lula—by emphasizing the success of the Plano Real (*Real* Plan) and making it seem like there was simply no other safe option for Brazil's political and economic future. In 2002, the strategy was to emphasize the economic danger of Lula's election over right-wing candidate José Serra. Every electoral year since then, Globo has progressively engaged more openly in the electoral process, attacking the Lula and Rousseff administrations consistently while strategically omitting the abuses of the judicial system in the process (Miguel 110).

Meanwhile, headlines in major newspapers emphasized the protests that supported Rousseff's impeachment, while diminishing the importance of those protests that opposed it (Moretzsohn 134). More recently, Globo contributed significantly to the spread of fear in the city of Rio de Janeiro without addressing the social inequality and historical causes of the violence that it reported (Astrolábio 186–87). The media coverage of the violence in Rio paved the way for Rousseff's successor Michel Temer to justify a military intervention in the city (Rossi).

A Consumer's Dystopia

In this way, while proposing an important critique of the deterioration of leftist ideals—a deterioration that includes the fact that the Workers' Party's administration did little to change the previously mentioned media monopoly—*Luxúria* reads as a rather reductive portrayal of the complexities of the socioeconomic and political context that it addresses.

In the face of such a catastrophic situation, whether or not taking antidepressants, the entire family in *Luxúria* surrenders to a state of ennui as the narrative progresses. The dialogue below encapsulates this state while showing the connection between the characters' mental health and their material possessions and desires to consume:

> *Eu ainda sou o melhor do mundo?*
> *A felicidade?*
> *É uma dúvida que eu tenho*
> *A infelicidade?*
> *É uma certeza, pelo menos*
> *O dinheiro. Acabou. Faz tempo.* (302)

> *Am I still the best one in the world?*
> *Happiness?*
> *This is a doubt I have*
> *Unhappiness?*
> *This is certain, at least*
> *The money. It ran out. A while ago.*

A linguistic indicator of the characters' surrender to numbness is the recurring answer that they provide when asked about bruises and marks of violence on their bodies. Instead of explaining what happened, they repeat an excuse conjugating the verb in the present, as if using drills to memorize content for a school test. The first instance in which this happens is when the couple's child arrives home after being beaten up by his classmates, who constantly bully him. When asked about what happened, he replies: "*eu caí na rua, tu caíste na rua, ele caiu na rua; nós caímos na rua, vós caístes na rua, eles caíram na rua*" ("*I fell on the street, you fell on the street, he/it fell on the street, we fell on the street, you [pl.] fell on the street, they fell on the street*"; 173). His strategy invokes a traditional pedagogical approach to content in Brazilian schools, by which students are expected to demonstrate empty memorization of, for instance, the conjugation of verb forms that have extremely limited use in contemporary Brazilian Portuguese, such as the form of "vós"

Chapter One

("you" [pl.]) conjugated in the passage above. This memorization, Bonassi's novel suggests, functions as a kind of drug, in a sense, maintaining characters disconnected from their reality and incapable of acting on the injustices of which they are victims.

The boy's father repeats the same mindless behavior when his co-workers beat him up in revenge for him siding with their boss against them. The man's explanation to his child about the bruises on his body is simply the following: *"eu escorreguei no óleo e caí na fábrica, tu escorregaste no óleo e caíste na fábrica, ele escorregou no óleo e caiu na fábrica, nós escorregamos no óleo e caímos na fábrica, vós escorregastes no óleo e caístes na fábrica, eles escorregaram no óleo e caíram na fábrica, compreende?"* ("*I slipped on oil and fell at the factory, you slipped on oil and fell at the factory, he/it slipped on oil and fell at the factory, we slipped on oil and fell at the factory, you [pl.] slipped on oil and fell at the factory, they slipped on oil and fell at the factory, do you understand?"*; Bonassi, *Luxúria* 285). Yet in another instance, it is the man's wife's turn to respond in the same fashion. Days after having been abused by her husband, her pastor asks her about all the bruises on her neck, chest, and legs, to which she responds that she tripped and fell at home (294). If these repetitive answers might sound strange in real life, the responses provided by the characters' interlocutors ("*Ah, bom*" ["*Oh, okay*"], "*Deus seja louvado*" ["*Praise to God*"], and "*Claro, boa noite*" ["*Of course, good night*"]) convey a sense of normalcy that renders the characters' lines even more disturbing for the reader. The responses, like the statements they address, are uttered in a seemingly mindless fashion, implying a sense of acceptance of or similar numbness to the everyday violence of which others are victims. These responses ultimately represent the characters' inability to break away from the violence produced by consumer capitalism, whether in the form of labor exploitation, unattainable consumption expectations, or the profound unhappiness that follows the realization that one no longer has money, as the novel's protagonist states.

The Factory and the Country: The Right Turn?

While the novel highlights the transformation of humans into machines that operate automatically, it also deals with the replacement of humans by machines in capitalism, by portraying the conflict between the protagonist and his fellow factory workers over

A Consumer's Dystopia

his support for the use of new, more "efficient" equipment. The conflict alludes to Lula's perceived betrayal of the working class, as suggested by the transformation of his image in the 2002 election, thanks to carefully planned marketing strategies.[8] In other words, the protagonist's support for changes in the factory that would negatively impact his co-workers but benefit him mirrors Lula's perceived abandonment of leftist values in order to ascend to power.

Although Bonassi states, in a 2015 interview with Simone Magno, that he used his own experience as a factory worker as inspiration for the construction of the protagonist (Bonassi, "Luxúria, de Fernando Bonassi"), the parallel between the protagonist and President Lula unquestionably stands out. Like Lula in his early adulthood, the protagonist works in the metallurgical industry as a lathe operator. He betrays his "companheiros" (comrades, as they refer to each other in the novel, evoking language used by Lula and the Left) in exchange for temporary and illusory power, which he acquires when his boss asks him to compile a list of fifty co-workers to be fired. The sacking happens because the company purchases a new machine, capable of doing the work performed by several workers at a time, thus increasing production, lowering costs, and raising profits. The machine represents the fast technological advancement that has at least partly contributed to cuts in manufacturing jobs at the company, a process that the man's boss describes as follows:

> *Éramos quase seis mil em mil novecentos e setenta. Depois éramos dois mil e quatrocentos no final dos anos mil novecentos e oitenta ... Em noventa e poucos já não passávamos de oitocentos e tantos e ao dobrarmos o milênio ... Acho que tínhamos nos reduzido a quinhentos ... Duzentos a mais do que somos hoje, não é mesmo?* (Bonassi, *Luxúria* 308)
>
> *We were almost six thousand nine hundred seventy. After that, we were two thousand four hundred at the end of the nineteen eighties ... In ninety something we weren't more than eight hundred and some and at the turn of the millennium ... I think we had been reduced to five hundred ... two hundred more than we are today, isn't it?*

The power that the protagonist feels when deciding who is going to lose their jobs, an opportunity that he uses to get rid of people he does not like, blinds him to the fact that his own employment might also be in jeopardy. An omen of his unfortunate destiny, as well as that of his co-workers, is his choking when toasting with his boss to the new machine: "*Um brind ... De ao fut ... Uro!*" ("*A toa ... st to the fu ... ture!*"; Bonassi, *Luxúria* 244). This future, as we have seen, brings nothing but destruction to the protagonist. The only one to prosper in this case is the boss, who increases his profits. The toast also invokes the well-known phrase coined by the Austrian writer Stefan Zweig, "Brasil, país do futuro" ("Brazil, country of the future") in his highly optimistic book *Brasilien: Ein Land der Zukunft* (*Brazil, Land of the Future;* 2014), thus ironically suggesting that this future will never come.

The protagonist's toast and its meanings resonate with post-2003 Brazil, when the country seems to have finally achieved this future of prosperity, which, however, starts to fade away in less than a decade, as an economic and political crisis sweeps the country in the 2010s. Specialists have noted that this crisis has many factors, including the dependence on China's own economic boom; the absence of countercyclical policies;[9] the complex tax system and labor laws that are unfavorable to business growth; and, perhaps the most visible factor of all, widespread corruption ("What went wrong" 00:25:32). The latter, along with questionable political alliances and concessions to neoliberalism that prevented the radical reform seen by some members of the Brazilian left as necessary,[10] has damaged the Workers' Party's reputation, casting doubts on its integrity.

The protagonist's father embodies this sense of deterioration of the country, linking past to present and announcing a future of collapse. His decaying body attests to the unfulfilled promises of prosperity from his past. He lives in a nursing home, where we meet him for the first time during one of his son's visits. The narrator depicts him as more dead than alive, clutching to the bars of the gate as he is shooed like an animal by one of the nurses (Bonassi, *Luxúria* 164–65). He and his fellow co-residents, former factory workers like himself, are described as being trapped or imprisoned within the confines of the bars that surround the property. Like the decaying building where he currently lives, the father's mental state seems to have deteriorated. The old man summarizes the old days in the factory as days of relative "permanência

A Consumer's Dystopia

e previsibilidade" ("permanence and predictability"), which are now almost entirely gone, as the current lay-offs at the factory indicate (34).

Another indication of current instability is the protagonist's ever more elusive retirement, as the clock at the factory seems to run backwards, taking away weekends, shortening boundaries between work time and leisure. This sense of increasing precariousness is also conveyed by the narrator's description of the nursing home as filled with "fedor de pele morta, de calçado gasto, de partes baixas e dobras úmidas que não são lavadas com frequência, de fraldas usadas, de meias suadas e de cobertores que não veem a luz do sol há muito tempo" ("the stench of dead skin, overworn shoes, body parts, and humid skin folds that haven't been washed very often, used diapers, sweaty socks, and blankets that haven't been exposed to the sun in a long while"; Bonassi, *Luxúria* 166). From the past, the only thing left is the assembly line efficiency with which the nurses take care of the retired workers, now symbolically treated as the products that they once assembled: "um velho desdentado é deixado nu, limpo com um pano úmido e vestido com o pijama padrão em trinta e sete segundos" ("a toothless old man is stripped of his clothes, cleaned with a wet cloth, and dressed in the [asylum's] standard pajamas in thirty-seven seconds"; 166). The asylum residents are subjected to capitalist time yet again: they are discarded as they are no longer capable of producing capital. As David Harvey states, in his analysis of Marx's 1867 *Capital*, "... asylums, prisons and clinics ... [can] be read as continuations of ... a disciplinary capitalism, in which workers have to be socialized and disciplined to accept the spatiotemporal logic of the capitalist labor process" (*A Companion* 149).

Time, indeed, is an important aspect of the novel not only in terms of what the future holds or of what is left behind in the past, but also with respect to the present management of the daily routine at the factory. In order to increase productivity, the company implements several time control strategies, such as having the bathroom light on a timer in order to prevent workers from staying away from their stations for too long. This measure, which actually does not allow enough time for the protagonist to urinate, as we find out in a scene, reduces time in the bathroom by 30%, thus increasing productivity and profits (Bonassi, *Luxúria* 59). The clock, according to the narrator, is a "ladrão do tempo e do espaço de sossego" ("thief of time and space for rest") within the factory, requiring persistence and youth from the workers in order to survive, in a Darwinian manner (237).

Bonassi's references to time in capitalism allude to Marx's *Capital*, which the Brazilian writer cites in the novel's epigraphs:

> Quanto maior a força produtiva do trabalho, tanto menor é o tempo de trabalho exigido para a fabricação de determinado artigo, tanto menor também a quantidade de trabalho nele cristalizada e tanto menor seu valor. Ao contrário, quanto menor a força produtiva do trabalho, tanto maior é o tempo de trabalho necessário para a fabricação de determinado artigo, e tanto maior seu valor. (Bonassi, *Luxúria* 5)

> [In general,] the greater the productiveness of labour, the less is the labor required for the production of an article, the less is the amount of labour crystallized in that article, and the less is its value; and *vice versa*, the less the productiveness of labour, the greater is the labour time required for the production of an article, and the greater is its value. (Marx and Engels 15)

The epigraph frames the reading of the novel as a critique to capitalist labor exploitation. Read in this context, the factory's control of its workers' time points precisely to the use of discipline to maximize profits, as the example of the bathroom light time illustrates. Bonassi's novel shows that, as Marx asserts, "capital oversteps not only the moral but even the merely physical limits of the working day. It usurps the time for growth, development and healthy maintenance of the body" (qtd. in Harvey, *A Companion* 144). To this control, Bonassi contrasts a kind of freedom, expressed by Jimmi Hendrix's song "Drifting" (1971), quoted along with the above-cited epigraph: "Drifting on a sea of forgotten teardrops / On a life-boat / Sailing for your love / Sailing home. / Jimmi Hendrix" (Bonassi, *Luxúria* 5). This freedom, however, is immersed in sorrow in the novel, for it means above all mere survival. It is a search for home in a world of despair, deteriorated by capitalist interests and the illusions of consumer culture.

While the factory, the nursing home, and the school appear in the novel as spaces of capitalist discipline, institutions that would provide some kind of protection for citizens and that would defend their interests appear to sell out to the new geopolitical and economic order in Bonassi's Brazil:

> O que foi feito do sindicato?
>
> *Está ocupado com as comissões do governo e dos empresários.*
> (Bonassi, *Luxúria* 79)
>
> Whatever happened to the union?
>
> It is busy with the government and businessmen's commissions [committees and dividends]

Passages such as the one above allude once again to the Brazilian Left's perceived betrayal of the constituency that it is meant to represent. Bonassi's novel refers to this betrayal once more in chapter 66, titled "Provérbios 6:16–19" ("Proverbs 6:16–19"). This chapter cites the very passage of the Bible referenced in the title, followed by a direct accusation of the protagonist of being a traitor:

> *Seis são as coisas que o Senhor abomina, e a sua alma detesta uma sétima: olhos altivos, língua mentirosa, mãos que derramam sangue inocente, coração que maquina perversos projetos, pés velozes para correr ao mal, testemunha falsa, e o que semeia discórdia entre irmãos. E por tudo isso eu te acuso, Judas traidor de sua classe!*
> (Bonassi, *Luxúria* 324)
>
> *These six things the Lord hates, yes, seven are an abomination to him: a proud look, a lying tongue, hands that shed innocent blood, a heart that devises wicked plans, feet that are swift in to running to evil, a false witness who speaks lies and one who sows discord among brethren.*[11] *And for all this I accuse you, Judas, traitor of your class!*

By the time this reference to the Bible appears in the narrative, the protagonist has committed almost all of the deadly sins referenced in the passage:[12] he has envied the dentist for what the latter possesses, he has lied to his boss, plotted against his co-workers, and started conflict in the factory. Furthermore, his association with evil is emphasized by the smell of sulfur that the metals in storage exhale when the protagonist and his co-worker have a confrontation about the protagonist's betrayal (Bonassi, *Luxúria* 328). In this chapter, the word "companheiro" ("comrade") appears yet again, reinforcing the link between the protagonist's actions and those of Lula's Left, steering the reader's attention to what some would consider the neoliberalization of Lula and his party.[13]

Chapter One

These allusions to the Bible also suggest the intertwining of neoliberal ideas and religious beliefs in Brazilian society today. These references appear when the couple's pastor is preaching at the church. His speech defends the accumulation of material goods as individuals' main goals in life and as a sign of having been blessed by God:

> *as riquezas e as bênçãos estão vinculadas. O dinheiro também é uma forma pela qual o Senhor nos abençoa, e quem aqui se dedica a vencer e progredir sabe muito bem que ser abençoado com o dom de ter e fazer mais dinheiro não torna tudo mais fácil, e sim o contrário: cria uma responsabilidade ainda maior para cada um de nós ...*
>
> *Quem aqui quer ser rico? Rico de coração, de espírito?*
>
> ...
>
> *E ter casa, carro do ano, televisão e telefone e computador de último tipo, tudo o que o Senhor de Deus nos deu o dom de descobrir? Alguém aqui é contra estar bem?* (Bonassi, Luxúria 48)
>
> *Riches and blessings are connected. Money is also a way by which the Lord blesses us, and those here who dedicate themselves to win and to improve [their financial situation] know very well that being blessed with the gift of having and making more money does not make everything easy, but quite the opposite: it creates an even bigger responsibility for each of us ...*
>
> *Who here wants to be rich? Rich in your heart, in your spirit?*
>
> ...
>
> *And to have a house, a brand-new car every year, a television and a phone and the latest computer, everything that the Lord, God, has given us the gift of discovering? Who here is against being well?*

As the passage above illustrates, neoliberal values of individualism and entrepreneurship permeate the preacher's speech in the form of self-improvement in economic terms. The church itself is run like a business, as the pastor's testimonial published in the fictitious *Jornal Nacional das Igrejas* (*National Church News*)—an allusion to the manipulative power of Rede Globo's long-standing prime time news program Jornal Nacional—indicates. According to the pastor, for as long as he was preaching a simple life of compassion and contained material desires, he was not successful:

> *O máximo que obtinha era um compromisso difuso, uma concordância de princípios, uma vaga promessa—e, desafortunadamente, baixíssima coleta de dízimos. As despesas do Templo se acumulavam: refeições de pastores e funcionários terceirizados; aluguel de imóvel, água, luz, gás, equipamento de som, material de limpeza, decoração. Crescia também a pressão do escritório central do ministério, que queria saber como as coisas iam tão mal em meio a tanto sofrimento ...* (153)

> *The most I got was a weak commitment, an agreement with the principles, a vague promise—and, unfortunately, extremely low tithing collection. The Temple's expenses were accumulating: pastors' and outsourced employees' meals; rent, water, electricity, gas, sound equipment, cleaning products, décor pieces. The pressure from the ministry's central office was also increasing; they wanted to know how things could be going so bad [for the church] amidst so much suffering.*

From then on, his discourse is filled with vocabulary that refers to profit and accumulation, such as "conferir ganhos" ("to make a profit"), "multiplicar" ("to multiply"), and "agregar valor" ("to add value"). As a result of this change, his church becomes one of the ten most lucrative churches of the year (153).

The pastor's case points to the recent growth of prosperity theology in Brazil, with its capitalist approach to faith, in which church members are expected to invest money into their relationship with God in exchange for blessings in this life in the form of commodities. In Brazil, prosperity theology has found fertile terrain since the late 1970s, when it became evident that the economic growth achieved during the dictatorship had fallen short of bringing about social equality. Abandoning the ideology of poverty preached by the Christian faith, Brazilian neo-Pentecostal churches imported North American prosperity theology, creating later on an entire gospel industry that includes music, fashion, television channels, among other products and services targeting its followers (B. Sousa 229). These churches have proven to be appealing to various segments of Brazilian society, with some catering predominantly to the middle and upper classes, such as the Igreja Bola de Neve (Snowball Church) in São Paulo, founded in 1999.

If the protagonist can be read as a portrayal of the fall of the Workers' Party and Lula into sin, the wife, as a woman, can be seen as a representation of the nation, cursed into eternal suffering for her lust and greed for consumer goods. The novel suggests this parallel by referencing Genesis 3:16, in chapter 60, as well as by quoting the positivist motto printed onto the Brazilian flag "ordem e progresso" ("order and progress"), two things that she is responsible for providing in the household, according to the narrator (Bonassi, *Luxúria* 299). The passage of the Bible in question, which refers to the curse of childbearing and labor pains bestowed upon women as a consequence of their lust, suggests that Brazil can be seen as the mother who will always suffer under the rule of her "husband," the (apparent) owner of capital. Read from this perspective, it is very symbolic that this mother (the nation) is murdered by her husband (the one which has betrayed his origins), along with their child (a potential future of prosperity).

Sant'Anna's *O Brasil é bom*: Federal Republic of Consumption

The cover of *O Brasil é bom* features the image of a rotten banana on a plate with a fork stuck to it. The rotten banana on the cover evokes the *tropicalidade* of a certain national identity, the one incorporated by icons such as Carmen Miranda dancing among giant plastic bananas and banana trees and singing "The Lady in the Tutti-Frutti Hat" in Busby Berkeley's film *The Gang Is All Here* (1943). Carmen Miranda and her exuberant bananas made up—and still do—an imagined geography south of the U.S. border, a Banana Republic, so to speak, an exotic and primitive land just waiting to be explored—and exploited—by foreign political and economic interests or simply by tourists in search of adventure. For President Getúlio Vargas (1930–45; 1951–54),[14] Carmen Miranda was part of strategic efforts to paint a picture of Brazil as an attractive country for foreign powers, namely, the United States. In the meantime, internally, the Vargas administration spread ideas of development, a discourse that crosses Brazilian history through the twentieth century and stretches into the twenty-first century, albeit taking various forms: President Juscelino Kubitscheck's 50 years in 5 platform during the 1950s,[15] the dictatorial governments' promises of "dividing the cake once it has risen" in the 1970s,[16] President Fernando Henrique Cardoso's (1995–2003) neoliberalism in the 1990s,[17] and the Workers'

Party's policies of social inclusion post-2003.

The image of a rotten banana on the cover of *O Brasil é bom*, therefore, signals the irony of the title, questioning the idea of development and pointing to the dystopic view of the country that the short stories in the book reveal. From this perspective, the 2010s would have been characterized by an only limited and temporary socioeconomic advancement, which would have been accompanied by the exacerbation of violence in interpersonal relations. These relations, as shown in the stories of *O Brasil é bom*, are fed by prejudice and hatred, sentiments largely expressed by an elite that is very much unhappy with any betterment achieved by the bottom of the social pyramid. The twenty-four narratives of the book, which are mostly snapshots of current daily life in Brazil in two to four pages, suggest that these relations derive from a socioeconomic development that has its roots in public policies only made possible by a perverse deal with neoliberalism. In this way, *O Brasil é bom* deals with some of the same issues addressed in Bonassi's *Luxúria*. Similarly, it presents a rather dystopic view of Brazil, which is perceived as having experienced a fragile socioeconomic growth starting in 2003 under the Workers' Party's leadership.

The first short story of *O Brasil é bom*, "Deus é bom nº 8" ("God is Good no. 8"), signals the sarcasm that permeates the entire book. The narrative tells the story of Jesus Cristinho's life, a character that is constructed so as to resemble Lula and his trajectory as a politician, referencing his political alliances in order to ascend to the highest office of the nation. Contrary to the Jesus Christ of the Bible, who combats the merchants of the temple, Jesus Cristinho allies himself with them. From the biblical Jesus's biography, the narrator borrows the humble origins, describing the place where his character would have been born as "um lugar bem pobrinho, cercado por vaquinhas, estrelinhas, uma lua sensacional" ("a poor little place, surrounded by little cows, little stars, and a spectacular moon"; Sant'Anna 7). Like Sant'Anna's Jesus, Lula also has humble origins in the backlands of the Brazilian Northeast. To the initial description of the protagonist, the narrator adds that Jesus would have been baptized by Brazilian soap opera star Glória Pires, who plays Lula's mother in the 2009 film *Lula, o filho do Brasil* (*Lula, the Son of Brazil*), which tells Lula's life story. These media references allude to the construction of

Chapter One

Lula's new image during the 2002 election, which became known as "Lulinha paz e amor" ("Peace-and-love little Lula"), a future president who would not "privatizar nada, … nos bancos, ó, na boa, paz e amor" ("privatize anything, … in the banks, look, cool, peace and love"; Sant'Anna 8). Later on, when another character of the story, Judas, talks to Jesus Cristinho in the name of international capital and the local elites, the narrator once again references Lula's renewed image:

> … pô, Jesus, em vez de eu acabar com a tua vida—tu vai ser crucificado e vai doer e o mundo vai continuar injusto—, a gente faz uns acordos, aceita um pecadinho ou outro da rapaziada, mantém a parada fluindo pros bancos, transforma esses paraíbas tudo aí em consumidor, resolve as parada toda com o mercado internacional de dinheiro, que é a coisa mais importante que existe, e, depois, até melhora a vida dos que mais precisam; na política não dá pra não fazer alianças estratégicas, arte do possível, etc. (Sant'Anna 8)

> C'mon, Jesus, instead of me ending your life—you will be crucified and it will hurt and the world will continue to be unfair—, we can negotiate, accept a little sin or so from the crowd, keep the stuff flowing into the banks, change these *paraíbas* into consumers, solve all this stuff with the international currency market, which is the most important thing there is, and, after that, we even improve the lives of those who need the most; in politics you can't avoid making strategic alliances, the art of the possible, etc.

Judas's speech suggests the articulation of a scheme to manipulate "paraíbas," a pejorative term used to refer to those native of the impoverished Brazilian backlands, the main beneficiaries of the programs of income distribution initiated in President Fernando Henrique Cardoso's administration and expanded during President Lula's years. Lula thus appears as a traitor of his own social class, ascending to power by appeasing the elite and by developing a program of social inclusion to keep up appearances. In another pejorative comment, the narrator suggests that Jesus/Lula would have maintained the "classe baixa-alta … sob controle comprando iogurte e batata chips" ("the upper-lower class … under control, purchasing yogurt and potato chips"; Sant'Anna 9). This perspective echoes the Brazilian elite's expectations with respect to the morality of working-class consumption. From this elite's point of view, industrialized products such as the ones mentioned in the quote above, yogurt and potato chips, are considered luxury items for the beneficiaries of the social programs in question. Purchasing them would, therefore, be considered inappropriate use of public money.

In this process of inclusion via consumption, the "classe baixa-alta" ("upper-lower class") or the so-called new middle class, now seeing itself wishfully as part of the elite and, therefore, reproducing its ideals, would eventually be responsible for the downfall of a Jesus/Lula that by any chance would come to have "alguma crise de compaixão, ou de esquerdismo" ("a crisis of compassion or leftism"; Sant'Anna 9). "Deus é bom nº 8" thus condemns the centrality of consumption in twenty-first century Brazilian society, alluding to the "Carta ao povo brasileiro" ("Letter to the Brazilian People") that Lula read during his campaign, in which he mentions the need for creating "um amplo mercado interno de consumo de massas" ("an ample internal market of mass consumption"; "Leia íntegra"). The short story in question suggests that driving consumption this way is a path of no return toward a socioeconomic and political abyss.

This opening story sets the tone for Sant'Anna's exploration of the impacts of consumption on current Brazilian society. For the sake of space, the following two sections will focus on a total of six of the most representative stories of *O Brasil é bom*. These stories address two major themes: the rise of a neoconservative subjectivity and the spread of daily microaggressions in today's Brazil. The third section presents some general conclusions about *O Brasil é bom*, drawing specific examples from other short stories in the book.

The Growth of Neoconservatism

Harvey contends that the rise of neoconservative forces in the United States in the early 2000s can be understood as a moralist reaction to the social instability caused by neoliberalism. In Harvey's view, the elite's desire to regain the power that they have lost generates this conservatism, whose growth reveals neoliberalism's authoritarian roots (*A Brief History* ch. 3). These roots can be seen in various narratives of *O Brasil é bom,* particularly in three short stories: "Nós somos bons" ("We Are Good"), "Pra ser sincero" ("To Be Honest"), and "Comentário na rede sobre tudo o que está acontecendo por aí" ("Online Comment on All That Is Happening Out There").

In "Nós somos bons," a first-person narrator, who includes him/herself in a collective "nós" ("we"), seems to speak for a segment of the Brazilian population that would have been responsible for a series of political decisions in the country's recent history. These decisions should have resulted in development for all, however, they have only yielded the maintenance of certain privileges held by a conservative elite who benefits from neoliberal practices. The "nós" of story claims, for instance, that "bom era no tempo da ditadura" ("good were the times of the dictatorship"), when the economy grew and, supposedly, there was no corruption (Sant'Anna 27).[18] It states, furthermore, that although torture "não tem nada a ver" ("is not good"), it was a reasonable price to pay in exchange for a government that "pelo menos governava bem," ("at least governed well"), guaranteeing a strong economy and a country free of corruption (27).

Expressing the elitist opinion of many Brazilian voters who rejected Lula in the 1980s and 1990s, this "nós" states that Lula is "um nordestino ignorante que não sabia falar inglês, que se vestia mal" ("an ignorant Northeasterner who could not speak English, who dressed poorly"), and therefore not well suited for the presidency (Sant'Anna 27). Afraid of losing consumer power due to the implementation of a communist regime in Brazil that would supposedly take place if Lula were elected, the "nós" evidences their hatred of those it holds responsible for Lula's election, calling them "pobres pretos vagabundos [que] não querem trabalhar o suficiente para comprar um Audi cheio de air bags, para comprar um iPhone para ligar para a esposa já meio passada da idade …" ("miserable lazy blacks [who] don't want to work enough to buy an Audi full of airbags, to buy an iPhone to call their over-the-hill wife …"; 28). This perspective reflects a belief in the myth of meritocracy, according to which those who succeed in life, which in consumer capitalism equals being able to accumulate material goods, do so because they deserve it. Conversely, those who are poor are believed to be responsible for their own demise, following the neoliberal logic.[19] "Nós somos bons" conveys a fear of communism that echoes that of many who participated in protests against then-President Rousseff and ex-President Lula starting in 2014, shouting a motto such as "a nossa bandeira jamais será vermelha" ("our flag will never be red"), in reference to the Workers' Party's flag color, which is commonly associated with communism.

The neoliberal conservatism evoked by "Nós somos bons" only accepts Lula when he is perceived to have surrendered to neoliberal capital, an attitude expressed, for instance, by protecting the economic status of the "nós" of the short story, allowing it to spend vacation time in Europe and at Disney World (Sant'Anna 28), like many upper-middle-class Brazilians at the beginning of the 2010s. In other words, the preservation of an elite's consumer power dispels this elite's fears of a communist future. With these anxieties put to rest, even the elite's linguistic prejudice against Lula diminishes, as the "nós" affirms that Lula's Portuguese seems to have "improved" (29). This change of mind is due perhaps to the fact that Lula now, from the perspective of the short story, speaks a language that this elite can understand: the language of consumer capitalism. The short story ends with an assertion that "[n]ós ainda vamos desenvolver o país, gerando empregos, gerando renda" ("we still are going to develop the country, generating employment, generating income"; 29). This assertion, when contrasted with the series of conservative political choices made by the "nós," renders the short story rather sarcastic, as it expresses a profound disillusionment with Brazilian society. After all, as the examples that the "nós" highlights indicate, only a small portion of the population—the one who can buy their own "Audi full of airbags"—has actually benefited from the development that has been promised so much to Brazilians.

"Pra ser sincero" is the transcription, so to speak, of a man's complaints about telemarketing. The short story portrays the contradictions of a self-proclaimed communist whose actions indicate that he has been engulfed by capitalism much more than he seems to realize. The story opens with the protagonist claiming that he received a phone call he initially assumed to be from a credit card company. Ready to fight, he was going to express his contempt for bankers, banks, and telemarketing, revealing to the woman on the other side of the line that he "only buys what he can pay for up front" and that he is "a communist" (Sant'Anna 17). However, he soon learns that that was a different kind of call. The person he was talking to was calling about donations for children with cancer. When she asks him about his Christmas and New Year's, the

Chapter One

character rants about the "classe baixa-alta" ("upper-lower class"), which according to him, is tacky, ugly, and desperate to consume all sorts of low-quality products (19). The classist view he conveys in this comment is further emphasized when he reveals his fear of the socioeconomic ascension of those whom he considers inferior to him. In a nostalgic remark about a past when the poor "knew their place," he confesses:

> eu que gostava daquela classe baixa que era baixíssima, daquela gente pobre e limpinha que, em qualquer praia desse litoral brasileiro que era lindo, estava lá, fritando peixe pra gente que viajava por essas praias maravilhosas do Brasil, até contava histórias do mar e era antigamente, nos bons tempos, essas paradas. (Sant'Anna 19)

> I liked that lower class that was really low, those poor but clean people who, on any beach of the Brazilian coast [,] which was pretty, would be there, frying fish for us, travelers through these wonderful beaches of Brazil; [they] would even tell stories about the sea and this was in the old days, this stuff.

Uncomfortable with having to share public spaces with those he considers beneath him, he blames them for the perpetuation of capitalism and transfers to them the responsibility to start "a communist revolution" (Sant'Anna 20). He complains about his fragile position as a member of the "middle-middle class," revealing again his fear of "falling into" the "lower-middle class." His comment suggests not only the highly unstable nature of current capitalism, but also his desire for the perpetuation of a class system, which is incompatible with his communist claims. Capitalism, the story indicates, has the power to become so entrenched in daily life that it produces contradictions such as the protagonist: a self-proclaimed communist who seems to have little interest in truly building an egalitarian society. Conservatism out of fear of losing one's social status engulfs even those who seem to have revolutionary intentions.

The narrator of "Comentário na rede sobre tudo o que está acontecendo por aí," in turn, is radically against advocates for human rights who, in his view, defend criminals who deserve the death penalty for the crimes they have committed against "cidadãos de bem" ("good citizens"; Sant'Anna 22). According to him, these "criminals" are living the good life in prison with free food paid for by taxpayers and it is people like the narrator himself who lack human rights.

He also blames human rights advocates for the increase of crime in the country, in part because they defend gun control laws, taking away the citizens' right to defend themselves (Sant'Anna 22). His opinion echoes the support of many Brazilians for taking the law into their own hands; support that in turn sounds familiar to those who follow the debate on gun safety in the United States. According to Universidade de São Paulo Emeritus Professor of Sociology José de Souza Martins, since World War II, the number of cases of lynching in Brazil has increased considerably, reaching an average of one case per day. He adds that periods of political instability have contributed to the rise in those numbers and cites three main peaks in the time in question: World War II, the military dictatorship, and the protests in 2013, just a year before the publication of Sant'Anna's *O Brasil é bom*. The most recent rise generated growing support not only for reducing the legal age for criminal responsibility from 18 to 16 ("Após Cunha"), but also for relaxing or altogether ending the Estatuto do Desarmamento (Disarmament Statute), approved during the Lula administration, which restricts possession of firearms. Per a proposal put forth by the so-called "Bancada da Bala"[20] in Congress, the Estatuto would be eliminated, allowing any citizen older than twenty-one to carry a gun, provided that they pass a psychiatric test and that they have not committed a crime (J. Carvalho).

The proposal, whose opponents denounced as benefiting firearms companies that have financed the electoral campaign of those who support it, was not approved ("Comissão rejeita"). However, it signaled the growing political prominence of extreme conservatism in Brazil, as represented in Sant'Anna's short stories under analysis, also evidenced by a reference to another *bancada*, the "Bancada da Bíblia."[21] The narrator of "Comentário na rede" uses the Bible to justify his rant against human rights groups, affirming that the situation should be handled in terms of "an eye for an eye."

In line with his ultra-conservative views, the narrator also blames sexual assault on the victims, suggesting that rape is a consequence of women's "devious" behavior when they imitate what they see on "degrading" soap operas (Sant'Anna 22). Lastly, recalling the slogan used by the dictatorial regime in the 1970s,

Chapter One

"Brasil, ame-o ou deixe-o" ("Brazil, love it or leave it"), the narrator suggests that those who are not "green and yellow"—an allusion to the colors of the Brazilian flag, which were appropriated by predominantly middle-class protesters who supported President Rousseff's ousting—should leave the country instead of criticizing the measures that he supports. He therefore demonstrates little openness to dialogue on controversial issues. His statements, which can be summarized as a series of repetitive and rather simplistic comments on the complex issue of violence in Brazil—an issue that has to do with socioeconomic, racial, and political factors—reflect a far-right discourse that one can encounter on social media in Brazil today. In this way, as the title suggests, the short story reads like online comments about the issues in question.

As these stories indicate, and as we would see a few years later with President Jair Bolsonaro's ascension to power, a neoconservative subjectivity has been on the rise in Brazilian society, dangerously questioning human rights, propagating nationalism and ideals of morality, and attempting to control the advancement of social equality. This neoconservatism that expresses neoliberalism's authoritarian roots, while certainly present among the Brazilian elite, has not, however, been restricted to them, as Pinheiro-Machado and Scalco demonstrate ("Da esperança"). According to these authors, this conservative subjectivity reveals itself among low-income segments of the Brazilian male youth, who see in Bolsonaro a symbol of power and the promise of reestablishment of morality in the face of so much corruption and violence. This explanation sheds light onto the spread of neoconservatism across social class in Brazilian society that we see in some of the short stories by Sant'Anna addressed in the section that follows.

Brazil, a Country of "Nice" People

In *O Brasil é bom*, one of the consequences of Brazil's pursuit of consumer dreams is the deterioration of social relations within and across socioeconomic boundaries, as portrayed in "Amando uns aos outros" ("Loving one another"), "Só" ("Alone"), and "Lodaçal" ("Swamp"). Similar to Bonassi's representation of everyday life as alienated and domesticated by capital, these stories propose that social relations are either rendered artificial or altogether eliminated by capitalist interests.

A Consumer's Dystopia

In "Amando uns aos outros," the reader goes into the thoughts of two characters, a man and a woman, who appear to be talking to themselves about whether or not they should go on a vacation to an unspecified location. Evidence that what we read corresponds to what the characters are thinking is a shift in the linguistic register when the focus of the story changes from the man to the woman. In the first case, the voice uses the second person pronoun "tu" to refer to his interlocutor, whereas the second voice uses "você." The shift in gender is indicated by adjectives in the masculine in the first part of the narrative and adjectives in the feminine in the second part, which are used by the characters, through free indirect speech, for self-description. Additionally, while the first voice uses words such as "cara" and "mané," the second voice uses a more "sophisticated" register, expressed by words such as "palidez" ("paleness"), "tom" ("tone"), and "espírito" ("spirit"; Sant'Anna 45). This distinction suggests a difference in social class, which is further emphasized by the experiences that each character would have during this vacation time: while he would be sharing a house with twenty people who would be getting drunk and "entupindo a única privada da casa" ("clogging up the only toilet in the house"; 44), she would rather enjoy a trip to Indonesia, away from people like him, "essa gente se esfregando pelas ruas, suada, feia, sem dente, vendendo coisa barata, comprando coisa que não devia ser vendida, bebendo pinga, berrando palavrão, ..." ("these people rubbing against each other in the streets, sweaty, ugly, toothless, selling cheap things, buying things that should not be sold, drinking booze, yapping swear words"; 45). The woman's high social status is further emphasized by her savoring of wine while listening to jazz at home. Different, modern, technological, with her skin exuding a "precise balance between tan and pale," the woman sees herself as superior. The man's lower social status, on the other hand, is indicated by his cheap tie and the fact that, unlike the woman, who seems to have plenty of free time, he has to work overtime during the weekend.

Separated by social status, the protagonists are, nevertheless, united in a world view informed by discourses on consumption. The man tries to convince himself that he, similar to Bonassi's protagonist, deserves to enjoy free time, a free time that would ultimately allow him to be able to return to the grueling work routine later, after having made memories with the family. At the same time, this voice reminds him of the challenges of traveling with the family and the things that he would not like about the experience. Nevertheless, according to that voice, the protagonist should go, for "todo mundo vai" ("everybody is going"), thus suggesting that he should conform to what everyone else is doing. Finally, the voice conveys a sense of social panic by pointing out to the protagonist that he must be careful with the violence that increases during that time of the year, for it would not be until they could get rid of "these human rights advocates" that this violence would come to an end. His attitude toward those who are socioeconomically below him mirrors the woman's attitude toward someone like him, thus revealing his reproduction of social class boundaries in which one attempts to separate him/herself from an "inferior" other. The woman, in turn, has incorporated discourses that equate happiness with consumption. She tells herself that she has everything that it takes to be a happy person: a mind open to new experiences, disposition to constantly create new trends, access to the most modern technologies, and a smile always on her face. This smile, however, seems only fake, for, as the voice tells her, being happy is an obligation in today's society (Sant'Anna 45). In this way, "Amando uns aos outros" reads almost as a commercial, in which we watch two characters on a split screen listen to their inner voices telling them what (not) to do as they confront the everyday problem of how to be happy in consumer society. The open ending of the short story suggests that, unlike in a commercial, there is no magical product that will solve the characters' problems.

The short story "Só" presents a radically bleak view of social relations, proclaiming that in capitalism there is only solitude. The narrator speaks to an unidentified interlocutor, who could be the reader, saying that he/she is alone in life, for everyone—his/her co-workers, school teacher, family members—is running after money, in a race to try to beat the insecurity caused by the increasing economic instability that affects the majority living under capitalism. This race turns life into a meaningless "amontoado de dias" ("pile of days"), rather than a steady line of progression toward a future goal (Sant'Anna 56). The short story denounces the superficial relations into which one is forced to enter in consumer capitalism. The law of the survival of the fittest demands that each person protect him/herself by avoiding getting to know others too closely and having their livelihood potentially threatened by association

(57). Everything in capitalist life is reduced to money, according to the narrator: you are money, education is seen as a means to find a job so that you can earn money, and the only goal of having a job is to earn money. There is, therefore, no space for personal fulfillment, collective projects, or the acquisition of knowledge beyond the mere goal of becoming rich. From the narrator's perspective,

> Você está só porque a imagem de uma criança toda queimada, toda suja de lama numa maca suja, cheia de moscas voando ao redor, é apenas uma imagem na televisão, patrocinada por um banco que finge ser seu amigo, finge estar à sua disposição no momento que você mais precisar dele, aquele banco legal, aquele banco amigão.
> Você está só porque tem dinheiro.
> Você está só porque não tem dinheiro.
> Você está só por causa do dinheiro.
> Só dinheiro.
> Só. (Sant'Anna 58)

> You are alone simply because the image on television of a child with burns all over her body, covered in mud, laying on a dirty stretcher, flies swirling around, is just an image on television, sponsored by a bank that pretends to be your friend, that pretends to be available to you any time you need it, that cool, buddy-like bank.
> You are alone because you have money.
> You are alone because you don't have money.
> You are alone because of money.
> Only money.
> Only [money] / Alone.[22]

In the quoted passage, the commercial's effort to mobilize the viewer's compassion fails due to the desensitization that the media creates by reproducing images of a reality that is elsewhere, far away from the viewer. The bank appears as a symbol of financial capitalism and the friendliness expressed in marketing campaigns hides the cruel reality of social inequality that the economic system in question promotes. The last lines of the passage denounce money as being the main problem of the world, whether for its presence (money does not necessarily bring happiness) or its absence (lack of money brings suffering). Repeating the word "só" ("only, alone"), the narrator emphasizes the emptiness of life in consumer capitalism: your life is empty if all you care about is material goods, on one hand; and your life is empty if your economically poor condition transforms you into a mere image on television for others to simply ignore. The primacy of money over compassionate human relations is in fact conveyed in practically every story of Sant'Anna's book, when characters or narrators repeatedly proclaim that money "is the most important thing there is."

The violence of consumer capitalism is brutally apparent in the story "Lodaçal," which follows the lives of two street kids, Chiquinho and Toninho. The protagonists live in Brejo da Cruz, described by the narrator as "uma aldeia, um lodaçal, é umas quatro/cinco casas, é nada ..." ("a village, a swamp, [it] is four or five houses, it is nothing ..."; Sant'Anna 69). The narrator emphasizes the idea of nothingness several times so as to point out the low capital value of the village, whose only "production" is a few children "ready for consumption," that is, ready to be semi-enslaved by nearby farm owners (71).

Chiquinho and Toninho, like their village, are thus judged by their potential productivity and the extremely low value of their labor. In a country where consumption, especially consumption of technology, is equated with progress, Chiquinho and Toninho have never seen a television. Drug use becomes their escape from the brutal reality of poverty and hunger, almost in a kind of replacement of the entertainment that the mass media to which they do not have access would provide (Sant'Anna 73). As they embark on a hallucination while smoking marijuana, the reader joins them in different scenarios presented by the narrator, in which Toninho and Chiquinho seem to follow different paths in life. In each scenario, either Chiquinho or Toninho reproduces certain discourses about the other's socioeconomic situation. For instance, in one of these scenarios, Toninho is a taxi driver. His opinion about street kids echoes that of characters from other short stories in *O Brasil é bom*. He states that Brazil's problem is that it needs the death penalty for kids who do drugs, who rape, and even kill, since, in his view, they commit crimes because they are protected for being underage (76). Toninho makes this comment in response to Chiquinho having stolen a necklace from a girl. Toninho is in favor of lynching Chiquinho and even steps on his head. In another scenario, Toninho is the door attendant of a theater where

A Consumer's Dystopia

Chiquinho is an actor. Toninho treats Chiquinho with prejudice, referring to him as "bichinha nordestina," ("little Northeastern faggot") and "paraíba viadinho" ("little *paraíba* faggot"; 88).

As these examples illustrate, the future that the two kids see when they hallucinate while on drugs is mostly bleak. Even when one or both of them are imagined as having attained some level of success, their views perpetuate certain capitalist ideas and/or convey prejudice. For example, in the scenario in which Chiquinho is an actor, he hopes to become famous one day and he works toward this goal in part by reading *Pense e fique rico*, the Portuguese version of Napoleon Hill's *Think and Grow Rich* (1937), a best-seller that claims to provide the secret to attain material and spiritual prosperity. In Sant'Anna's story, the protagonist is meant to stand as an example that hard work leads to success. According to the narrator, Chiquinho dreams of the day when he will give an interview and his story will be revealed, for he

> tinha tudo para dar errado, uma criança que só tinha sapo para comer, que trabalhou honestamente como criança escrava cortando cana, sem reclamar, sem roubar, sem vender o próprio corpo, estudando muito, lendo muito, sempre disposto a aprender porque quem tem garra e força de vontade, quem trabalha com afinco, quem nunca se acomoda sempre alcança um lugar ao sol ... (Sant'Anna 97–98)

> had everything against him, a child who only had frogs to eat, who worked honestly as a slave child harvesting sugar cane, without complaining, without stealing, without becoming a prostitute, studying a lot, reading a lot, and always willing to learn because those who have determination and will power, those who work hard, who never settle for less always find a place in the sun ...

At first sight, Chiquinho's story values the image of the docile poor, who "does not complain about anything," while reinforcing the idea that one's success or failure is their own responsibility (Bauman, *Liquid Modernity* 68). Nevertheless, the sarcasm in the narrator's language, revealed by the uncomfortably awkward use of "honestly" to qualify slave work, points out not only the oppression of which Chiquinho is a victim, but also the absurdity of a neoliberal discourse of self-entrepreneurship that erases the impact of one's socioeconomic background on one's chances to succeed.

Chapter One

As "Lodaçal" progresses, the different scenarios and the back-and-forth between several Chiquinhos and Toninhos create confusion, hinting at the chaos that permeates the reality represented in the narrative. The Chiquinhos and Toninhos can be interpreted not just as possible versions of the protagonists' future selves, but also as the many Chiquinhos and Toninhos that inhabit Brazil today, and the potential socioeconomic and ideological divides between them.

Brazil Isn't Too Bad. Or Is It?

As the stories analyzed so far suggest, and another short story in the collection, "Use sempre camisinha" ("Always wear a condom"), corroborates, the aggressive competitiveness of consumer capitalism spreads as Brazilians are encouraged to be violent in their relationships, from sex to work, beating up others, and profiting as much as they can from every situation (Sant'Anna 24–25). In such a toxic environment, it seems that one of the few possible solutions according to *O Brasil é bom* is that people with attitudes like those of the protagonists of these stories simply do not reproduce, possibly leading to the extinction of Brazilians as a people altogether.

The short story that perhaps most radically questions Brazil is "O Brasil não é ruim," ("Brazil is not bad"), in which a narrator strings a sequence of sentences in the negative form about Brazil, such as "Os deputados brasileiros não são vagabundos, não ganham quase vinte e cinco mil reais por mês mais uma série de ajudas de custo como passagens aéreas, casa, comida, roupa lavada, etc." ("Brazilian congressmen/women are not lazy, they do not make almost twenty-five thousand *reais* a month, plus a number of bonuses for air travel, housing, food, clothing, etc."; Sant'Anna 11). The narrator denounces corruption among politicians (financed campaigns, political alliances); claims that hosting the Olympics and the World Cup is evidence that Brazil is a rich country; comments on the number of street kids and on violence, ending the short story with the sentence, "Por isso que o Brasil é bom" ("That is why Brazil is good"; 13). The latter sentence, which is essentially a slightly modified version of the title of the short story in question, is the only affirmative sentence in the narrative. The "não" that is missing in it is exhaustingly repeated in every single sentence of the story. If we invert this syntactic structure, that is, if we remove all the "náos" in the text and add a "não" to the last sentence, turning it into "Por isso que o Brasil *não* é bom," the narrator's sarcasm turns into direct and acidic criticism to Brazilian society, especially with regard to the rampant political corruption, and the prioritization of capital and private interests over human rights.

Everything seems to be wrong with this Brazil. Such a country, the short story "O juízo final" ("Judgment Day") indicates, perhaps can only be successful in the future if it can erase itself and its history and start from scratch. In this story, Jesus says to an interlocutor on the day when he descends upon Earth that he will reward those who have been good and punish those who have misbehaved. In his monologue, he condemns capitalism and consumer culture, denouncing the incredible distortion of his teachings by those in power. He complains about having been transformed into an instrument of banal oppression, a guardian of others' masturbation and the controller of women's skirt length (Sant'Anna 66). Moreover, he points out the transformation of God into the "God of Money," highlighting the sinful behavior in which his "followers" incur by driving "aqueles automóveis com vidro preto para que os mendigos, os leprosos, as adúlteras, os filhos de Deus não possam olhar vocês nos olhos …" ("those cars with windows tinted so that beggars, lepers, and adulteresses, the children of God are not able to look you in the eye …"; 67). Finally, he declares that those "without a car or a credit card" will inherent the kingdom of God, for they are like Jesus: "cabeludo meio hippie, meio mendigo, meio comunista, com essa mania meio hippie, meio comunista, meio maluca de repartir o pão e compartilhar o amor" ("hairy, a bit hippie, a bit beggar, a bit communist, with these a bit hippie, a bit communist, a bit crazy habits of sharing bread and love"; 67). Jesus then denounces capitalism as non-Christian-like and, after declaring that only about half a dozen people will be saved—capitalism is so encompassing, after all!—detonates everything, as suggested by the last word of the short story, "Bum" ("Boom"; 68). This is, then, the destiny that Brazil and Brazilians—and by extension anyone who aligns themselves with capitalist values—deserve according to *O Brasil é bom*: annihilation. These short stories by Sant'Anna, like Bonassi's *Luxúria*, declare that there is no way out of consumer capitalism, as one moves from total alienation to total destruction.

Chapter One

Policing Consumption

As my analysis has shown, *Luxúria* and *O Brasil é bom* make a harsh critique to post-2003 Brazil, portraying the country as sinful and delusional, as it witnesses the collapse of its unsustainable socioeconomic growth. While Bonassi's and Sant'Anna's critiques are in many ways valid and to some extent even prophetic, given the aggravation of the political and economic crisis that followed the publication of the books in question, their portrayal of working-class consumers' role in Brazil's doom deserves some careful consideration.

In the case of Bonassi, the narrator often quite explicitly describes working-class characters as irrational. This irrationality comes across, for instance, when the man and his wife approach Paraíso das Piscinas for the first time, "atraídos, incomodados, cegados, excitados e hipnotizados pelo barulho das cascatas, dos refletores e dos holofotes apontados diretamente para eles" ("attracted, bothered, blinded, excited, and hypnotized by the sound of the cascades, by the reflectors and the spotlights pointed directly at them"; Bonassi, *Luxúria* 64). The store is similarly described as a place conducive to irrationality, for it displays a

> confusão de números, letras e slogans determinada por economistas e publicitários, para que todos sejam levados a um único pensamento:
>
> (...) (65–66)
>
> confusion of numbers, letters, and slogans devised by economists and marketing agents so that everyone is taken over by one only thought:
>
> (...)

As the use of ellipsis within parenthesis in the passage above suggests, ads at the store are designed to restrict or even eliminate consumers' abilities to think critically, in efforts to make them easy to manipulate into buying anything.

Besides being portrayed as easy to seduce, characters are also sometimes described as animalistic in *Luxúria*. For example, the factory workers are said to "[raciocinar] precariamente" ("reason precariously") when hungry (Bonassi, *Luxúria* 101); every day at lunch time, they "saltam desembestados uns sobre os outros para agarrar talheres e bandejas de metal, palitos de madeira e guardanapos de papel" ("jump haphazardly over one another in order to grab utensils and metal trays, toothpicks, and paper napkins"; 102). In another instance, the narrator uses the verb "to growl" to describe the way that the boy, the wife, the housekeeper, the contractor, and the construction workers speak (201–02). Lastly, characters' attitudes toward their peers' ability to acquire goods is described as one of jealousy and repulsion, with no sign of any kind of feelings of solidarity or happiness for others' accomplishments (206).

In Sant'Anna's case, although he does direct plenty of criticism to the middle and upper classes, the contrast between the different points of view of the stories suggests the reproduction of some the same prejudices against working-class consumption that we see in Bonassi's novel. There is a moral judgment that attempts to negate the right to pleasure to this class and that blames their "excesses" as consumers for the downfall of the country. Meanwhile, middle- and upper-class consumption appears problematic insofar as it is seen as empty, elitist, or a vehicle of prejudice, but not so much as responsible for the socioeconomic crisis that the country faces. If the stories narrated in first person can be read as transcriptions or snapshots of certain social types, thus offering some critical distance from their points of view, the stories narrated in third person or in which the point of view seems rather ambiguous are open to a different type of interpretation. The latter stories leave the reader with the impression that a kind of master-narrator that sews the stories together—and that is characteristic of Sant'Anna's work—reproduces, rather than questions the same elitist view mocked in other stories of *O Brasil é bom*.

While one can appreciate Bonassi's and Sant'Anna's use of caricature for the purpose of criticism, and their suggestion that in the end, working-class individuals are the ones most negatively affected by consumer capitalism, their representation of this segment's behavior as consumers comes across at times as rather simplistic and even prejudiced. Anthropological research suggests that reality is much more complex. Although it is true that the Brazilian working class has incorporated certain values of neoliberalism, these values have not been necessarily incorporated as neoliberal per se, but rather as an understanding that one should have the *right* to improve one's social condition. According to William Nozaki (2017), the consumption of many goods and services that are perceived by the middle class as a luxury, are often solutions that working-class families find to replace the safety net that they lack. He cites the example of a woman he interviewed for his research, who used the money she received from the income distribution program Bolsa Família to pay for cable television so that her daughter can be left at home alone watching the Cartoon Network channel while she is out working. As Nozaki points out, for this woman, cable television is not a luxury, but rather a way to deal with the unavailability of daycare.

Furthermore, as Pinheiro-Machado and Scalco note, it is important to keep in mind that recent working-class consumption in Brazil is informed by a context in which capitalism tells individuals that goods are for all while controlling access to such goods and thus contradicting its claims to democratic access to commodities and rights. As the authors in question point out in their presentation "The Right to Pleasure: Poverty, Politics, and Consumption in Neoliberal Brazil":

> Consumption enables imagination of a better life (Appadurai 1996), but in a highly segregated country this dream is experienced in a way that society makes several contrary efforts to put "the poor in their place," making the oppression noticeable. Low-income groups face the contradiction of unequal neoliberal societies: while the market and policies say "buy things," a discriminatory backlash culture delegitimises their autonomy.

While certainly emphasizing the pressures of consumer capitalism on their working-class characters, Bonassi's and Sant'Anna's negative portrayal of these consumers seems to suggest that the consumption by the "poor," and the consumption by the poor only, needs to be controlled. While deeming any kind of consumption as simply irrational is problematic in itself, their choice of treating consumer habits among working-class members as such while leaving out, for instance, the middle-class' shopping sprees in the U.S. that occurred during the same period, reinforces the prejudiced idea that the poor must, indeed, "be put in their place."

To conclude, in both Bonassi's and in Sant'Anna's portrayals of Brazil, a dystopic nation emerges, where relations of solidarity disintegrate. The overall image of Brazilian society is one of temporary and illusory progress. The writers criticize the Workers' Party's administration for what they perceive as a problematic path to social equality. For them, stimulating consumption leads to stimulating greed, individualism, and irrationality and eventually brings self-destruction, as tension accumulates though everyday (micro)aggressions. Consumer culture appears as deeply embedded in Brazilian everyday life, informing several spheres, including religion, as prosperity gospel gains much ground in the country.

In these narratives, Brazilians as consumers simply reproduce a deeply ingrained social hierarchy that has roots in slavery and that was promoted by authoritarian regimes. Brazil comes across as a nation that still lacks a plan to develop *values* about equality and human rights (Pinheiro-Machado "A falência"), a project that the Workers' Party had the opportunity to take up, but instead, appears to have sold out to neoliberalism and given in to corruption, having had its ethics questioned and its public image damaged. While Sant'Anna emphasizes the oppressive and prejudiced values of the middle and upper classes, Bonassi suggests that low-income sectors are bound to aspire to become oppressors one day, as they gain more access to consumer goods. Consumer culture is thus seen as highly corrosive of social relations. In this Brazil, therefore, there seems to be no way out. Everyday life has been conquered by consumer capitalism once and for all and there is no hope for the future.

Bonassi and Sant'Anna, therefore, paint a rather totalizing picture of consumer capitalism. In their narratives, *homo oeconomicus* seems to have, for the most part, prevailed over *homo politicus*, fulfilling Brown's prophecy (39). Their protagonists are a kind of entrepreneurs of themselves. Consequently, their relationship with others is one of competition rather than solidarity. The vast majority of Sant'Anna's characters seem to have been completely conquered by the neoliberal logic. Incapable of seeing the social structures that generate the socioeconomic imbalances around them—or perceiving some of them when it is too late, in the case of Bonassi's protagonist—, they see those who have "failed" as deserving of their fate. The *homo politicus*, characterized by "deliberation, belonging, aspirational sovereignty, concern with the common and with one's relation to justice in the common"

(Brown 94), has practically disappeared from the world portrayed by the authors in question. Even when some of this conscience seems to be there, there is total disillusionment and a sense that characters have simply given up.

In the next chapter, I will look into two novels by two other writers who, like Bonassi and Sant'Anna, speak of this dystopic environment. Their characters are equally entrepreneurs of themselves, who have been completely overtaken by neoliberal ideas that permeate all spheres of their daily lives. While there is clearly no hope for these characters in particular, the novels analyzed in Chapter 2, nevertheless, envision a possible way out of this consuming world, albeit a rather utopic one, from the perspective of the fictional environments that they create.

Chapter Two

The Consuming Self

In the best-selling self-help book *The Secret* (2006) by Australian Rhonda Byrne, self-described teachers with credentials that include "personal coach," "moneymaking expert," and "visionary," ask the reader: "What kind of a house do you want to live in? Do you want to be a millionaire? What kind of a business do you want to have? Do you want more success? What do you really want?" A few pages later, they explain:

> Why do you think that 1 percent of the population earns around 96 percent of all the money that's being earned? Do you think that's an accident? It's designed that way. They understand something. They understand The Secret, and now you are being introduced to The Secret.

The book's contributors affirm categorically that the secret to success is within you, that all you need to do to achieve what you want is to think positively. According to them, this is the law of attraction, which is "as impartial and impersonal as the law of gravity is. It is precise, and it is exact" (27). In other words, if you do not get what you want, it is because you did not picture yourself enough as a successful person. The book and the homonymous film were certainly successful, for, combined, they generated $300 million dollars in revenue just three years after the initial release of the film in 2006 (Lidner).

The rhetoric of self-help books such as *The Secret* taps into one's wish to be visible, desired, talked about. It promises you the secret to unlock success in all areas of your life. As the quotes above illustrate, this success often entails owning commodities. The book's rhetoric goes hand in hand with what Bauman calls the commodification of the self, that is, the attempt to sell oneself as desirable

Chapter Two

by displaying commodities that make one look more socially attractive (*Consuming Life* 6). The process of commodification of the self is characteristic of what Bauman calls liquid modernity (*Liquid Modernity* 1), a term that he uses to refer to the current stage of capitalism. This stage is characterized by a liquid quality, which permeates all spheres of social life. Bauman contrasts this "liquid" society to that of "solid" Fordism. In the latter, capital was fixed, individuals started and ended their careers in the same job, and had a clear idea of what personal success meant and how to achieve it. In contrast, in the liquid society, job security and ideals of personal success float along with capital, generating a race toward a blurry future of instability and uncertainty (58). This instability calls for a search for anchors, one of which is the commodification of the self. In order to stay in the race, individuals are pushed to turn themselves into attractive and efficient products. In this process, we are led to turn even our behavior and our personality traits into commodities, often quite literally, as our electronic footprint allows corporations to profit on our personal data, which covers anything from our taste in music to our political leanings (Pariser 45).

In contemporary Brazilian fiction, the work of Lísias and B. Carvalho in *O livro dos mandarins* (*The Book of Mandarins*) and *Reprodução* (*Reproduction*), respectively, helps us think through this process of commodification. These narratives look into how the commodification of the self translates into everyday practices, criticizing its potential consequences, and reflecting on literature's role as a possible antidote to this commodifying process. *O livro dos mandarins* tells the story of Paulo, who works for an international bank. He is obsessed with professional success, which he measures by criteria such as how much networking one is capable of doing, or how closely one follows the model of his idol, former president of Brazil, Fernando Henrique Cardoso (1995–2003). The title of the novel references Paulo's homonymous book, which is written by his ghost writer, named *poeta* (poet) Paulo, based on Paulo's scattered notes about how to be successful in the corporate world through strategies that he develops as he attempts to climb the corporate ladder. As described early on in the narrative, the book is "uma espécie de guia para jovens executivos com análises financeiras, geopolíticas e dicas de gerenciamento" ("a kind of guide for young executives, with financial and geopolitical analyses and tips on management"; Lísias 72). *Reprodução*, in turn, follows a man, who is simply identified as "o estudante de chinês" ("the student of Chinese"), as he is stopped and interrogated by the police when trying to check in for a flight to China. The goal of the interrogation seems to be to catch the student's teacher of Chinese, who was supposed to take the same flight to China and is suspected of being involved in some kind of international trafficking scheme. As we follow the interrogation, we learn about the protagonist's arrogant and prejudiced personality, which is built on the less than reliable sources of information that he consumes online.

Both novels denounce their protagonists' failure to be the successful individuals that they believe themselves to be. We find out that instead of smart, well informed, and highly successful, Paulo and the student of Chinese are actually misinformed prejudiced men, who have achieved nothing but delusional views of themselves and of the world around them. By unveiling the failure behind the narratives of only apparent success that their protagonists attempt to tell, the novels in question ultimately denounce the pitfalls of the neoliberal thought that shapes the protagonists' experiences, while unveiling the subtle ways in which this thought permeates daily life in the twenty-first century. Through a language of excess, which piles up clichés, disconnected information, and often just plain nonsense, the novels expose the empty promises of the capitalist utopia and caution against the dangers of self-commodification, the most troubling of which, the novels suggest, is the breakdown of democracy. These novels' critique of authoritarian figures relying on superficial knowledge acquired within their bubbles—corporate culture, in the case of Lísias's protagonist; the blog sphere and social media, in the case of B. Carvalho's—conveys to us the urgency with which these issues need to be addressed.

From this perspective, consumption appears in the novels as an alienating force that blinds characters to social injustices and turns them into oppressors. Both characters are so immersed in consumer culture, so mesmerized by it, that there seems to be no way out of this alienated state for them. Nevertheless, unlike Bonassi's and Sant'Anna's take on the alienating powers of consumption, Lísias and B. Carvalho contemplate a possible solution, one that appears rather difficult to be achieved in their narratives: the reading of literature. I call this representation of existing in consumer culture *utopic reinvention*, for it is only in a realm beyond everyday life—one which these writers' protagonists are not capable of achieving—that change seems possible in the narratives in question.

Lísias's *O livro dos mandarins*: What Is in a Name?

The name of the protagonist of *O livro dos mandarins* is one of the most striking features of the novel. It takes reading no more than a few pages of the narrative to realize that almost every character holds a name that is in some way a variation of Paulo's. For example, his mother is Dona Paula; his secretary is Paula; her nephew is Paulo; her father is Seu Paulo. One of the bank employees from Scotland is Paul; the director of the bank's London branch is Paulson; a vice president of the Chilean branch is Paulino; an Irish employee of the corporation is Pauling. An Eastern European waitress who helps Paulo in London is Paulina; a Swedish woman that Paulo encounters in Sudan is Pauline; Pauline is married to a Paul; the "passport controller" in Sudan is Pauli; Paulo's ghost writer is known as "poeta Paulo"; and several other employees of the bank where Paulo works are also named either Paulo or Paula. Therefore, from the start, the reader learns that this novel revolves around one person and one person only, Paulo.

This repetition of names reflects consumer culture's subjectivity fetishism, which Bauman defines as a process by which consumers are dissolved into a sea of commodities and are imposed the task of "lifting themselves out of the grey and flat invisibility and insubstantiality making themselves stand out from the mass of indistinguishable objects" (*Consuming Life* 12). Read from this perspective, Lísias's choice to name almost everyone a version of the name Paulo not only points to the self-centered nature of the protagonist, but also emphasizes his commodity status and amplifies his need to stand out in a sea of "Paulos." In response to this need to make the character stand out, Paulo's name will change fifty times throughout the novel, with a unique identity—oftentimes based on his supposedly distinguished abilities—assigned to him with every name change. These identities, albeit specific to each context in which they are assigned in the narrative, are yet generic, for they could technically apply to anyone else with the same

The Consuming Self

characteristics. Many of these names are noun phrases that replace Paulo's name as the subject or object of several sentences, for paragraphs or even multiple pages, until he earns another designation, which will then become the new name used by the narrator to refer to Paulo. In this way, Paulo is named "o profissional brilhante" ("the brilliant professional"), "Versati" (a reference to the brand of clothes that he wears), "o samurai chinês" ("the Chinese samurai"), "homem feito" ("distinguished man"), "muito detalhista e metódico" ("very detailed and methodical"), "o homem realizado" ("the accomplished man"), and "o homem mais inteligente do mundo" ("the most intelligent man in the world"), among others. However, as the narrative constantly creates tension between the image of the perfect man that Paulo has of himself and how others actually see him, some of his names point to quite the opposite of success. This is the case, for example, of the derogative nickname he receives in Sudan "branquelo" ("whitey"), and other names by which his colleagues call him, such as "o torto" ("the warped"), "seu bobo" ("you fool"), or simply "aquele cara que foi pra China" ("that dude who went to China"). Paulo's name changes mark the oscillation of his identity between a generic unimportant or even worthless object and a commodity to which certain positive values are attached in order to make it more marketable.

Paulo's name changes convey his value to the bank specifically as, according to the narrator, Paulson's impression of the protagonist becomes progressively positive while he reads his application to participate in the company's "China Project," of which Paulo hoped to be the leader. As Paulson reads the application documents, he replaces each letter of Paulo's name with a star supposedly to indicate Paulo's outstanding qualities. The main criteria for using the stars seems to be Paulo's degree of loyalty to the bank. He receives the first star when Paulson reads Paulo's note that a company's employee "jamais [deve revelar] os segredos de uma empresa, [e sim levá-los] para o túmulo" ("must never reveal a company's secrets, but rather take them to the grave"; Lísias 47). Paulson adds two more stars to Paulo's name after a preliminary interview, as he notices more signs of Paulo's loyalty to the bank. A fourth star is added when Paulson decides that Paulo deserves to move on to the second phase of the competition after he shows absolute fidelity to the bank by firing his own girlfriend for what they claim to be good cause. Finally, the last letter of Paulo's name is replaced by a star after he impresses Paulson while giving a presentation in London. This presentation prompts the director to designate Paulo as the leader of the China project in what is supposedly a secret mission. While the stars are meant to represent Paulo's excellence—only to the extent to which he puts the bank above everything else in his life—they also represent the increasing effacement of Paulo's identity as an individual and his reification, that is, his transformation into a tool completely at the service of the company.

In the neoliberal environment in which Paulo lives, his quest for perfection translates into an obsession with cultivating an image of strength and success that aligns with consumer society's values. One of these values is the same idea that some of Sant'Anna's short stories criticize, which is that one's success or failure is entirely up to them. Paulo's book, titled *O livro dos mandarins*, like the homonymous narrative in which he is a character, reproduces these values of self-entrepreneurship, like self-help books such as the aforementioned best seller *The Secret*, as well as the tenets of prosperity theology that we addressed in Chapter 1. According to him, his book intends to help readers avoid falling short of a successful life by "taking control of their own destiny."

Among the many ways in which this operation must take place, Paulo notes that networking is essential. He explicitly says that if you do not make as much money as you deserve, it is your fault because it is the result of you not networking properly. His comment references the Chinese practice of *guanxi*, which is the use of personal ties for economic purposes that is part of China's current capitalist practices (Pinheiro-Machado, "Fazendo guanxi" 99). On the other hand, his comment also evokes the philosophy of Multilevel Marketing companies (MLMs). These companies have recently acquired much visibility in Brazil. Like their American counterparts ("Multilevel Marketing"), they focus heavily on a rhetoric of consumption in order to convince people to join in the business. For instance, they bring in members who have achieved success to tell the stories of how they were able to afford the house and the car(s) of their dreams. Hashtags on social media such as #anovaeconomia (#theneweconomy) encapsulate the branding of these MLMs in Brazil as the most promising way to reach financial stability in the twenty-first century. The use of other hashtags such as #lawofattraction (a reference to Byrne's book, *The Secret*) on social media by members of MLMs both in the United States and Brazil, along with their comments attributing their financial prosperity to God, indicates a close connection between MLMs and the tenets of the prosperity gospel.

Drawing on a rhetoric similar to that of these organizations about one's responsibility for their own success, Lísias's protagonist later on blames employees again for being fired, saying that only idiots lose their jobs because they do not manage the situation well, thus making themselves unemployable. The "unemployment paradox," he says, explains that if people who lose their jobs knew how to manage challenging situations through networking, they would not have lost their jobs in the first place (Lísias 158). Likewise, it is imperative for one to be self-confident because someone who lacks confidence will never be promoted (63). As an indication of the spread of the ideas of success propagated by Paulo, his book is said to be intended for "um público mais amplo, simplesmente todas as pessoas que estão atrás de exemplos de sucesso, inspirações para uma postura diária mais enriquecedora ou um pouco de filosofia que sirva para a vida" ("a broader audience, simply anyone who is looking for examples of success, inspiration for a more enriching everyday behavior and a little bit of philosophy that is useful for life"; 207). Paulo's description of his book's target audience, which encompasses virtually everyone, points to the pervasiveness of neoliberal principles in twenty-first century Brazilian society. These principles, the novel suggests, apply to individuals' lives from the very moment they are born, as exemplified by Paulo's secretary's family's plans for her nephew's future. When the child is born, the first thing that everyone in the family agrees on is that the best way to start building a future of success for him is to make sure that he will have his own business (42). In the novel, one's identity is thus inescapably shaped by neoliberal capital.

Of Great Leaders and Neoliberal Thought

Much of Paulo's philosophy comes from a, to say the least, questionable appropriation of Confucian thought, as evidenced by the protagonist's multiple references to the Chinese philosopher in question. Confucius, who was also a teacher and a politician, developed ideas of personal growth through morality.

Chapter Two

Confucius's China, of around 500 BC, bore some resemblance to the context of consumer culture in which Lísias's novel takes place. That was a period of conspicuous consumption, displayed by nobles' and rulers' way of life. China was steeped in war, treason, passion for money, and self-interest. After the breakdown of feudalism, as a consequence of the end of the Zhou dynasty, the rules regarding the right to be a lord became complex because there was no longer one single way in which someone could claim political power. Consequently, several plots to claim the possession of land were set in motion within and across families, resulting in the reduction of the number of feudal states from one hundred twenty to only seven in a span of about five hundred years (Rainey 3). Given such a context of violence and selfishness, Confucius considered it necessary to develop through education virtues such as filial piety, honesty and sincerity, dutifulness, loyalty, and rightness, which would in turn lead to what he called Humanity, an umbrella term for all virtues, which was understood as the opposite of self-interest. For the philosopher, Humanity is to be expressed through rituals as a way to achieve a state of Gentleman. The latter term is defined by Confucius as an example of moral behavior, and is presented in contrast to the petty man, whom Confucius characterizes as arrogant, but never grand (42).

Paulo's version of Confucius's ideas are to be spread with the publication of his book, which reads like a cross between Byrne's *The Secret* and Confucius's *Analects*: decontextualized rules of behavior that, if followed, are supposed to guarantee the achievement of success. However, in spite of his seeking inspiration in Confucius, Paulo's behavior, as well as the behavior that he encourages in his teachings about corporate culture, actually coincide, for the most part, with that of Confucius's notion of the petty man. Unlike Confucius's *Analects*, which strongly opposed "greed for money, possessions, and power ... [as well as being] desperate to be famous and to indulge in sensual pleasure" (Rainey 35), the fictitious *O livro dos mandarins* values quite the opposite. The latter is meant to be a kind of bible of corporate culture, that is, a set of guidelines whose goal is to help alleviate the uncertainties of everyday life and to build employees' identities within the company, so that they will work more, better, and be more competitive. Paulo's book, therefore, reinforces corporate culture values such as ambition, efficiency, profitability, the creation of wealth, and, indirectly, the transformation of each individual's life into a mini-business in itself, generating stress and contaminating social relations (L. Barbosa). These values clash in many ways with Confucius's ideals, thus transforming Paulo's book into a guide to commodifying oneself in order to (supposedly) thrive in consumer capitalism.

Confucius's work "inspires" not only Paulo's book, but also a business of his own, which he claims to be a consulting firm for executives. He names the firm Confucius and describes it as:

> uma consultoria que traz ao Brasil, pela primeira vez, os valores com que a moderna China tem enfrentado o mundo contemporâneo, casando-os com as ideias do sociólogo e ex–presidente Fernando Henrique Cardoso. Qualquer pessoa que passe uma semana que seja em Pequim percebe como os antigos comunistas souberam se adaptar às regras do mercado, e inclusive transformaram diversos pontos negativos em conquistas próprias. (Lísias 314–15)

> a consulting firm that brings to Brazil, for the first time, the values with which modern China has faced the contemporary world, marrying them to the ideas of sociologist and former president Fernando Henrique Cardoso. Anyone who spends even just one week in Beijing notices how old communists [there] were successful in adapting to the rules of the market, including how they turned various negative aspects [of their culture] into achievements of their own.

Paulo thus chooses a name for his firm as homage to someone who, in fact, would likely be very much against many of the precepts of consumer culture that the protagonist's company means to emphasize. Indeed, a closer look at Paulo's philosophy reveals that it is more in line with a more recent version of Confucianism. This version, which was established in 1958 and named New Confucianism, supports capitalism and intends to combine traditional Chinese values with a modernizing Western mentality (Rainey 188). However, while New Confucians argue that bringing Confucius's ideas back—which had been practically extinguished since Mao Zedong's Cultural Revolution[1]—would prevent some of the negative consequences of capitalism, such as individualism, selfishness, and materialism, Paulo finds inspiration

Chapter Two

in Fernando Henrique Cardoso's policies in line with neoliberal thought, which is at the heart of some of these very consequences.

Paulo develops an obsession with ex-president of Brazil Fernando Henrique Cardoso, commonly known by his initials, FHC. He refers to Cardoso countless times throughout the novel as a model for those who want to achieve professional and personal success. He describes President Cardoso as "o cara que mudou a história do país" ("the guy who changed the country's history"; Lísias 36), the one who had a "governo insuperável" ("insurmountable administration"; 65), and who was responsible for a "transformação histórica" ("historical transformation"; 53) of the country.

The historical transformation to which the protagonist refers is Cardoso's success in turning Brazil into a neoliberal state. Cardoso believed that Brazil would achieve economic growth through the privatization of industries, the cutting of regulations, and the opening of the market to foreign investment (Goertzel 128). During his first term, he significantly expanded the privatization process that had started with his predecessor, impeached President Fernando Collor de Melo (1990–92), in order to include utility companies, railways, and banks. He then used part of the revenue to pay short-term government debts (131). In addition, he increased taxes, cut government spending, particularly retirement benefits, in response to the business sector's complaints that government regulations that guaranteed benefits such as pensions and leaves made national businesses less competitive in the international scene. FHC also pushed for subcontracting to nongovernmental agencies in order to increase efficiency. In other words, despite his reluctance to admit it,[2] FHC closely followed the tenets of neoliberal thought, which Harvey defines as

> a theory of political and economic practices that proposes that human well-being can best be advanced by liberating individual entrepreneurial freedoms and skills within an institutional framework characterized by strong private property rights, free markets, and free trade. The role of the state is to create and preserve an institutional framework appropriate to such practices ... if markets do not exist (in areas such as land, water, education, health care, social security, or environmental pollution) then they must be created, by state action, if necessary. But beyond these tasks the state should not venture ... Neoliberalism has ... pervasive effects on ways of thought to

the point where it has become incorporated into the common-sense way many of us interpret, live in, and understand the world. ("Introduction," *A Brief History*)

Lísias's protagonist exemplifies this (extreme, in his case) incorporation of neoliberal thought as common sense, for his life, both professionally and personally, is guided by these neoliberal principles. It is no surprise, then, that FHC becomes such an idol for Paulo, to the point of a simple glance at a picture of the ex-president—which Paulo carries with him like many Brazilians would carry a picture of a saint in their pockets or wallets—gives him strength to continue to pursue his corporate career. The picture even has the power to nearly bring the protagonist to tears. Repeating the discourse of those who defended FHC's candidacy against former union leader Luís Inácio Lula da Silva, who was painted as unprepared to become president allegedly due to, among other reasons, his lack of formal higher education, Paulo considers FHC a "verdadeiro intelectual" ("true intellectual"; Lísias 87) and a "verdadeiro conhecedor da alma humana" ("true expert in the human soul"; 94). For Paulo, FHC has a "espécie de luz que emana das pessoas que se acham importantes e torna seus olhos meio opacos, o rosto cheio de nuances e o corpo um pouco mais alto" ("a kind of light that emanates from those people who consider themselves important and that makes their eyes look somewhat opaque, the face filled with nuances and the body a bit taller"; 135). This description shows a god-like FHC, a savior. Indeed, Cardoso ascended to power mainly thanks to his ability to do what seemed impossible at the time: pull the country out of a deep recession. His success in the elections stemmed, in part, from the creation of the *Real* Plan, developed when he was Minister of Finance during the Itamar Franco administration (1993–94). Strategically, the plan was launched with the goal of bringing inflation down just at the time when voters, feeling its positive effects, would be compelled to vote for Cardoso in the upcoming presidential elections. With the help of communications giant Globo Television's massive publicity on the success of the plan, Cardoso was elected president in 1995 and reelected in 1999 (Goertzel 119).

Although Paulo does not refer to the Cardoso campaign's use of marketing strategies, FHC appears in the novel as a model for anyone concerned about their own image and the value that this

Chapter Two

image projects. Besides their neoliberal perspectives, Lísias's protagonist and President Cardoso share some of the same physical traits and business-oriented mindset. For example, it has been pointed out that FHC, similar to Paulo, often appears stiff and formal, an image that had to be softened when he was running for president because he "usually dresses like a corporate executive" (Goertzel 113). In addition, FHC had close ties to the business sector during his academic career as a sociologist. For instance, he secured funding from a businessman, Fernando Gasparian, for his research about business people in the 1950s, when he co-created and directed the Centro de Estudos de Sociologia Industrial e do Trabalho (CESIT—Center for the Studies on the Sociology of Industry and Work) (Sorj and Fausto 36). He also founded Centro Brasileiro de Análise e Planejamento (CEBRAP—Brazilian Center for Analysis and Planning) with the financial support of the Ford Foundation, which his colleagues were hesitant to accept, given the symbolic meaning of surrendering to North American capitalism (46).

Beneath the protagonist's portrayal of FHC's tremendous success, however, lies a narrative of shortcomings. Paulo admires the former president for having been able to consolidate the banking system in Brazil and having led the best administration in the history of the country (Lísias 132), but a closer look at the banking crisis of 1996 reveals some of the shortcomings of the *Real* Plan and, ultimately, of neoliberal practices in general. As Edmund Amann and Werner Baer note in their article "A ilusão da estabilidade: A economia brasileira no governo FHC" ("The Illusion of Stability: The Brazilian Economy in the FHC Administration"), although initially successful, the effectiveness of the *Real* Plan depended on controversial long-term reforms that could only come to be partially implemented in 1998 when the IMF (International Monetary Fund) intervened. The banking crisis was set in motion in great part by the waning of the consumption expansion that the *Real* Plan initially granted the working class, when inflation and high interest rates made it more difficult for private debt to be paid off (Amann and Baer 152–53). To respond to the crisis, the government created a series of measures that resulted in the consolidations to which Paulo refers, with private banks buying public ones. While the crisis was tamed and the banking system became more efficient, once again it was the low-income population who paid the price: popular sectors considered less attractive to private banks were left unassisted when some of the public banks that used to serve them were wiped out (154).

Lísias's novel mocks the Cardoso administration, making the former president the idol of a pathetic businessperson who only *appears* to be successful—as we will see in the next section—, thus suggesting that FHC was a flawed and unsustainable model of a leader. By tracing a parallel between the protagonist's story of apparent success and that of FHC's, the novel hints at narratives of failure underlying both of these individuals and, ultimately, points to the distance between neoliberal discourse and neoliberal practice. In other words, the novel unveils the fiction of the neoliberal narrative, which promises a chance of prosperity to all, but in practice delivers prosperity to some at the expense of others (Harvey, *A Brief History* ch. 3).

Lísias continues to question apparent narratives of success that have points of convergence with neoliberal thought by referencing another political figure that Paulo considers a good example for those who want to understand the corporate world and attain success in it (127). That second "icon" is Chinese dictator Mao Zedong. For Paulo, Mao was a great leader, who made sure that the country was ready for the implementation of a market economy by his successors (44). China is for Paulo a "great country" for having adapted so well to a market economy, thanks, according to him, to Mao's leadership, which prepared the Chinese for this economic transition, in the protagonist's view. Paulo believes that Mao's successful model comes from the "absolute trust" that the Chinese have in their government, which has aided the country in "straightening itself up" while "benefiting the entire population" (66). Paulo's recipe for success in the corporate world includes modeling within one's business the Chinese attitude of "absolute trust and loyalty" toward leaders such as Mao.

Yet again, what Paulo's opinion of Mao ignores is the fact that many of Mao's policies led China into a massive crisis that impacted the population to varying degrees,[3] resulting in starvation in certain rural areas (Teiwes 138). Thanks to political propaganda, Mao's image maintained some degree of positivity until his death. Close Mao followers saw him as wise, gifted, masterful, history itself. They approached him in awe and admired his persona for combining "the talents of a political thinker, philosopher, general, poet, and perhaps a Chinese sage, someone with grand vision and practical skills that held out hope for achieving the promised land of a new China" (31–32). Others credited Mao with overcoming issues such as corruption, unemployment, and inflation (32). This description resembles Paulo's view of FHC, thus creating a parallel between Mao and the Brazilian former president. Paulo elevates FHC to the level of myth that Mao acquired. Of course, there are more differences than similarities between these two historical figures, although the changes in their political paths have in common the moving away from certain socio-political values. Mao was a communist leader who turned into a bloody dictator, whereas FHC was a leftist sociologist who pushed neoliberal policies during his time as a democratically elected president. However, by approximating these two figures, Lísias's novel suggests that there are some rather not so visible points of convergence between these models of leadership. These points of convergence lie in the authoritarian qualities that neoliberalism shares with dictatorial regimes. Neoliberalism tends to use authoritarian state power while claiming to be acting in the name of democracy. In the words of Harvey:

> To guard against their greatest fears—fascism, communism, socialism, authoritarian populism, and even majority rule—the neoliberals have to put strong limits on democratic governance, relying instead upon undemocratic and unaccountable institutions (such as the Federal Reserve or the IMF) to make intense state interventions and government by elites and "experts" in a world where the state is supposed not to be interventionist … Faced with social movements that seek collective interventions, therefore, the neoliberal state is itself forced to intervene, sometimes repressively, thus denying the very freedoms it is supposed to uphold. (*A Brief History* ch. 3)

For Harvey, the neoliberal state is authoritarian when it comes to market enforcement. Furthermore, neoliberalism can lead to the revival of authoritarian forms such as fascism and nationalism, as a response to the loss of social order that results from the destruction of social solidarity, unstoppable commodification, and excessive individual freedoms (*A Brief History* ch. 3). By putting Mao and FHC side by side as myths of communism and neoliberalism respectively, Lísias prompts readers to reflect on the hidden contradictions and dangers of neoliberal thought.

The Consuming Self

Like Mao's China and FHC's Brazil, Sudan appears in the novel as a deceivingly prosperous country, thanks to the work of another leader that Paulo comes to admire, the country's seventh president, Omar Hassan Ahmad al-Bashir (1989–2019). According to the protagonist, "no Sudão as coisas funcionam direito porque o governo está atento a tudo o que acontece. Muitos países por aí, inclusive na África, têm políticos desleixados, o que acaba prejudicando os interesses do próprio povo" ("in Sudan, things work well because the government is aware of everything. Many countries out there, including African countries, have lazy politicians, which ends up jeopardizing the interests of their own people"; Lísias 134). Paulo admires al-Bashir because, in his view, the Sudanese leader was able to govern effectively without resorting to terrorism. Furthermore, Paulo affirms that the Janjaweed—actual armed militia supported by al-Bashir—are the government's secret agents, who are in charge of border control to ensure that foreigners do not destabilize the area. Paulo believes that, if the president were to send the army, that action would stain the country's image of an orderly nation.

Obviously, Paulo's portrayal of Sudan is far from accurate. In reality, al-Bashir took over power after a military coup ousted the previous democratically elected government. He was elected president three times in allegedly corrupt elections and was indicted in 2010 by the International Criminal Court (ICC) for genocide (Lynch and Hamilton). The Janjaweed systematically raped, slaughtered, starved, and displaced the population of Darfur. An estimate of over 400,000 people died because of the government's and the militia's actions in Sudan (Prendergast).

In spite of all of Paulo's praising for Sudan and its government, the narrator points out that the country is not perfect and that the protagonist comes in as the foreigner who, according to a taxi driver that takes the protagonist through Khartoum, will help make Sudan the first African nation of the developed world (Lísias 146). The taxi driver's comment, along with the supposed financial intention of Paulo's mission, hints at foreign influence in Sudan's economy, namely that of the IMF and the World Bank. Sudan's negotiations with the IMF first started in 1978, aiming, as elsewhere, at the acceleration of economic growth and the reduction of poverty. However, as Lísias's novel suggests, behind the promises of neoliberal development lie international interests that bring violence rather than positive change to the majority of the

Chapter Two

population. In Sudan's case, John Prendergast shows in his 1989 assessment of the consequences of the IMF's policies, following the usual neoliberal recommendations—which included currency devaluation, liberalization of trade, cuts to social spending, and increasing privatization of the economy—Sudan was driven into starvation, increased deficit and instability, and redistribution of income that favored the rich (47).

Paulo's role as a representative of a Westerner posing as a foreign savior suggests that, as has tended to be the case with neoliberalism, international pressures justify themselves, even if their justification clashes with basic neoliberal principles, that is, even if it means supporting an authoritarian regime in the name of "individual freedom" (Harvey, *A Brief History* ch. 1). Lísias's novel suggests that these international interests have little regard for the drastic consequences they leave behind when Paulo dismisses the possible involvement of his bank in facilitating the Iran-Contra affair[4] and funding the IRA (Irish Republican Army) as "alguns deslizes involuntários" ("some involuntary slips"; Lísias 91).

Lísias's protagonist aspires to become the intersection of these three political figures, that is, FHC, Mao, and al-Bashir, a combination that is depicted in the novel as not just pathetic but also dangerous. As the analysis has shown thus far, Paulo serves as an example of neoliberal thought run amok. His obsession with corporate success leads him into extreme competition, isolation, an unhealthy fast-paced routine, and even paranoia. His everyday life is completely overtaken by the neoliberal vision of individual entrepreneurial freedom in the sense that anything that can help him climb the corporate ladder is fair game for him, regardless of the consequences for others or even for himself. His idea of relaxation is the feeling of having finished a project for the bank. He does not worry about having friends, but rather about building a network of people whom he can use to achieve his professional goals. One of his rituals is to make lists of what he calls "magic words," which include words from the language of capital such as "enriquecer" ("to become rich") and "produzir" ("to produce/be productive"; Lísias 135), painting mental pictures of a successful future, much in the way that Byrne advises in *The Secret*.

The way that Paulo treats those who work for him at Confucius is also revealing of the exploitative quality of the neoliberal practices he stands for. The company, which is advertised as a space that provides training for businessmen, with special services for high-end executives who need to de-stress, is in practice a brothel in which women live in quasi-slavery conditions. The main employees at Confucius are women taken by Paulo to Brazil from Sudan, who have undergone genital mutilation. Their services are described as massages and, according to Paulo, are meant to respond to his clients' needs. As Paulo himself puts it, "a Confucius ... não pode deixar de ouvir as críticas dos clientes e tentar se ajustar aos anseios deles" ("Confucius cannot ignore its clients' criticism and [must] attempt to adapt to their desires"; Lísias 315). After all, in consumer capitalism, the (powerful) consumer is always right. It is in order to respond to his clients' "needs" that Paulo forces one of his female employees, who is actually Brazilian, to undergo a mutilation operation by a doctor who engages in illegal medical practices. The novel ends with the woman going into the clinic for her operation. This scene immediately follows the narrator's report on Paulo's success, thus suggesting the link between the two events. Paulo's success, as well as that of the doctor himself, who proclaims "se cheguei aqui onde estou hoje, foi depois de muita seriedade e esforço" ("if I got where I am today it was because of much commitment and effort"; 324), depends on the exploitation of these women. Paulo's company's foundation, thus, lies on human trafficking, exploitation of labor, a total lack of regulation thanks to the bribery of politicians and police, and marketing that aims to hide the real goal of the business. The company, run by an individual who defends neoliberal principles with such fervor, and who has leaders that range from elected democratic supporters of neoliberalism to bloody dictators, stands for the possible extremes that private interests can reach in today's world.

Failure: The Narrative Behind the Narrative

As we have seen, while being evaluated by the bank, the letters in Paulo's name are changed into stars, in a process that is meant to indicate his ascension in the company at the same time as his transformation into a mere object that exists at the service of the bank. This transformation casts doubt on his status within the corporation, which is further emphasized by several signs that the bank, rather than promoting him, appears to be relieving him of his duties.

Chapter Two

One of such signs is the fact that, later on in the novel, the reader finds out that Paulo is actually never sent to China, but rather to Sudan. At the same time, the bank severs Paulo's ties with it, in a move vaguely justified by the narrator as a way to keep Paulo's trip somewhat a secret for reasons that are unclear in the novel. There is also a sense that Paulo may have psychological issues such as compulsion and paranoia, both expressed in terms of his socioeconomic ambitions, and potentially linked to his apparent dismissal from the bank. These psychological issues manifest themselves, for example, in rituals that Paulo creates, such as retracing President Cardoso's official trip to China or mentally repeating mantras associated with corporate culture, as ways to soothe himself when he cannot sleep at night. Some of his behavior also indicates that he believes people are persecuting him in an attempt to impede his professional ascension.

Although there is little information about his childhood, Paulo's disorders seem to be connected to his quest to be the perfect child, which turns later on into his quest to be the best employee in the bank. Acceptance during his childhood comes from his imaginary friend, the extraterrestrial Rincão, whose name is phonetically similar to the augmentative form of the Portuguese word *rico* ("rich"). The friend comes to visit him and promises to take him to his planet, where he would find the cure to the back pain that will plague Paulo his entire life as a kind of somatization of his emotional challenges (Lísias 113). Paulo's obsession with a Chinese piece of equipment that, according to what he has heard, would finally cure him, suggests that China takes the place, psychologically, of Rincão's planet in the protagonist's adulthood. In the meantime, Paulo's efforts to learn Chinese in order to achieve success mirror his earlier learning of *rinconês*. As a word derived from the name of the imaginary friend, *rinconês* sounds like a neologism for "the language of the rich." Perhaps here lies a psychological (and metaphorical) explanation for why Paulo's trip to China is associated with professional and personal success.

In light of Paulo's apparent failure to go to China, the narrator's obsessive insistence on Paulo's brilliance throughout the entire narrative comes across as an attempt to mask the protagonist's probable career failure. There is a sense of pathological anxiety in much of the language of the novel, which goes hand in hand with Paulo's apparent psychological issues. As the narrative progresses, it becomes evident that the protagonist inhabits a world of appearances. It is a world of simulacra, that is, a world that Baudrillard defines as filled with signs, images of an absence, of a non-existing reality that one desires and projects onto objects meant to represent this reality (6). By revealing this world of simulacra, the narrative of success turns into a narrative of failure, in the sense that everything that the protagonist conquers is much more modest than what he tries to make it seem or, at best, it is achieved through questionable means.

The importance of appearances in Paulo's life is evident even in the most banal aspects of his job, such as the strategically crafted emails that he sends out to all employees with the purpose of portraying himself as a "tolerant man," completely dedicated to increasing productivity, "a big concern" for all (Lísias 29). However, his lack of tolerance is evident when the narrator reveals his opinion about the secretary's reaction to him firing her, an instance in which he even convinces the secretary that he was actually doing her a favor. As she cries over being fired, he thinks

> Pois então, é por isso que esses funcionários nunca conseguem nada na vida. Diante de uma pequenina dificuldade, em vez de se reerguer, começam a chorar. Por que essa retardada, por exemplo, não pergunta os seus defeitos, pede algumas dicas e, quem sabe, até não admite os problemas e diz que está disposta, na próxima oportunidade, a fazer melhor? (79)

> So, that is why these employees never get ahead in life. In the face of a small obstacle, instead of overcoming it, they start to cry. Why doesn't this retard, for example, ask about her weaknesses, ask for tips [on how to improve], and, maybe, acknowledge the problems and say that she is willing to, on the next opportunity, do better?

Examples of mismatch between appearance and reality such as the one above abound in the narrative. The passage above, in particular, unveils the weakness of systems of protection in the workplace such as the bank's Human Resources, which is described in the novel as not playing any actual role in the bank, but rather just being an annoyance to the directors (Lísias 82).

Paulo's excellent sense of style—or rather a sense of style perceived as such—provides another contrast between appearances and reality. Due to his polished look, the government of Sudan

Chapter Two

invites him to give a presentation on male elegance so that the attendees would "fazer bonito" ("impress/look good") at the next summit of African countries (Lísias 185). However, this sense of style is actually shaped by Paula, Paulo's girlfriend, who takes the back seat in the protagonist's sexist world. Upon receiving the invitation, Paulo immediately calls Paula for advice, reminding us of her earlier intervention before he leaves for London. On that occasion, she points out that his clothes are embarrassing for such an important training. She subsequently takes Paulo shopping for "quatro ternos, dois Armani e dois Ralph Lauren, alguns paletós Ermenegildo Zegna e um sobretudo da mesma marca ... [doze gravatas], todas Bulgari ou Hermès ... três pares de sapato Bally ..." ("four suits, two Armani and two Ralph Lauren, a couple of Ermenegildo Zegna jackets and a coat of the same brand ... [twelve ties], all Bulgari or Hermès ... three pairs of Bally shoes"; 70). Paula's advice to Paulo clearly reflects an understanding of the language of success in Paulo's business world, which is expressed by the branded items that he acquires. A Sudanese taxi driver's response to Paulo after being given the latter's Ermenegildo Zegna's coat attests to the international standing of this language. The driver is happy because he is sure that everyone will bow down to him when he wears his new garment. He even becomes emotional when people compliment him on his new clothes and thinks that they will make him the king of Port Sudan one day (148).

Paulo's time abroad is riddled with signs that the experiences that he describes do not quite correspond to reality. His experiences are often narrated in ways that collapse Sudan and China into one space. When Paulo arrives in the destination of his mission, the narrator underlines the hyperreal quality of the trip by describing the foreign space where Paulo is as both China and Sudan, often within the same sentence, stating that the Hilton where Paulo would stay in China was very close to the Nile (Lísias 115). In the hotel, Paulo builds a stereotypical mini-China, with bedding, spades, kimonos, and other items. This mini-China, a simulacrum, can be read as a representation of his professional shortcomings; a hyperreality that replaces the reality of failure to have the successful career that he so vigorously pursues. His time in China (actually Sudan), as the business trip for which he worked so hard, represents his greatest success so far. Yet, the fact that he actually spends time in Sudan rather than in China serves as evidence of his failure to achieve his goal.

The most significant simulacrum in the novel is Paulo's first book, whose title coincides with that of Lísias's novel itself: *O livro dos mandarins* (*The Book of Mandarins*). As the narrator notes, in spite of being such a great intellectual, who can express himself remarkably well both in spoken and written language (Lísias 37), Paulo hires a ghostwriter, *poeta* Paulo, to put the protagonist's brilliant ideas in writing. According to the narrator, Paulo needs this "assistance" because he lacks the adequate amount of time to do it himself due to his busy life as a businessperson.

Poeta Paulo, in turn, is described as a frustrated writer whose poetry fails to catch the attention of literature professors (Lísias 176). Tired of the petty disputes that he considers characteristic of the academic and literary circles, *poeta* Paulo accepts Paulo's offer and becomes his ghostwriter. As a character, *poeta* Paulo serves as a vehicle of criticism to the commodity nature of literary writing in twenty-first century Brazil. From the perspective of the novel, becoming a professional writer of what one would consider "good quality" literature is not an easy task, for one has to deal with the requirements of consumer appeal and taste expectations that do not always coincide with what is at least assumed to be appealing to a rather large group of readers/consumers. Similarly, *poeta* Paulo's comment about literature professors suggests his disapproval of the power of an elite to determine what is deserving of becoming canonical.

The fictional *O livro dos mandarins* represents Paulo's achievement of ultimate personal and professional success, a goal he has long visualized achieving. However, as the product of someone else's writing, Paulo's book is like Paulo's mini-China in Sudan: a sign replacing an absence; the absence of what it claims to represent, that is, actual success. Furthermore, it can be argued that Paulo, as the persona that the protagonist projects to his peers in the business world, is a simulacrum himself. Behind the strong, bright, highly accomplished image, lies a physically weak and psychologically disturbed victim—and at the same time perpetuator—of corporate culture. The latter image is what the other *O livro dos mandarins*, the one written by Lísias, reveals. It peels off the layers of Paulo's rhetoric of success in order to reveal its emptiness. Lísias accomplishes much of this work through narrative techniques that indicate disruption, superficiality, and breakdown, such as the use of fragmented sentences (e.g. "o governo acha que a imagem do Sudão no exterior e por isso" ["the government thinks that Sudan's image abroad and because of this"] 219); clichés ("a soma dos valores é o que traz o verdadeiro sucesso" ["the sum of one's values is what results in true success"]; 23); and repetitions that eventually become empty of meaning. These repetitions stall the narrative several times while also expressing the obsessive-compulsive nature of the character's behavior and, by extension, the obsessive-compulsive nature of our times. As Bauman notes, we live in a world in which "the hunt [for anything that makes us successful, famous] turns into a compulsion, an addiction, and obsession" (*Liquid Times* 107). Expressions used *ad nauseum* in the novel, such as "a bem da verdade" ("the truth is"), contrast with the character's misguided interpretation of the reality around him. Together, these stylistic choices, which Lísias uses elsewhere for similar purposes,[5] result in a long 339-page book that conveys the excess and the waste of consumer society, leaving the reader with the impression, at first glance, that she has perhaps wasted time on a rather unsubstantial narrative. Words, sentences, paragraphs accumulate into a pile of what often looks like mere nonsense, such as chapter XXVI, which is a two-page list of random words separated by commas. This chapter illustrates the protagonist's habit of "collecting words" as he routinely starts his day with a fifteen-minute "meditation" session, in which he repeats five words that he believes to be capable of bringing inspiration into his day ahead (Lísias 289). Nevertheless, as the present analysis has shown, Lísias's narrative is quite the opposite of this apparently empty novel. It presents substantial critical reflections on consumer culture, corporate culture, neoliberal thought, and the liquid nature of the time in which the narrative is written and which it addresses.

Bernardo Carvalho's Reprodução: Information in the Era of Reproduction

In *Reprodução*, B. Carvalho addresses the shifts in communications that have deeply marked the first decades of the twenty-first century, suggesting that they can lead to the reproduction of oversimplified and potentially dangerous ideas. The novel's protagonist, like Lísias's Paulo, attempts to build an image of self-confidence by boasting pridefully not only of having a large number of followers on social media, but also, and especially, of the "wisdom" he displays via less than well-informed views of the world. The knowledge that he claims to have accumulated comes from the Internet, especially blogs that he follows religiously. The result of this consumption of information is prejudice and ignorance, as *Reprodução* shows in its representation of a rather bleak world.

This world resembles that which media scholar Postman describes in *Amusing Ourselves to Death* (1985). Departing from Marshal McLuhan's argument that the medium is the message, Postman asserts that media transform not only our perceptions of reality, but also a society's intellectual and social preoccupations (9). Studying the shift from print to electronic culture, Postman argues that public discourse has become progressively simplified, as new, fast, and segmented forms of communication such as television have become part of our daily lives. For him, the everydayness of television, in particular, has made us expect discourse in general to be packaged as entertainment, thus changing the way in which we talk about spheres of social life such as religion, politics, and education. In other words, both the production and reception of discourse within these spheres has come to reflect an epistemology made possible by the advent of a fragmented culture of entertainment. For Postman, the epistemology of a rational public conversation encouraged by print media has been replaced with one that favors simple, shallow ways of thinking, and that has changed our notions of truth and intelligence (43).

This transformation, Postman notes, began with the invention of the telegraph, which exposed us to information about distant realities, thus creating a sense of disengagement by changing the relationship between information and action (68). Once decontextualized, information became increasingly conveyed through the language of headlines, which Postman characterizes as sensational, fragmented, and impersonal. While the amount of information increased, its depth was progressively reduced, creating an atomized world, in which "there is only a present and it need not be part of any story that can be told" (74). In the second decade of the twenty-first century, we can see this world, for instance, in many complexity-reducing memes about political issues on social media, in the popularity of reality television epitomized by the

Kardashians and their empire, in the marketing of products as providers of "experiences," and in pedagogical expectations that content be delivered in a fun way.

The commodification of information that began with the invention of technologies such as the telegraph has reached new heights since the advent of the Internet, as activist Eli Pariser shows in *The Filter Bubble. How the New Personalized Web is Changing What We Read and How We Think*. A few years ahead of the public debate that was ignited in the aftermath of the 2016 presidential election in the U.S., Pariser argues that, while algorithms help us sift through ever-increasing amounts of online data, they create a filter bubble that is changing our culture. Through personalization, that is, through the tailoring of content to one's likes and dislikes, algorithms restrict access to certain ideas as they end up determining our preferences, reducing exposure to opposing views and thus limiting our understanding of the complexity of real life. Their capacity to determine individual preferences is also changing the economy of the production of content in the sense that the latter is becoming increasingly more targeted as a means to expand sales of any given product. In other words, personalization "is changing the economics that determine what stories get produced" (69). Personalization, Pariser argues, is restricting serendipity, which poses a threat to human creativity, given that, once in the bubble, an individual is unlikely to be confronted with knowledge from different areas, an encounter that has made possible some of the biggest inventions of humankind (96). Furthermore, personalization threatens democracy, given that, as Pariser notes,

> [d]emocracy requires citizens to see things from one another's point of view, but instead we're more and more enclosed in our own bubbles. Democracy requires a reliance on shared facts; instead, we're being offered parallel but separate universes. (5)

The filter bubble becomes particularly dangerous when coupled with authoritarian responses to neoliberalism. The promotion of individual liberties and the devaluing of societal solidarity have produced a return to older political ideologies such as nationalism and fascism (Harvey, *A Brief History* ch. 3). These ideologies have advanced in Europe and in the United States recently, as evidenced, for instance, by Brexit and Donald Trump's election, two events fueled by, among other issues, xenophobia.

In the case of Brazil, neoconservative ideas have become more prominent since at least the 2013 protests,[6] which started a long and complex process of expression of discontent that ended with the controversial impeachment of Brazil's first female president, Dilma Rousseff. As Pinheiro-Machado summarizes in a piece published in the Brazilian newsmagazine *Carta Capital* in 2014 titled "O Reich tropical: a onda fascista no Brasil" ("The Tropical Reich: The Fascist Wave in Brazil"): "o germe do ódio está à solta no Brasil pronto para linchar física e moralmente todo aquele que não se enquadra no establishment masculino, branco, heterossexual, rico, bem-sucedido e cheio de bens de consumo" ("the seed of hatred has found fertile soil in Brazil, and is ready to lynch, both physically and morally, anyone who does not fit into the male, white, heterosexual, rich, well-accomplished, consumerist establishment"). A demonstration of the affirmation of the establishment to which Pinheiro-Machado refers is the fact that Rousseff's successor, Michel Temer, chose an overwhelmingly white and male cabinet of ministers and secretaries, while proposing a myriad of controversial measures that directly affected the strides that Brazil had made toward inclusion and diverse representation. The power of conservatism became even clearer in Brazil after the 2016 local election, which put the administration of cities like Rio de Janeiro in the hands of conservatives such as Marcelo Crivella, bishop of the Universal Church of the Kingdom of God. The church in question was founded in the 1970s by his uncle, billionaire Edir Macedo, who envisioned the advancement of his church into Brazil's political scene, with the goal of implementing a "project of nation," which he describes in his book *Plano de poder: Deus, os cristãos e a política* (*Power Plan: God, Christians and Politics*). The ascension of ultra-conservatism culminates in 2018 with the election of far-right candidate Jair Bolsonaro to the highest office in the nation.

An important factor in the rise of neoconservative ideas worldwide is the Internet, which has provided a platform for far-right speech to spread rapidly. The medium in question allowed this kind of speech "to circumvent national prohibitions on anti-Semitic materials, and to inspire right-wing revolutionaries" (Berlet and Mason 30). In Brazil, according to Adriana Silva et al., research shows that between 2002 and 2009, the number of websites that contain neo-Nazi content increased 170%, while the number of comments on the content in question in online forums increased 42.585% during the same time. The number of blogs dealing with the issue, in turn, grew more than 550% (431). For A. Silva et al.,

> A mídia patronal e alguns agentes "independentes" cumprem um papel funcional à reprodução de visões que alimentam o campo ideológico da extrema-direita. O poder de comunicaçao—a fala fácil, direta, pouco aprofundada, parcial e saturada de sensacionalismo explorador das mazelas cotidianas—tem grande receptividade num contexto social despolitizado e cindido entre os projetos de aspirações individuais e genéricas. (442)
>
> Mainstream media and some "independent" agents play an essential role in the reproduction of views that feed far-right ideology. The power of communication—a discourse that is easy, direct, shallow, partial, and saturated with sensationalism that exploits everyday social ills—is well received in a social context that is depoliticized and split between projects of individual and generic aspirations.

Published in 2013, *Reprodução* by B. Carvalho, as the title itself suggests, tackles this reproduction of conservative discourse online and its potential impact on the shaping of individuals' perceptions of social reality. The novel's structure conveys the challenges in communication in the twenty-first century created by the abundance of information and the decreasing reliability of news sources. B. Carvalho's linguistic explorations present a reflection on the pitfalls of communication in general and the challenges posed by the commodification of information in the twenty-first century, specifically. By consuming increasingly targeted content, Internet users such as the protagonist inadvertently allow their personal preferences and online behavior to become a commodity, which is, in turn, shaped by an algorithmic culture that contributes to divert the focus away from larger social issues and/or to reinforce segregationist behavior. Attempting to go beyond denouncing the problem, *Reprodução* provides some insights on the role of literature in the face of these challenges.

The Consuming Self

Talking to Oneself

B. Carvalho's *Reprodução* is divided into three parts: "The language of the future," "The language of the past," and "The language of the present." Each part consists of a long dialogue, in which the words of only one of the interlocutors are "transcribed" onto the pages of the novel, thus mirroring the disjunctures of communication that the novel addresses. Without having access to what the other interlocutor said, the reader is left with an incomplete and often incoherent version of the conversation that took place. Moreover, the reader is led to question whether the interlocutor even exists.

According to the characters, these dialogues supposedly allude to the structure of Incan comedies, which "baseavam-se no diálogo. Mas em um diálogo no qual só um dos lados tinha o direito de falar. Era uma comédia do massacre das outras línguas" ("were based on dialogue. However, a dialogue in which only one person had the right to speak. It was a comedy of the massacre of other languages"; B. Carvalho 114). This characterization signals the novel's intent to speak about a contemporary "massacre" of communication, in the terms proposed by Pariser. The technique used by B. Carvalho shrinks the characters' bubbles to a minimum, in that their monologues read as if they are talking to themselves, regurgitating random pieces of information that cannot be verified.

The first dialogue in the novel takes place between the protagonist and a police officer. The second dialogue involves, supposedly, a female police officer and the first officer who interrogates the protagonist in the first dialogue. The third and last dialogue has the protagonist and the first officer again as participants. A third-person omniscient narrator remains mostly silent throughout the narrative, giving us direct access to the dialogues, which are, however, filtered by the perception of the protagonist. The latter is a middle-class man, whom the narrator simply calls "o estudante de chinês" ("the student of Chinese"). We find him at the beginning of the novel being stopped by the police while standing in line to check in for a flight to China. The police interrogate him regarding his links to a Chinese woman named Liuli and referred to in the novel simply as "the teacher of Chinese," who was also checking in for the same flight as her former student, the protagonist.

Chapter Two

From this opening scene on, the reader learns pieces of disconnected information about the characters' past and their personal relationships. In order to piece the story together, it is necessary to deal with frequent ambiguity, repetition, false starts, in addition to irrelevant and mostly untrustworthy information filtered by the protagonist. The structure of the novel therefore places the reader in the uncomfortable position of having to not only sift through an insurmountable amount of chaotic data, but also to doubt everything she reads, for the protagonist mostly narrates what he *imagines* to have happened, as the narrator points out. Among the data made available by the protagonist are numerous references to news and random pieces of information, ranging from the discovery of the God particle[7] to the television coverage of the birth of the grandson of a famous member of a *sertanejo*[8] duo. By creating a narrative that reads like a chaotic and inconclusive assembly of pieces of information, mostly taken from various media, *Reprodução* reproduces, so to speak, the information overload that characterizes communication in the twenty-first century, highlighting the fragmentation and oversimplification that can stem from the way in which we consume information today.

The novel's characters live in a world that Postman would characterize as Huxleyan: where individuals become alienated not because their access to information is restricted—in the sense of being scarce—but rather because it is widened and, in the process, made simplistic and non-contextual (141). While the protagonist claims to be "um cara hiperinformado" ("a hyper-well-informed guy"; B. Carvalho 53), his rather superficial statements on various issues paint him as highly prejudiced, racist, sexist, homophobic, and xenophobic. For instance, he defends torture as a way to protect democracy, he mocks Jewish children's looks, and supports the extermination of the elderly. He feels uneasy when he sees a woman in a burka and insulted when the police officer insinuates that he might be gay, to which he reacts by saying that he would rather be black. He claims to be objective, and states that he is not judgmental, but rather that he simply describes what he sees (40). In other words, to use a phrase often repeated these days, "he tells it like it is."

His compulsive insistence on prejudiced opinions demonstrates the result of the sort of "invisible auto propaganda" that characterizes the filter bubble. This propaganda makes it harder for him to deviate from his cognitive path as it reinforces his schemata, that is, concepts that result from the compression of information that one hears and sees and that tend to be strengthened once acquired (Pariser 15). His incapacity to learn anything in depth is evidenced, for instance, by his inability to communicate minimally in Chinese even after six years of studying the language (B. Carvalho 12). He also expresses superficiality by repeating, out of context, sayings and clichés that are common in Brazilian culture, such as "Não deixe pra amanhã o que pode fazer hoje" ("don't leave for tomorrow what you can do today"; 15) and "Na Arábia Saudita, ladrão é amputado; aqui é deputado" ("in Saudi Arabia, thieves are amputated, here they are made representatives of the people"; 19). In addition, his superficiality becomes evident when he expresses his belief that concerns about global warming are mere manipulation of facts aimed at impeding the economic growth of countries such as Brazil and China, a view espoused, for instance, by Donald Trump with respect to the U.S. (Wong).

The protagonist's enclosure in his bubble leads him to live in a kind of schizophrenic state, in which he talks to nobody but himself. As he himself notes, in an allusion to the progressive loss of common ground necessary for public debate that we have experienced in recent years: "[n]ão tem interlocutor. Ninguém sabe nada" ("[t]here is no interlocutor. No one knows anything"; 37). At times, characters' responses to "ghost" comments and questions by their interlocutors read as episodes of mental breakdown, as the passage below illustrates:

> O senhor devia se informar melhor. Os elefantes estão morrendo. O Talmude está por trás do tráfico internacional de entorpecentes. E o senhor acha que eu tenho cara de jihadista? Eu, não. O vice-presidente do Irã, aquele que comprou o Corão faltando uma página. Logo aquela em que Alá dizia que Israel era a terra dos judeus. Curti. E pra onde o senhor acha que vai o dinheiro do tráfico internacional de entorpecentes? Pra onde? Pros bancos! (38–39)

> You should get better informed, Sir. The elephants are dying. The Talmud is behind drug trafficking. And do you think that I look like a jihadist? Not me. The vice-president of Iran, the one that bought the Coran that was missing a page. It had to be the page in which Allah says that Israel was the land of the Jews. I liked it. And where do you think the money made in the international drug trafficking goes? Where to? To the banks!

Chapter Two

Passages such as the one above also resemble the fragmentation of online news or even of comment sessions available on social media, when users talk past each other or when account owners delete parts of conversations, leaving behind only the responses to absent statements or questions. Furthermore, these passages allude to how our consumption of information today may affect our notion of what constitutes a fact. The protagonist's bias and incoherence denounce the information that he consumes—and by extension the reader's own consumption of information—as distorted, and its dissemination as normalizing of this incoherence. This normalization, the protagonist suggests, is characteristic of what he calls the language of the future: "Nenhuma contradição. Está aí uma palavra que não vai existir na língua do futuro. Coerência também não. Na língua do futuro, o senhor vai poder dizer o que quiser, sem consequência, nem responsabilidade, nem contradição" ("No contradiction. That's a word that will not exist in the language of the future. Neither will coherence. In the language of the future you will be able to say whatever you want, without consequences, responsibility, or contradiction"; 52). The protagonist's behavior is telling of Postman's prediction of the results of television culture. According to him,

> embedded in the surrealistic frame of a television news show is a theory of anticommunication, featuring a type of discourse that abandons logic, reason, sequence and rules of contradiction. In aesthetics, I believe the name given to this theory is Dadaism; in philosophy, nihilism; in psychiatry, schizophrenia. In the parlance of the theater, it is known as vaudeville. (105)

In fact, the protagonist's response to the officer's comment on his mental health references the link between information overload and psychiatric imbalances that Postman mentions: "É claro que estou louco. E o senhor queria o quê? Muita informação. Ninguém aguenta" ("Of course I am crazy. What did you expect, Sir? Too much information. No one can handle it"; B. Carvalho 49). Later on, he affirms once again: "E o senhor me pergunta se eu estou louco? É claro que estou. Completamente louco. Porque o que está acontecendo comigo não passaria pela cabeça de nenhuma pessoa normal. Só posso estar delirando" ("And you ask me if I am crazy? Of course I am. Completely crazy. Because what is happening to me wouldn't occur to any normal person. I must be delirious"; 150).

Mental breakdown also seems to characterize the behavior of the female officer, whose conversation with another officer the protagonist supposedly overhears. Her mental health is called into question when the existence of a report to which she repeatedly refers is denied. Her interlocutor seems to suggest that her impression of its existence must be the result of the effects of antidepressants (B. Carvalho 73), thus suggesting that she suffers from a mental illness. An explicit reference to schizophrenia appears in the novel when a question is raised regarding an officer who is supposedly on the run with the teacher of Chinese: "Você não concorda, então, que o agente é fruto da loucura? Mesmo se esquizofrenia não for hereditária, ele não é fruto da loucura dela?" ("Don't you agree, then, that the agent is the fruit of madness? Even if schizophrenia is not hereditary, isn't he the fruit of his [mother's] madness?"; 90). As these examples demonstrate, not only the protagonist, but others of B. Carvalho's characters are immersed in a world that seems to have ceased to make sense; where a schizophrenic state becomes a metaphor for the breakdown of dialogue.

The (Dis)Information Era

In *Reprodução*, B. Carvalho questions the possibility of an objective account of reality in an information era when individuals are sold the promise of impartial reporting, but instead tend to consume chaotic unreliable piles of disconnected information. Mirroring this social reality, the novel constantly questions its own plot, leading the reader to wonder about how much to trust what she reads or whether to trust it at all. B. Carvalho's novel represents the role of language in conjuring up realities, whether through the misunderstandings that its precariousness in communicating meaning may cause, or through its manipulation by certain individuals to gain and/or maintain power.

Revisiting an issue that philosophers and linguists have grappled with for centuries (Taylor 4), namely, what it is exactly that explains how we communicate effectively, B. Carvalho's novel puts into question the very idea that we ordinarily understand each other when we communicate, especially given the current context of information dissemination and linguistic exchange in the virtual world. Part Two of *Reprodução* highlights everyday

Chapter Two

communication challenges by providing, on nearly every page, examples of linguistic mechanisms that indicate breakdown in communication between the characters. These mechanisms include:

a. Rewording: "Você sempre contou com o meu apoio—apoio não é a palavra—, com a minha discrição" ("You have always counted on my support—support is not the right word—with my discretion"; B. Carvalho 59)

b. Comprehension checks: "Oi?" ("Excuse me?"; 65), "Confirma?" ("Can you confirm it?"; 83)

c. Comments on linguistic differences between interlocutors: "Você tem um vocabulário engraçado! Minha avó falava assim" ("You have a funny vocabulary! My grandmother used to talk like that"; 66)

d. Corrections: "é isso que ele está querendo dizer" ("that is what he was trying to say"; 78), "Não foi isso que você me disse" ("That was not what you told me"; 87)

e. Verbs that indicate vagueness and uncertainty such as "alegar" ("to allege")

f. Imprecisions: "Eu não disse *própria*, eu disse *uma* família" ("I didn't say [his/her] *own* [family], I said *a* family"; 95)

g. Ambiguity: "Vai se foder! Não o senhor. Vai se foder, em geral, sem sujeito" ("Fuck you! No, not you. Fuck you in general, without a subject"; 138)

h. Failure to account for tonality (in Chinese) appropriately: "Eu já disse. Depende do tom. Pode ser um monte de coisa" ("I have already said it. It depends on the tonality. It can mean a bunch of different things"; 139)

i. Lack of cohesiveness: the female officer jumps from one random subject to the next, talking about how long it has been since it rained, then the percentage of trash produced in the entire world that ends up in the oceans, and language death rates today. She explicitly says: "Eu sei que não tem nada a ver uma coisa com a outra" ("I know that one thing doesn't have anything to do with the other"; 99)

j. Inadequate translations: the student of Chinese doubts his translation of Chinese proverbs, which appears indeed inaccurate, for different parts of the proverbs do not seem to relate. For instance: "Enquanto passam as nuvens, os irmãos vão à igreja. Nem eu. Talvez não seja exatamente assim. Não faz sentido, né?" ("While the clouds go by, the brothers and sisters go to church. Neither do I. Maybe it is not quite like that. It doesn't make sense, does it?"; 152)

k. Polysemy: play with the various meanings of the word *reprodução* (reproduction) in Portuguese. These meanings include, for instance, the idea of procreation, in reference both to humans and living organisms of different types. Here reproduction is equated with both destruction, on one hand, and resistance, on the other hand. The protagonist notes that humans are the only animals that continue to procreate even though they understand that this act will ultimately lead to their extinction. He also points out that just like the bacteria that reproduce in our throats, we reinvent ourselves through our speech. Like bacteria, ideas become more resistant as they reproduce (97).

The two meanings of the word *reprodução* in the last example are particularly important in the novel because they point to the unbalanced attention given to different points of view within an information bubble. This reinforcement of some ideas over others, in turn, may ultimately extinguish not only entire ways of conceptualizing reality, but humanity itself. The many examples of linguistic barriers in *Reprodução* suggest that the information era is, ironically, also the miscommunication era. With these various examples of contradiction, imprecision, and linguistic precariousness, B. Carvalho's novel turns into a confusing, convoluted text that often frustrates the reader, who is lost in translation, as she is likely to be in the real world when attempting to follow the various news cycles that bombard her daily.

The veracity of the chaotic assembly of "facts" presented to the reader in Part Two, in particular, is in the end questioned by the female officer, who asks her interlocutor, regarding rumors pertaining to her: "E você acreditou?" ("And you believed [it]?"; 132). Her question, placed emphatically as the last line of Part Two, casts doubt onto everything that she said up to that point, which will be even further disputed in Part Three, when the very existence of the female officer is denied by her interlocutor during the latter's interaction with the student of Chinese. The female officer's last words in the novel, thus, reinforce the sense of distrust in the entire narrative. Earlier on, in a complex play with the limits between reality and fiction, she triggers this sense of distrust when she states: "Eu imito. Não sou personagem de romance" ("I imitate. I am not a character in a novel"; 69). Her words paradoxically both confirm and deny her realness in the fictional world of *Reprodução*. On one hand, *is* she real in the fictional world of the novel, or is she created by the protagonist's imagination? On the other hand, she points out that her realness in the novel depends on the imitation of something else, in a reference to both other characters in her fictional world and to her shared traits with real-life individuals from the world of the reader, which would have inspired her creation by B. Carvalho. In an intricate puzzle condensed in two short sentences, B. Carvalho both affirms and denies the reader's reality, as if asking "what *can* you trust, not just in the novel that you are reading right now, but also in the real world around you?"

The novel further confronts communication challenges by commenting on the human desire to communicate perfectly through artificial languages that would be, in principle, capable of conveying what culturally constructed languages cannot. The female officer describes such an ideal language as one in which

> tudo estivesse dito e não sobrasse nenhum espaço nem pra imaginação nem pra mal-entendido. Ninguém ia precisar explicar nada. Bastava ler. Na minha língua, você ia entender tudo o que lesse. Se eu quisesse ser irônica, bastava dizer *ironia* depois da frase, pra pessoa entender. Ironia! Pronto. (B. Carvalho 114)

> Everything would have been said and there would not be room neither for the imagination nor for misunderstandings. No one would need to explain anything. All you'd have to do is read. In my language, you would understand everything that you read. If I wanted to be ironic, I would just need to say *irony* after a sentence and you would understand. Irony! That's it.

In her reflections about communicating via a perfect language, the female officer references twelfth century abbess Hildegard von Bingen's *lingua ignota*, which is considered the first artificial language and would have been capable of expressing precise meanings in the way that the officer envisions it. It is said that von Bingen's purpose was to create an ideal universal language. However, it appears that she never shared this language with anyone else, thus failing to accomplish the alleged purpose of the language. By referencing this apparent failure—interestingly enough, one that cannot be confirmed, much like the facts presented by his characters—B. Carvalho suggests the impossibility of achieving transparent communication.

A Time of Crisis

The world of B. Carvalho's protagonist is, thus, a world in crisis. This crisis extends to the notion of time as well, which is embedded in the very title of each one of the three parts of the novel: "A língua do futuro" ("The Language of the Future"), "A língua do passado" ("The Language of the Past"), and "A língua do presente" ("The Language of the Present"). The parts appear in this particular order, with past, present, and future out of a chronological sequence. In this way, the novel opens with a reference to the future and ends referencing the present, with the past filling the majority of the pages in between. This particular sequence mirrors our anxiety about an uncertain future and our sense of living in an eternal present, while stressing the importance of remembering our past.

The first part, "A língua do futuro," starts with an epigraph that alludes to twentieth century English poet and novelist Malcolm Lowry's short story "China." In this short story, the narrator speaks of his experience as a traveler to the eastern part of the world. He notes that to him China seemed unreal, a dream, "a muddle," even after he finally arrived there (Lowry 21). The closer he got to the country, the less he believed in its existence. Language fails him when he tries to convey his experience and his feelings about China:

> What I want to convey to you is that to me it was not China at all but right here, on this wharf. But that's not quite what I wanted to say. What I mean is what it was not was China: somewhere far away. What it was here, something solid, tactile, impenetrable. But perhaps neither one thing nor the other. (Lowry 25)

B. Carvalho quotes one of the first lines of this short story by Lowry: "I don't believe in China" (8). His reference to Lowry's China evokes the intangible, uncertain, questionable nature of the reality of the world in which B. Carvalho's protagonist lives. This intangibility translates into what the protagonist calls the language of the future, which is characterized, as he states, by its ability to avoid any kind of contradiction. He notes that "no fundo, o que vai dizer é outra coisa, o contrário, na língua do futuro. Uma palavra pela outra, na língua do futuro. A língua do futuro vai dizer sempre o contrário" ("ultimately, what one says means something else, the opposite, in the language of the future. One word in place of another word, in the language of the future. The language of the future will always state the opposite [of what one means to say]"; 52). Immediately following this statement, the protagonist goes on to tell his interlocutor that everything that he just said about being of Chinese heritage is false (53), thus proving to be a proficient speaker of the language of the future, which is, ultimately, a language that cannot be trusted; one that goes in the opposite direction of the precision that artificial languages have sought to achieve.

This language, the protagonist suggests, is rooted in capitalist culture. For him, the language of the future can be learned in any MBA course, that is, it is the language of business, of commodification. Racing toward the future, much like Lísias's protagonist, B. Carvalho's "estudante de chinês" believes that "[o] passado não existe. Só o futuro" ("the past does not exist. Only the future does"; 53). On one hand, this comment underscores the importance of chasing unattainable goals in capitalist culture because there is always more to be wanted and achieved. On the other hand, the comment in question, which appears on the last page of Part One, signals a postmodern disregard for the past.

The next part of the novel, titled "A língua do passado," signaling a desire to negate the aforementioned culture of capitalist accumulation, rescues the past by telling the story of a native Brazilian, to which I will return in the next section of this chapter. This part opens with a quote by the Spanish philosopher Ortega y Gasset, which serves as an epigraph: "Todo povo cala uma coisa para dizer outra. Porque tudo seria indizível" ("Every people silences something in order to say something else. Because saying everything would be impossible"; B. Carvalho 55). This attempt to make the past speak—in what is the longest part of the novel—brings to the fore a time of domination through physical and cultural violence that repeatedly emerges throughout history in different cultures and different geographies. At the same time, this attempt calls the attention of the reader to the fact that the past exists as the constructed narrative that is memory, in which the possibility of silencing and/or being silenced is always present, for better or for worse.

The last part of the novel, "A língua do presente," reinforces the idea of uncertainty developed in Part Two, portraying the present as eternal alienation, as suggested by the narrator's characterization of today's world as a "mundo de crentes" ("world of believers"), a reference to a (sometimes blind) faith in this or that perspective of reality (B. Carvalho 167). For him, today, individuals are easily manipulated by those who hold the power of language, such as religious leaders (167). The idea of an eternal present is further emphasized by the protagonist's allusion to the developmentalist discourse of the 1950s that imagined Brazil as "the country of the future."[9] He asks his interlocutor: "Sabe o que é viver no país e na cidade da possibilidade? ... Quer pior horror do que viver onde ainda parece possível mesmo se já não é possível há muito tempo?" ("Do you know what it is like to live in the country and the city of possibility? ... What could be worse than the horror of living where things still seem possible even if they haven't been so for a long time?"; 141–42). Like Lowry's character, the narrator pronounces his profound disbelief in the reality around him and in this promised future that has never arrived for Brazil. From this perspective, the country remains in an eternal present that expects a never-attainable future of prosperity.

B. Carvalho's portrayal of time, with its alteration of the temporal order between past, present, and future, its characterization of the future as disbelief, the past as extermination, and the present as eternal alienation, signals a contemporary response to what Andreas Huyssen characterizes as a crisis of the temporality that was predominant in the age of modernity (*Twilight Memories* 6). For Huyssen,

> The jumble of the non-synchronous, the recognition of temporal difference in the real world thus clashes dramatically with the draining of time in the world of information and data banks. But the borders between real world and its construction in information systems are of course fluid and porous. The more we live with the new technologies of communication and information cyber-space, the more our sense of temporality will be affected. (*Twilight Memories* 9)

Chapter Two

The temporality of B. Carvalho's novel establishes a link between the crisis of modernity with its promise of a linear move toward progress, and the chaos of information overload that we experience today, which negates this promise.

Language and Power

In *Reprodução*, B. Carvalho reflects about the power of language to both create and burst an information bubble. The novel establishes that language is power(ful). It is both creation and destruction. These two facets are addressed by B. Carvalho in an episode involving the encounter between a young officer and a native Brazilian from some remote tribe. According to the female officer, this native Brazilian would have been killed by a missionary because the latter would have wanted to become the only person in the world capable of speaking a language that could express "God." This language would have been the one spoken by the native Brazilian's tribe, and would have been exterminated with his death. The episode in question, which alludes to the colonization process of the Americas, characterized by the decimation of peoples, languages, and cultures, serves as a metaphor for the destructive power of language, when the power to speak allows one to also silence others.

The story of the native Brazilian can be linked to communication in the twenty-first century via a comment by one of the characters, who points out that "God" in Hebrew is "The Word," thus evoking the idea that God would have created the universe by bringing things into existence through utterances.[10] Curiously, this relationship between God and The Word also evokes a programmer's first experience when learning how to code. According to Pariser, the first sentence that programmers ever code is "Hello, world!" This gesture suggests a power of creation similar to that of God's: a sense that one can create entire universes on the screen. For Pariser, that is the moment when one senses that "if you're clever enough, you can make and manipulate anything you can imagine" (166). The story of the native Brazilian and that of the protagonist, albeit radically different, evoke the relationship between language and power throughout history. Just as the missionary conquers a sense of power by eliminating the other, the protagonist feels empowered by a process of information consumption that is highly excluding, for it leads to the disregard of the complexity of reality by restricting access to points of view that would challenge his perspective. Both of them acquire power by silencing others. Language, therefore, is seen in the novel as an extraordinarily potent and potentially dangerous tool.

A proof of this danger is the fairly narrow-minded and superficial nature of the protagonist's statements that we have seen so far, which raises questions about the early belief that the Internet would open up channels of democratic expression by decentralizing the power of information dissemination. As B. Carvalho himself notes in an interview by Raquel Cozer published in the Brazilian newspaper *Folha de São Paulo* in 2013, *Reprodução* presents an account of the only apparent freedom of the online world, in which users exchange free access for information that corporations gather about their everyday lives, without realizing the degree of asymmetry involved in this exchange. Indeed, we have witnessed an increase in the concentration of power in the hands of a few companies operating without much regulation (Pariser 141).

In *Reprodução*, the very acquisition of a language appears as the first step toward becoming enclosed in an information bubble: "quando a gente se conecta com uma língua e passa a usar os dez por cento de sons correspondentes a essa língua, perde a capacidade de ouvir os noventa por cento restantes" ("when we connect with a language and start using only ten percent of all the sounds that we can produce, we lose the capacity to hear the remaining ninety percent"; B. Carvalho 116). The acquisition of one linguistic code to the detriment of our capacity to speak other languages, viewed from this perspective, is paradoxically[11] akin to language death, at an individual level, in that it restricts our linguistic expression, which in turn results in the withering of possible ways of conceiving reality, as well as in the silencing of other worldviews. By drawing a parallel between language extinction and the shrinking of the protagonist's filter bubble, B. Carvalho cautions readers about the troubling consequences of consuming information like his protagonist does. The most serious of such consequences, according to Pariser, is the end of democracy itself:

> Ultimately, democracy works only if we citizens are capable of thinking beyond our narrow self-interest. But to do so, we need a shared view of the world we cohabit. We need to come into

> contact with other peoples' lives and needs and desires. The filter bubble pushes us in the opposite direction—it creates the impression that our narrow self-interest is all that exists. And while this is great for getting people to shop online, it's not great for getting people to make better decisions together. (164)

A possible answer to this rather dystopic future, B. Carvalho's novel suggests, lies in language itself, specifically, literary language. In fact, some of the same linguistic features used in *Reprodução* to represent the shrinking of our filter bubbles are also some of the novel's main strategies for potentially expanding our information horizon as readers. Let us take, for instance, B. Carvalho's use of monologues. While his strategy of giving us access to only one side of a dialogue represents our progressively single-minded views and somewhat schizophrenic reproduction of the information that we consume, it also challenges us to move in quite the opposite direction. On one hand, the limited access to the content of the conversations in the novel creates confusion. On the other hand, it also creates curiosity. As readers, we are prompted to wonder about what was left out, that is, the utterance to which a character is responding. The novel creates a knowledge gap that pushes us to inquire, to question, to want to learn more, and to be able to "listen" to the other interlocutor, whose words are missing from the text. In other words, it creates the kind of gap that can push someone like the protagonist out of his or her bubble.

Literature is explicitly mentioned in the novel several times when characters emphasize that they do not read novels because they "não pass[am] a vida fora da realidade" ("do not spend their lives outside of reality"; B. Carvalho 77). This statement is another of the many playful ways in which B. Carvalho juxtaposes reality and fiction. On one hand, the statement calls our attention to the fact that we are reading fiction that, nevertheless, so much resembles reality. On the other hand, the novel provides a good dose of the reality experienced by B. Carvalho's readers, as it cautions them about the dangers of said reality.

The novel references literature in a less explicit way when it introduces us to a character about whom we barely hear in the novel: *escrivã* Márcia. An *escrivã*, as the root of the Portuguese word indicates, is someone who *escreve*, that is, writes or records legal documents in courts. Márcia's job is in many ways the opposite of the job of a writer of fiction: rather than creating with language, she is expected to simply transcribe, in the most accurate and objective way possible. Nevertheless, Márcia is the only character who seems to be interested in literature, for she is the only one in the novel who reads fiction. Interestingly, she is also the only one who has a name, signaling her uniqueness in a story filled with characters named after generic descriptions of their attributes (the student of Chinese, the teacher of Chinese, the female officer, etc.). This uniqueness implies that literature serves as a kind of escape from the information bubble, to which Márcia is the only one who has access. Her wisdom comes across in a statement that she would have made, according to the female officer, that "os escritores procuram uma palavra mais forte que a morte" ("writers seek words that are stronger than death"; B. Carvalho 98). Her statement suggests the power of literature to make a profound, earth shattering even, impact on individuals. While Márcia *reproduces* speech in her reports, B. Carvalho *creates* speech in his novel, which is seemingly "transcribed" onto the pages that we read. The parallel between Márcia's work and that of her creator hints at the documentary nature of B. Carvalho's novel. In other words, the novel is, in a way, a (fictional) reproduction of behaviors and beliefs that we see in real life. Unfortunately, Márcia never really appears in the novel, but is rather spoken of by unreliable characters. This fact makes her existence questionable, casting doubt, by extension, on the possibility of the concrete realization of the power of literature that her character represents.

The novel suggests that other art forms besides literature can function as antidotes to the world of appearances and uncertainties that it portrays. It does so by referencing Brazilian singer and song writer Caetano Veloso's "Um índio" ("A Native"; *Bicho*). According to B. Carvalho's narrator, the power of the word will be delivered by a futuristic, science-fiction type of character, who will announce potentially life-altering perceptions of reality. This is a reference to Veloso's indigenous figure, who is expected to descend upon Earth in a shiny object, in the "heart of the Southern hemisphere" in Latin America. The song predicts that this indigenous figure will come after the last indigenous nation has been exterminated, to make revelations that will astonish humankind: "E aquilo que nesse momento se revelará aos povos / Surpreenderá a todos não por ser exótico / Mas pelo fato de poder ter sempre estado oculto / Quando terá sido o óbvio" ("And that which at this moment will be revealed to the peoples of the world / Will astonish all not for being something exotic / But for having always been able to stay hidden / While it will have been obvious"). Like B. Carvalho's indigenous character, Veloso's speaks a language that has a unique power: that of expressing the astonishingly obvious. This is, in fact, what B. Carvalho's novel itself does: it defamiliarizes the prejudiced and harmful discourses that permeate contemporary society, which are proclaimed by some as unquestionable truth, spreading daily in different types of media. In this way, the novel's message, like that of Veloso's futuristic indigenous figure, is quite simple. The novel shakes its readers by pointing out the pervasiveness and problematic nature of discourses that may hide behind their mindless repetition within the bubbles that we inhabit.

Of Utopic Futures

Both *O livro dos mandarins* and *Reprodução* depict what Bauman calls the "society of hunters," characterized by the end of utopia in the modern sense, that is, the end of utopia as an imagined future prosperity that we aim to reach through progress. For Bauman, "instead of living *towards* utopia, hunters are living *inside* utopia" (*Liquid Modernity* 109; italics in original). In other words, in a society of hunters, there is no future common goal to be reached, but rather an individual rush to stay in the race.

In their eternal quest for more, Lísias's and B. Carvalho's protagonists embody this very feeling of living in an endless utopia of a dystopic world. This quest is expressed in *O livro dos mandarins*, for instance, by Paulo's plans after the publication of his book: "… aquele é apenas o começo. Não tem por que parar agora. Só com outro, um verdadeiro escritor como ele preenche o vácuo que um livro deixa" ("… this is just the beginning. There is no reason to stop now. Only with another [book] can a true writer like him fill the void that a [finished] book leaves"; Lísias 337). As he repeatedly advises his customers and readers, it is essential to continue to succeed and to overcome more "challenges." In *Reprodução*, the never-ending nature of the quest for more is conveyed by the protagonist's obsessions with learning Chinese in order to stay ahead of everyone else. Paulo and "the student of Chinese" can both be described as hunters in Bauman's sense (*Liquid Times* 107). Hunting—for a promotion, fame, recognition, etc.—demands their full attention and much energy, leaving time for virtually nothing else.

Structural elements of both novels convey this end of the modern utopia as well. As we have seen, B. Carvalho's novel reflects about the crisis of the modern notion of time. In the case of *O livro dos mandarins*, this crisis is conveyed by the narrative's constant switches between past and future tenses, as in the following passage: "Ele ainda não sabe, mas a sua transferência para a China além de tudo ainda vai fazer com que ele conheça a cama Ceragem" ("He doesn't know yet, but his transfer to China, on top of everything, will allow him to find out about the Ceragem massage table"; Lísias 57). Many of these predictions presented as facts of which the character is yet unaware, actually do not come true. Paulo never travels to China, as we have seen, and, as the narrator indicates later on, he never really finds this massage table (183). The narrations in the future, while highlighting the race to stay ahead in today's liquid society, point to the challenges of such a culture of accumulation, hinting at the impossibility of sustaining such a state of utopia.

With this endless utopia, the novels suggest, comes not only an obsession with success, but polarization and lock down as authoritarian thought seems to become the norm, as the possibility of civil and rational democratic debate appears to fade away and as every corner of our lives becomes commodified. The kind of self produced in this world of apparently boundless commodification is one characterized by pettiness, selfishness, lack of empathy, and a dangerous sense of knowing everything without actually understanding much at all. Both *O livro dos mandarins* and *Reprodução* depict characters that are, like many individuals today, at the same time the embodiment and victims of consumer culture's values. While Paulo desperately tries to market himself as a successful man, "the student of Chinese" becomes a commodity to the companies that own information about him and sell him news as entertainment, shrinking his perspective rather than expanding his participation in the public sphere. The hyperreal conditions of these characters represent the hyperreality of consumer capitalism itself, in which success is often measured based on appearances. Like those who reproduce the neoliberal narrative, with its justifications to legitimize anything deemed necessary to achieve the restoration of class power that hides behind a promise of progress (Harvey, *A Brief History* ch. 1), Lísias's and B. Carvalho's protagonists reproduce discourses used to justify almost anything in the name of reaching a goal other than the one promised at the surface.

Both *O livro dos mandarins* and *Reprodução* propose a critique of this world reproduced by their protagonists. Caricatures portrayed via unreliable narratives, the novels' protagonists turn out to be flawed, pathetic, and delusional, yet they seem so real in so many ways. As the novels reveal the stories of failure that lie beneath an appearance of success, they make a case for the power of fiction in a world where ultra-conservatism has hijacked the criticism to mainstream media and turned it against those very sources of criticism, labeling everything that goes against its narratives "fake news."

Both novels also make the case that fiction can serve as an antidote to the deep alienation of the world they portray. In the case of Lísias, *O livro dos mandarins* is at once the book of neoliberal norms (Paulo's version) and the critique to neoliberal thought (Lísias's novel). With respect to B. Carvalho, *Reprodução* both reproduces the information overload that leads to the oversimplification of social reality by electronic media, and combats this oversimplification by posing a highly challenging linguistic exercise to the reader. Paradoxically, the way out of the new utopia that the novels denounce seems to be what is ultimately another utopia in the context of the novels: these characters' engagement with art. This solution seems utopic because, within their fictional worlds, these characters seem far from being open to ever reading the narratives in which they are protagonists. The only one who has potential, Márcia, has her existence questioned by the fact that all we know about her comes from unreliable characters, as we have seen.

According to contemporary Brazilian fiction that deals with consumer culture, is there hope for transformation within rather than beyond the everyday? Or is it all lost? Have we reached a point of no return? Has capitalism already "swallowed humanity" (Brown 44)? The narratives analyzed in the following chapters of this book paint a different picture. They point to the possibility of breaking away from the forces of consumer culture that target us every day. Albeit momentary, the very possibility of this break renews the hope that there is still a chance to do things differently. In the next chapter, I discuss Ana Paula Maia's representation of working-class consumers in three of her narratives. I show that these narratives, albeit still relatively bleak, envision the possibility of change in the realm of everyday life under consumer capitalism.

Chapter Three

Consumer Culture's "Collateral Damage"

On November 5, 2015, the Brazilian city of Mariana in the state of Minas Gerais was swallowed by mining waste after the collapse of a dam in the nearby sub-district of Bento Rodrigues. In the worst environmental disaster Brazil had ever seen, the waste left a death toll of at least nineteen people, destroyed the wildlife, displaced families, and polluted the Doce River for years to come. Hundreds of documents were submitted by prosecutors showing evidence that Samarco, the mining company that owns the dam, was aware of the potential failure of the structure. Nevertheless, more than three years later, the company continues to dodge its responsibility in courts, responding to the damage with either timid or rather questionable measures such as changing the course of a river (Phillips and Brasileiro).

While mainstream media certainly covered the collapse of the dam as the catastrophe that it was, the underlying neoliberal structure that sustains the power of companies such as Samarco goes largely uncontested by these news outlets. Little questioning is directed toward what leads up to disasters such as the one in Mariana and significantly less explosive coverage is given to their aftermath as time goes by. In other words, while much attention is paid to the immediacy of the disaster, the gradual and disperse destruction surrounding it tends to be much less visible. Rob Nixon calls the latter "slow violence," which he defines as "a violence that is neither spectacular nor instantaneous, but rather incremental and accretive, its calamitous repercussions playing out across a range of temporal scales" (2). Nixon points out that there is a representational challenge here: how do we convey the drama of slow violence in a society that is used to engaging with spectacle? How do we make these narratives visible?[1]

Chapter Three

This chapter departs from these questions as it examines three narratives by Ana Paula Maia: *O trabalho sujo dos outros* (*The Dirty Work of Others*), *Carvão animal* (*Animal Charcoal*) and *De gados e homens* (*Of Cattle and Men*). In these narratives, which tell the stories of firefighters, coalminers, slaughter men, trash collectors, and crematory workers, Maia focuses on the consequences of the slow violence of consumer capitalism for the environment. This violence includes not only the pollution of air and rivers, and the killing of animals, but also the exploitation of individuals made invisible by society. In other words, she takes the reader into the world of those who suffer what Bauman calls the "collateral damages" of consumer capitalism, that is, the failed consumers, who he describes as

> people with no market value; they are the uncommoditized men and women, and their failure to obtain the status of proper commodity coincides with (indeed, stems from) their failure to engage in a fully fledged consumer activity. (*Consuming Life* 124)

In all three narratives addressed in this chapter, Maia unveils the slow violence behind consumption by taking the readers behind the scenes of the production of energy and meat, specifically, and of a culture of disposal more broadly. Maia's work has been frequently described as pulp, brutal, and scatological; her pages filled with blood, violence, and destruction (Barbarena; Cruz; Garbero, "A brutalidade"; Martinho-Ferreira; Pietrani; Quandt; Valente Jr.). Indeed, these elements are present in the novels under analysis. However, these narratives also contain a kind of turning point, in which practices of consumer capitalism are either challenged, threatened, or interrupted. Particularly in *De gados e homens*, Maia evokes the possibility of a severe disturbance to the capitalist order, precipitated in the narrative by a mysterious fantastic event, which I will address in detail later. For this reason, I propose a reading of these works by Maia as narratives of *temporary radical suspension*, in the sense that they envision a halt to consumer capitalism that suspends production and/or consumption in the fictional universe that she creates. In this case, unlike in B. Carvalho's and Lísias's narratives, change is envisioned within rather than beyond the realm of everyday life. Maia's confrontation of the sustainability of consumerism suggests the urge to rethink what we understand as

Consumer Culture's "Collateral Damage"

human prosperity, as the latter has resulted in much decay caused by our over-consumption. Furthermore, her narratives bring to the fore the fact that the highest price of our consumerist culture has largely been paid by the invisible individuals that she portrays and that this cost is reaching other segments of society as cities become nearly uninhabitable, as *O trabalho sujo dos outros* suggests. Novels such as the ones analyzed in this chapter offer what Kate Soper would describe as a "dialectical insight into the displeasures of the consumer lifestyle and its possible transcendence [that] can help to keep alive that needed imagination [of alternative notions of progress and development]" (171).

Invisible Lives

Unlike the other novels analyzed so far in this book, Maia's narratives feature characters who consume very little, often just enough to stay alive. Instead of focusing on conspicuous consumption, Maia turns her attention to the consequences of consumer society for the exploited workers who do "the dirty work of others," that is, the kind of work that nobody wants to do, but that needs to be done in order for society to function the way that it does today. This work includes activities such as slaughtering animals, cremating bodies, collecting trash, and coal mining. In an interview by Christian Grünnagel, Maia notes the invisibility of this type of work in the face of the banality that the products and services provided by workers in these sectors acquire through our daily consumption rituals:

> O trabalho sujo é o desse sujeito que abate o boi para virar hambúrguer e ser comido. Você come ali, em cinco minutos, em pé, sem nem se dar conta. Você está ali falando no celular e comendo um hambúrguer. Aquele hambúrguer era um boi. Para matar um boi, você fica ensanguentado da cabeça aos pés. É um banho em sangue. Você não tem noção de quanto sangue sai de um boi, quantas vísceras são necessárias para você comer o hambúrguer ali em pé. Não me interessa contar a história do sujeito que come o hambúrguer, mas do sujeito que mata o boi … Eu quero ficar sempre nesse homem comum, quer dizer, nas atividades que, por sua vez, mantêm a ordem. A ordem da sociedade. Trabalho sujo dos outros. ("Ir" 364–65)

Chapter Three

> The dirty work is that of this guy who slaughters the cow that becomes the hamburger that gets eaten. You eat [the hamburger] there, in five minutes, standing up, without even realizing it. You're there talking on the cell phone and eating a burger. That burger one day was cattle. In order to kill cattle, you get bloody from head to toe. It's a blood shower. You have no idea how much blood drains from a cow, how much gut it takes for you to eat that burger there, standing. I'm not interested in telling the story of the man who eats the burger, but of the one who kills the cattle … I want to always focus on this ordinary man, that is, on these activities that, in turn, maintain order. Society's order. The dirty work of others.

Maia explores the theme of the dirty work of others as early as 2006 in a narrative titled precisely *O trabalho sujo dos outros*, which was initially published online in seven installments. In 2009, the narrative in question appears in print in a volume that also includes her novel *Entre rinhas de cachorros e porcos abatidos* (*Between Dogfights and Slaughtered Hogs*). In *O trabalho*, Maia addresses consumption both as lack and as excess. On one hand, the novel unveils the excesses of consumer society by portraying the aftermath of our daily consumption: piles and piles of discarded items, from food to human bodies whose organs have been harvested for sale. On the other hand, Maia zooms into the daily life of garbage collectors, who consume very little while risking their lives to pick up the remainder of other people's consumption, riding the back of trash trucks and handling all types of garbage without wearing much protective gear. These characters are dismembered in accidents involving trash compactors; they become contaminated by syringes they accidentally touch when collecting the trash; they lose their sense of smell; some of them die from falling off the trash truck. As the narrator points out, society does not even notice that, like cheap merchandise, they are easily replaced after they die. For society, they seem to have no recognizable value.

The value of the garbage collectors' work only becomes visible when their strike turns the entire city into a giant dumpster. The strike also makes painfully visible how much the city consumes, as evidenced by the amount of trash that it produces, which accumulates in the streets at an astonishing rate. As the narrator notes about the protagonist's job:

> No itinerário de Erasmo Wagner são recolhidas mais de vinte toneladas de lixo por dia. A riqueza de uma sociedade pode ser

Consumer Culture's "Collateral Damage"

medida pela sua produção de lixo. Vinte toneladas num itinerário consideravelmente pequeno o faz pensar no tanto que se gasta. No tanto que se transforma em lixo. Mas tudo vira lixo, inclusive ele é um lixo para muitas pessoas, até para os ratos e urubus que insistem em atacá-lo. (*O trabalho* ch. 1)

In Erasmo Wagner's itinerary, more than twenty tons of trash are collected daily. A society's wealth can be measured by its production of trash. Twenty tons in a considerably short itinerary makes [Wagner] think about how much is wasted. About how much becomes trash. But everything turns into trash, including himself, who is garbage for many people, even for the rats and vultures that insist on attacking him.

The trash collector's strike, therefore, makes the aftermath of consumption visible. The impressive amount of waste produced by consumer society, and which, almost like magic, disappears into the night once it is collected, now confronts middle- and upper-class consumers. They are forced to face some of the negative consequences of their own consumption, which are usually transferred to low-income workers such as the garbage collectors themselves. In this way, the hidden violence of consumption becomes exposed: not the shocking violence of robbery or mugging showed by the media and feared by the upper classes, but the violence of decay, of the "state of putrefaction" of what is discarded and comes back to haunt consumers, polluting the environment, generating disease (*O trabalho* ch. 5).

Part of this waste, nevertheless, becomes commodity again as other consumers repurpose some of the discarded items. Such is the case of mattresses, box springs, doors, armoires, and chairs that one of the protagonists, Erasmo Wagner, collects in order to sell later (*O trabalho* ch. 1). This waste generates another level of commerce, the only one that seems possible for these "failed consumers," who cannot afford to participate in more visible consumption. Some of them cannot even spare the price of food and have to search for it in a landfill; a precarious condition portrayed in the 1989 Brazilian film *Ilha das Flores* (*Isle of Flowers*) by director Jorge Furtado.[2] Playing with the expression "our daily bread," the narrator says that the people scavenging food in the trash waited for "our daily sewage," evoking a feeling of repulsion and discomfort. Readers are thus forced to confront the social inequalities generated by the capitalist system in which they participate as consumers.

Chapter Three

Differences in socioeconomic power manifest themselves even in scatological ways in *O trabalho*. Erasmo Wagner, continuing to force the reader to confront this abject reality, points out these social differences when he comments that "[d]inheiro sempre vira lixo. Lixo e bosta ... Meu primo Edivardes trabalha desentupindo esgoto. Isso sim é um trabalho de merda. Você precisa ver o esgoto das áreas mais ricas. Ele diz que é uma bosta densa ... Comida boa faz isso" ("money always turns into trash. Trash and shit ... My cousin Edivardes works unclogging sewage systems. This is for sure a shitty job. You need to see the sewage of the wealthiest areas. He says the shit is dense there ... Good food does that"; ch. 1). Erasmo Wagner further comments that he does not like the rich because they have a lot of money to spend and, consequently, they produce more trash (ch. 1). His comment inverts the social value of commodities. Instead of indicating a high social status, excessive consumption is portrayed as an abjection when the emphasis is placed not on the item as shiny and new, but on its state of putrefaction. The epitome of this abject state of consumer goods is embodied by a lake called *chorume*, from the verb "chorar" ("to cry"). This site, located by the nearby landfill, is "o fim de todas as coisas" ("the end of all things"), where anything from leftover food to human bodies is dumped (ch. 4). *Chorume* represents, by extension, the entire city, for the latter appears in the novel as an apocalyptic site when it is taken over by waste during the trash collectors' strike. The city becomes an immense dumpster itself, exposing the waste and the social exclusion that is made invisible to its middle- and upper-class inhabitants (ch. 5). Maia's novel recreates a universe that confronts us with the opposite of the dreams of consumer society. It operates in a similar way to Vik Muniz's recreations of canonical paintings from garbage, which according to Lúcia Bettencourt prompt us to face the other side of our consumption, by taking us to a site where

> Quase que num simulacro (*perverso*) do paraíso consumista moderno, ali estamos rodeados por todos os (não)objetos e, ao invés dos corredores climatizados e dos cenários elaborados para um show de propaganda, temos a temperatura insuportável, o cheiro desagradável, o ruído das máquinas ao invés da harmonia da música, numa (*sub*)*versão* que revela como somos todos igualmente infelizes perante o lixo e, portanto, como a felicidade obtida com o consumo não passa de uma ilusão, se, em última análise, consumir é produzir cada vez mais lixo. (10–11)

Consumer Culture's "Collateral Damage"

> Almost as in a (perverse) simulacrum of a modern consumer paradise, there we are, surrounded by all the (non)objects and, instead of the air-conditioned hallways or the elaborate sets of an advertisement, we have the unbearable temperature and the unpleasant smell; the noise of the machines instead of the harmonic sound of music, in a *(sub)version* that reveals how we are all equally unhappy when confronted with garbage and, therefore, how the happiness that we obtain from consumption is no more than an illusion, if, ultimately, to consume is to produce ever more garbage.

This apocalyptic scene, however, represents positive change by forcing an interruption of daily life. This interruption, in turn, highlights socioeconomic tensions. Although trash collectors go back to their dangerous and exploited routines and to their state of invisibility after the strike is over, there is a very symbolic moment of confrontation between them and those who ignore them. This moment takes place in the last few pages of the narrative, in which Erasmo Wagner, soaking wet from being in the rain and smelling rotten due to his contact with the trash, taps on the window of a "pale and perfumed" middle-class woman's car. She seems terrified of him and, hesitantly, asks him if they are collecting the trash again, to which he responds: "Sim. E é esse o nosso trabalho: recolher a sua merda porque a senhora não pode recolher sozinha. É isso que fazemos aqui" ("Yes, this is our job: to collect your shit because you can't collect it yourself. That's what we do here"; Maia, *O trabalho* ch. 7). This is the only direct class confrontation that we see in the novel. This confrontation suggests that, although Erasmo Wagner "permanecerá recolhendo o lixo dos outros, como uma besta de fardo, estéril, híbrida, que não questiona" ("will continue to collect other people's trash, like a domesticated beast, sterile, hybrid, who doesn't question"; ch. 7), "successful consumers," to play on Bauman's term, have now seen his face. There has been a moment of disruption, if not suspension, of social order that leaves its mark on that woman, on the society that ignores the dirty work of others. This presence, this appearing before the society that rejects them, confers an identity to these workers, which is also conveyed by the names that Maia chose for them. Erasmo Wagner's initials, E. W., which are the same initials of other characters in her novels (Elvis Wanderley, Ernesto Wesley, Edgar Wilson), are a reference to Edgar Allan Poe and his short story

"William Wilson" (1839).³ While their names remove them from an anonymous mass of "others," they also connect them as some sort of alter egos of the same individual, much like Poe's Wilson. Their names signal their shared background as inhabitants of the underworlds that Maia portrays, who emerge to disturb those who live on the surface.

Everyday Death

Also belonging to an underworld, many of the characters of *Carvão animal* literally spend most of their time below ground level, as is the case of the coalminers and the cremators—who work in the basement of the crematory—of the fictitious city of Abalurdes, where the story takes place. The novel explores the relationship between death and consumption—which also appears in *De gados e homens*, as we will see later in the analysis—by portraying (dead or dying) bodies as commodities. In the case of the workers, their bodies suffer the slow violence of their poor work conditions, which exposes them to toxic elements. The novel also highlights how socioeconomic differences extend beyond life, as evidenced by the differential treatment given in the crematory to the dead bodies of the rich versus the bodies of the poor. Yet, the novel makes the argument that, in spite of these differences in life and in the rituals surrounding our passing, death ultimately transforms us all into the same organic substance. Our bodies, commodified throughout our lives and the rituals surrounding death, will eventually end in dust. Opening with a quote from Genesis 3:19, "tu és pó e ao pó retornarás" ("for dust thou art, and unto dust shalt thou return"), the novel indirectly confronts the capitalist race to get ahead with the ephemeralness of life, thus rendering that race meaningless. In the novel, the fire is the ultimate "consumer," for it consumes everyone in Abalurdes, either in sudden fires or by the slow consequences of pollution. Beyond that final consumption, all are equal, reaching an after-life state that transcends consumer capitalism.

In the city of Abalurdes, the commodification of dead bodies, which are called "mercadoria" ("merchandise") several times throughout the novel,⁴ is made explicit from the very beginning, when we enter the local crematory with some of the main characters. On the wall of the facility, families find a list of rules that alerts that "Os restos mortais só serão recebidos mediante o recibo de pagamento" ("The remains will only be received upon proof of payment"; 26). This alert takes Bauman's notion of the commodification of the self described in Chapter 2 to yet another level, suggesting that, in consumer society, individuals are treated as commodities not only in life but also after death, through rituals. The commodification of the dead body becomes evident again when the workers of the crematory prepare for the visit of investors who want to transform Abalurdes into a "polo nacional de morte" ("national center of death"), according to the manager (Maia, *Carvão* 113). Following an accident with one of the crematory machines not too long before the investors' visit, the workers are forced to illegally cremate over eighty bodies at the local coal mine in exchange for allowing its owner to sell charcoal in which plant and human remains are mixed together. Like mass-produced goods in a factory, the bodies become valuable commodities, generating profit for the city by providing energy that keeps the town running.

In contrast with the deceased whose families can afford a ceremony, unclaimed bodies are dumped in the polluted stream behind the crematory, like defective goods. For those whose families do not have the means, there is little ceremony in honor of their passing. Such is the case of Palmiro, an elderly man well beyond retirement age, who is forced to continue to work in the crematory due to his financial situation. Palmiro lives in rather precarious conditions. He shares a room in the back of the crematory with J. G., another employee of the establishment in question. The room, as the narrator describes,

> é mínimo: uma cama de solteiro, um armário embutido de duas portas, um fogão de duas bocas, uma pia encardida e um velho criado-mudo com uma televisão de vinte polegadas sobre ele. A televisão é nova. Palmiro pagou quatrocentos reais em dez parcelas sem juros. (*Carvão* 62)

> is minimal: a twin bed, a two-door armoire, a two-burner stove top, a dirty sink and an old nightstand with a twenty-inch television on top. The television is new. Palmiro paid four hundred *reais* in ten installments without interest.

Chapter Three

Palmiro's precarious financial state has consequences beyond his death. Due to his lack of means, his body is only transported in a coffin—rather than cremated in it, as is the case for deceased ones whose families can afford the cremation—and is subsequently transferred to a tray on which it is cremated clandestinely (*Carvão* 99). His co-workers take the coffin from the funeral home without permission and return it as quickly as possible. Palmiro's only valuable possession is his gold teeth, which his co-workers remove after his death, as Palmiro had requested, and make sure that the teeth are delivered as inheritance to his daughter. Besides Palmiro, other characters living in precarious conditions emphasize the low value of their few possessions. For example, Dona Zema, a neighbor of one of the main characters, notes that her chickens are "o que tenho de mais valioso na vida. Nem essa casa aqui é minha, é do meu irmão. Só tenho as galinhas pra me valer" ("the most valuable things that I have in life. Not even this house is mine, it is my brother's. The only thing I can rely on is the chickens"; 92). In an even more precarious position is J. G., whose sole material accumulation is said to be his body fat, which is "o reverso de todas as suas perdas, amarguras e sofrimentos" ("the reverse of all his losses, bitterness, and suffering"; 31–32).

Countering consumer capitalism's false promise of expressing one's individuality through ownership of commodities, the novel emphasizes that, after death, the only thing that actually sets us apart from one another and that allows our bodies to be recognized after they have decomposed is our teeth. The story opens with the narrator pointing out that, "sua profissão, dinheiro, documentos, memória, amores não servirão para nada" ("your profession, money, documents, memory, love stories, won't make any difference"; *Carvão* 9). It closes in a similar way, reaffirming the value of one's teeth over everything else that one may own, by stating that identifying one's teeth is the only way to tell a human being apart from mere ashes if one dies in a fire (158). Both the opening and the closing of the novel feature firefighter Ernesto Wesley, whose body appears as fragile and invincible at the same time. Wesley, who lost his daughter in a car accident and later on also lost his wife, suffers from a congenital disease that prevents him from feeling any physical pain. On one hand, this condition allows him to deal with circumstances that his peers would likely be unable to face (50). On the other hand, the condition makes him highly vulnerable to dying without even realizing that anything is wrong with him. Throughout the novel, we see Wesley entering buildings on fire to rescue agonizing victims or cutting through metal and body parts in order to remove people from cars smashed in road accidents. Wesley, thus, represents strength and fragility, invincibility and ephemeralness at the same time. Read against the novel's representation of consumer capitalism, he stands for both vulnerability and defiance of the slow violence that "the dirty work of others" impinges on his body.

The slow violence of which Wesley and the other characters of *Carvão animal* are victims runs deep into the environment that they inhabit. As in *De gados e homens*, in which the Rio das Moscas (River of the Flies) is contaminated by the blood and remains of the cattle, and as in *O trabalho sujo dos outros*, in which the *chorume* reeks of decomposing material, death contaminates the soil and the water of Abalurdes with toxic substances (*Carvão* 59). As a solution to the excess of dead bodies buried in its soil, the city turns their diseased into charcoal, an experiment that Maia affirms to have actually been carried out in a small town in Germany ("Ir" 366). For Abalurdes, however, this solution only brings more death, for it is anchored in capitalist exploitation and relies on yet another process that causes environmental destruction through water and air pollution. The narrator's description of the city itself evokes death and decay:

> O rio é morto e espelha a cor do sol. Não há peixes e as águas estão contaminadas. O céu, mesmo quando azul, torna-se carvoento nos fins de tarde. Uma região lamacenta e gelada nos dias de inverno. Nas áreas mais afastadas, ainda existem casas de alvenaria que são simples e desbotadas, a pavimentação é precária em algumas partes isoladas da cidade, com resquícios de um antigo asfalto. A estrada principal é mal iluminada, sem sinalização e com curvas acentuadas que margeiam longos despenhadeiros. (*Carvão* 71)

> The river is dead and reflects the color of the sun. There are no fish and the waters are contaminated. The sky, although blue, becomes coal-like at dusk. A muddy area, cold during the winter. In more remote areas, there are still simple faded brick houses; pavement is precarious in some isolated parts of the city, where there are traces of old asphalt. The main road is poorly lit, without signage and with sharp curves that border long cliffs.

Chapter Three

And later on in the narrative:

> O aspecto carvoento do céu se intensificou. A impossibilidade de os raios de sol atravessarem tanto a camada de fuligem que cobre o teto da cidade quanto as nuvens carregadas transforma Abalurdes num lugar desolador. Uma espécie de deserto de cinzas; com o céu pesado, formado por blocos de nuvem que aparenta concreto. Um céu sem dimensões. (*Carvão* 94)

> The coal-like look of the sky intensified. The impossibility for sunrays to go through both the layer of soot that covers the roof of the city and the dark clouds make Abalurdes a desolate place. It is a kind of desert of ashes; with heavy skies formed by blocks of clouds that look like concrete. A sky without dimensions.

With descriptions such as the ones above, among others that highlight the poor health of Abalurdes's working class,[5] the narrator unveils how that which is extraordinary has become ordinary for the town's population. Read against the everydayness with which the coal miners, the firefighters, and the crematory employees go about their work, passages such as the ones above highlight how one, in the words of Phaedra Pezzullo and Stephen P. Depoe, can become accustomed to *anything* (103). Throughout the narrative, we see characters eating lunch while hoping for bodies to burn fast so that they can go home and rest after a long work day, approaching the challenge of cremating tens of bodies merely as a task that will allow them to keep their jobs and to get a raise, or yet not worrying about the thick dark mucus that they spit out as a consequence of breathing in the toxic air from where they work. The everydayness with which these actions are portrayed in the novel demonstrates not only that workers become conditioned to see death as business and tragedies as mundane, but also that they simply *have to* approach their reality in this manner. Only in this way can they survive their grueling invisible routines in dark and damp coal mines and crematory basements.

Of Meat Consumption

De gados e homens similarly brings to the fore other segments of society that, like the trash collectors of *O trabalho sujo dos outros* and the characters of *Carvão animal*, can be considered "failed consumers" for their extremely limited consumption and their consequent social invisibility. The novel highlights the everyday life of slaughter men, following the process of meat production and its environmental and socioeconomic costs. *De gados* denounces the slow violence of capitalism that results in the pollution of the local river, the impoverishment of the community that lives near the slaughterhouse, and the disposability of the slaughter men.

The main characters of *De gados* work for Seu Milo, the owner of the slaughterhouse, who is portrayed as a self-centered voracious capitalist who regards his employees as disposable merchandise. This aspect of Seu Milo's character becomes evident when, upon learning about the death of Burunga, who is one of his employees, he promptly forces everyone else to work through the night in order to make up for the deceased worker's hours. Burunga dies accidentally while trying to raise money to buy glasses for his daughter. His death is "collateral damage" of Seu Milo's exploitation, given that the little amount that he earns as a slaughter man forces him to resort to another way of making money that ends up costing his life. The fact that two weeks after Burunga's death, "it feels as if he had never been there," conveys his low value for Seu Milo, which in turn stands for the low value of the many lives that are exploited at the slaughterhouse, as elsewhere in consumer society. Burunga and his coworkers work six days a week, slaughtering more than one hundred cows per day, making only a few cents per cow (Maia, *De gados* 13). They are hardly ever consumers of the meat that they produce simply because they cannot afford it. The indifference with which Seu Milo treats Burunga's death represents capitalism's systematic indifference toward those deemed redundant, that is, those with little to no consumer power, who are allowed to die for the sake of profit (Tyner 208).

De gados highlights that the exploitation that takes place at the slaughterhouse extends to the cows that are slaughtered there. As the title itself suggests, Maia traces a parallel between the slaughter men and the cattle in the novel, connecting the capitalist violence against animals to the violence committed against those considered "devalued humans" (Nibert 117). This parallel is conveyed, for instance, by the way in which the narrator describes characters' actions using words like to growl, to howl, or to ruminate, thus portraying them as somewhat animalistic, much in the way of John Steinbeck's characters in *Of Mice and Men* (1938), to which

Chapter Three

the title of Maia's novel alludes.[6] The cows, on the other hand, are described as having human cognitive abilities, such as thinking and planning, a point to which I will return later. A similar parallel appears again in Maia's most recent novel, *Enterre seus mortos* (*Bury Your Dead;* 2018), which features Edgar Wilson—one of the main characters of *De gados*—as a protagonist, and takes place after *De gados*. In *Enterre*, Wilson works picking up dead animals from highways. Along the way, he ends up collecting human bodies as well because the latter "[valem] tanto quanto um abutre e [merecem] ser recolhid[os] como o resto dos animais mortos" ("[are worth] as much as a vulture and [deserve] to be picked up as much as the remains of dead animals"; 48). On one hand, his comment implies that, for society, these human lives are perceived as being worth less than those of vultures, that is, than those of animals that humans consider the most repugnant. On the other hand, by affirming that all of these dead bodies, human or otherwise, deserve attention, he values both types of life equally, dissolving any hierarchy between human beings and other animals, no matter how devalued by humans these lives might be. Even in life, humans are treated like dead animals in the novels, as when Edgar gives a ride to the hospital to a couple with their dying daughter. The couple, who has no one else to turn to because of the state of total abandonment in which the population of the area finds itself—there is no ambulance that can take them—join the dead animals in the back of Wilson's truck (28–29). The animalization of humans and humanization of animals that we see in Maia's novels suggests their shared condition as victims of the same oppressive system in which the many are exploited in order to advance the goals of the few.

The connection between cattle and men established by Maia is also suggested by a comment made by one of the workers of the slaughterhouse, Helmuth, about the cattle, which could just as easily be applied to himself and his coworkers: that the animals live and die "under man's power," existing merely to serve them (*De gados* 94). The connection between men and cattle reinforced by this comment is also implied by a slip of the tongue by another character, a university professor who declares, in a visit to the slaughterhouse with his students, that they will visit "a fábrica de hamburger que processa a carne de vocês" ("the hamburger factory that processes your meat"; 67). In the professor's statement, the word *meat* can be read as either the cow's meat that the men produce or their own flesh, suggesting that both men and cattle are reduced to a product upon which Seu Milo builds his capital. Besides the workers, prostitutes who exchange sex (their own flesh, in a sense) for cuts of meat at the slaughterhouse are also portrayed as "devalued humans," becoming both commodities and consumers of what is, metaphorically, the same.

Maia takes the parallel between the exploitation of humans and other animals even further by using as one of the epigraphs of the novel a quote that has been attributed to German philosopher Theodor Adorno, although this authorship is open to debate. The quote—"É apenas um animal ... somente um animal" ("It's just an animal ... only an animal")—appears both in German and in Portuguese in the novel and would have been extracted from a longer sentence that compares animals to the victims of the Holocaust: "Auschwitz begins whenever someone looks at a slaughterhouse and thinks: they are only animals."[7] The comparison in question, which has been made by the organization for animal rights PETA (People for the Ethical Treatment of Animals), and which has caused much controversy, contributes to establishing the link between the cattle and the men who slaughter it as beings who are perceived as inferior and are, for this reason, considered disposable.

The epigraph that opens Maia's novel appears along with Leviticus 17:11—"Porque a vida da carne está no sangue" ("For the life of the flesh [also *meat*, in Portuguese] is in the blood")—, which references sacrificial rituals as atonement. The idea of sacrifice is central to the representation of change in *De gados e homens*, for the novel depicts a sacrifice that, contrary to its meaning in many societies, suspends rather than renews social order. According to anthropologist Daniel Miller, the renewal of social order is a common theme in rituals such as Vedic and some contemporary African sacrifices (*Theory* 80). He further notes that sacrifice is tied to consumption in the sense that

> ... the defining feature of sacrifice is the moment in which the object of sacrifice is literally consumed. Most commonly it is livestock or plants that have been up to that point the focus of labour and production. The act of sacrifice then takes the moment at which production is transmuted into consumption and appropriates it for the purpose of sanctification and receiving the powers of transcendent objects of devotion on behalf of individuals and society. (83)

Chapter Three

On one hand, the daily killing of cows in the novel evokes the sacrifice of one hundred oxen to the gods in Ancient Greece. The word for the ritual, hecatomb, came to mean, both in Portuguese and in English, catastrophe. From this perspective, the literal slaughtering of the cows and the metaphorical slaughtering of the men would represent the hecatomb of consumer capitalism: the sacrifice of the many so that the few can prosper. On the other hand, a mysterious mass suicide committed by the cattle can be interpreted as a sacrificial ritual transmuted into transgression. In a final symbolic gesture, the cows' (self-)sacrifice transfers the power from Seu Milo to a starving population that lives nearby, not only because the cows become meat for this population but also because their sacrifice interrupts the chain of exploitation at the slaughterhouse.

This sacrifice is foreshadowed by the cow's unusual behavior throughout the novel, starting with a high number of miscarriages, followed by the cows no longer facing north when they graze, which Edgar Wilson, in a conversation with his coworkers, notes to be strange. Next, cows start to commit suicide individually by running into walls and trees. Then, the water of the river, which is polluted with the cows' blood from the slaughtering, turns salty. This incident is followed by the heaviest rain ever seen in the area where the slaughterhouse is located. The rain pours over the characters as they search for twenty-two cows that disappeared overnight, only to find them dead at the bottom of a cliff, by the river. Looking for evidence that someone or an animal had pushed the cows down the cliff, the workers of the slaughterhouse watch, astonished, another group of thirty-five cows simply walk off the precipice on their own. The heavy rain represents a kind of cleansing of the dirty work that takes place at the slaughterhouse. Along with the actual rain, the narrator describes the cows' suicides as a "rain of cows" or a "rain of meat" for the poor people who live at the bottom of the cliff. Previously in the narrative, we learn that there is a group of famished men, women, and children who come to the slaughterhouse periodically in the hopes of claiming meat from cows that fail to endure the conditions under which they are shipped—in crowded and unsanitary trucks that take them on long trips from the farms to the slaughterhouse. Seu Milo's employees, following his orders, attempt to drive the starving population away. When the cows throw themselves down the cliff, about fifty men, women, and children rush onto the dead animals and cut pieces out for their own consumption. Interpreting the cows' suicides as a divine intervention, one of the men says to Seu Milo's employees: "As vacas se jogaram lá de cima. Nossas preces foram ouvidas" ("The cows jumped off the cliff. Our prayers have been answered"; Maia, *De gados* 118). By committing suicide, the cattle brings to the starving population the prosperity that The Charging Bull, the massive sculpture sitting on Wall Street, symbolizes and that capitalism has yet to deliver to these segments of society. As the novel's reference to Leviticus suggests, the cows' suicide is the "atonement for the souls" of the starving. As a transgressive act that destabilizes the capitalist order at the slaughterhouse, it represents the reparation that the starving population deserves as victims of consumer capitalism. According to what the narrator indicates, death in this case provides life to the famished population:

> O suicídio das vacas jamais poderá ser explicado. Talvez tenha sido Providência Divina atendendo aos pedidos dos moradores da região que ansiavam por comida, especialmente carne. Assim como os peregrinos do deserto foram atendidos com uma chuva de codornas, os povos de outros desertos receberam uma chuva de vacas: a carne proveniente dos céus; a morte que dá vida. (*De gados* 123)
>
> The cows' suicide will never be explained. It might have been divine intervention, an answer to the prayers of the locals who longed for food, especially for meat. Like the pilgrims in the desert whose prayers were answered with a rain of quails, the people from other deserts received a rain of cows: the meat that came from the heavens; death that generates life.

The reference to Exodus 16 in the passage above evokes the idea of communal and equal share of food/goods, when the Israelites were sent the manna of quails from God while in the desert. On that day, the Israelites are said to have been likewise granted enough provisions to satisfy everyone's hunger. Maia makes further reference to this biblical passage by introducing into the story cows that are supposedly from Israel, and seem to have initiated the cows' rebellion against the slaughterhouse that culminated with the suicides and, consequently, with the feeding of the starving population.

After the cows' suicide, order is apparently re-established at the slaughterhouse. However, the narrator's use of verbs in the future,

Chapter Three

rather than the past, to describe what happens next ("em poucos meses a produção aumentará" ["in a few months production will increase"; *De gados* 123]), Seu Milo's fear regarding the future, and the equally mysterious disappearance of cows in a nearby farm that shuts down for good, hint at the possibility of an equally permanent interruption of the activities of the slaughterhouse. From this perspective, the cows' suicide can be read as a metaphor for the possibility of interruption of capital exploitation via disrupting the consumption of products such as meat produced in such cruel conditions. The challenge that the cows' unexplained behavior poses to the human characters can be interpreted as a representation of the unsustainability of consumer society. As Edgar Wilson comments when he learns that the cows have jumped off the cliff, quoting the Book of Psalms 42:7, "Um abismo chama outro abismo" ("Deep calleth unto deep"; 112). In other words, the perpetuation of atrocities such as the animal cruelty, the human exploitation, the greed, the environmental damage, and the social injustice that happen around the slaughterhouse can only result in self-destruction. As Seu Milo and his employees are challenged to understand the cows' suicide, readers are prompted to think about the "immeasurable horror," as Edgar Wilson characterizes it, behind the "delicious and delicate" things that daily consumption tends to obscure (21).

In this moment of interruption of the established order caused by the suicide of the cows, Edgar Wilson appears as a kind of mysterious and perceptive agent of change. From the beginning, it is clear that he has a special connection with the cattle. He demonstrates compassion for each cow that he stuns, producing a hissing sound that calms the animal down (*De gados* 11). An ambiguous character, Wilson is capable of brutally murdering as an expression of compassion. This is evident when he kills Zeca, a young man who takes pleasure in making the cattle suffer before slaughtering it (38), and subsequently makes the body disappear. Edgar Wilson, thus, echoes Edgar Allan Poe's William Wilson, after whom he is named.[8] Two opposing forces drive him. When the cows start to commit suicide, he is the only one who senses that there is no plausible explanation for the cows' behavior. According to the narrator, he has a special connection with the animals: "Edgar sente-se tão afinado com os ruminantes, com seus olhares insondáveis e a vibração do sangue em suas correntes sanguíneas, que às vezes se perde em sua consciência ao questionar quem é o homem e quem é o ruminante" ("Edgar feels so connected with the ruminants, with their unfathomable gaze and the vibration of their bloodstream, that sometimes he loses his conscience when questioning who is the man and who is the ruminant"; 68). In this description, Edgar becomes one of the cattle.

His identification with the cows is further suggested by his satisfaction when the students who visit the slaughterhouse demonstrate extreme discomfort as they become familiar with the process of slaughtering. When asked by a student about whether what he does is a crime and whether he is ashamed of doing his work, Edgar Wilson replies: "A senhora já comeu um hambúrguer? ... E como a senhora acha que ele foi parar lá?" ("Ma'am, have you ever had a burger? ... And how do you think it ended up there?"; *De gados* 71–72). Handing the student the hammer that he uses to "put the cows to sleep," as he prefers to think of his task, he adds: "A senhora pode descobrir se quiser. Desde o início. Conhecer todo o processo, não foi pra isso que vocês vieram? Se quiser fazer seu próprio hambúrguer, o processo começa aqui" ("Ma'am, you can find out for yourself, if you want. From the beginning. You can learn about the whole process, isn't this what you came here for? If you want to make your own burger, the process starts here"; 72). Edgar Wilson's comment denounces consumers' indirect responsibility for the killing of the cattle, making visible the death and cruelty behind the banal act of eating a hamburger and suggesting a relationship between consumption and crime. The woman ends up crying after that response while another student in the group vomits. During this visit, Edgar Wilson declares: "Eu sou o atordoador" ("I am the stunner"; 69), in a symbolic moment that suggests his connection with the cattle and their rebellion, so to speak, in the narrative. The word *atordoador*, which is used to refer to the person responsible for stunning the animals in the first phase of slaughtering, comes from the verb *atordoar*, which also means to disturb, to cause discomfort. Edgar, indeed, disturbs the students, as we have seen, by calling their attention to the fact that they partake in a crime when they consume meat. His close identification with the cows, who also *atordoam*, that is, disturb the order at the slaughterhouse, suggests his underlying role as an agent of change in the chain of exploitation that sustains the meat industry.

Chapter Three

It is also by following Edgar in his visit to the hamburger factory to which Seu Milo sells meat that we are further exposed to the connection between death and consumption in the novel. By establishing this relationship, the novel reconstructs the path of killing and exploitation that is mostly erased in the process of meat production. Along this path, there is a sort of "cleansing" of this process, which becomes evident in a contrast between the dirty space of the slaughterhouse and the cleanliness and whiteness of the hamburger factory. When Edgar Wilson visits the factory to run an errand, the narrator notes how the office to which the receptionist takes the protagonist is "limpo, arejado e iluminado" ("clean, airy, and bright"; *De gados* 18). As Edgar walks through the factory, he passes by men wearing perfectly white overalls, which contrast with the filth at the slaughterhouse, where one can find "uma quantidade excesiva de sangue e pedaços de crânio esfacelado" ("an excessive amount of blood and pieces of destroyed skulls"; 20). The slaughterhouse is further described as a space where one can witness the exsanguination and slaughter of the cattle. Further descriptions of the slaughterhouse provide a rather vivid and gruesome picture of the activities that take place there: "Depois da sangria e da remoção da pele, o gado, suspenso por correntes, é empurrado por uma carretilha até chegar a Helmuth, o desmembrador, que usa uma motosserra para remover a cabeça e partir a carcaça ao meio" ("After the exsanguination and the removal of the skin, the cattle, hanging from chains, is pushed along a roulette until it gets to Helmuth, the employee responsible for dismembering the cows, who uses a chainsaw to remove the head and to cut the carcass in half"; 24). Later in the narrative, the narrator explicitly notes the effacement of the dirty work required to produce meat once the latter reaches the factory: "Lá na fábrica de hambúrguer a brancura reflete uma paz que não existe, um clarão que cega a morte. Todos são matadores, cada um de uma espécie, executando sua função na linha de abate" ("Over at the hamburger factory, the whiteness of the place reflects a peace that does not exist, brightness that blinds death. Everyone is a killer, each one of a different kind, executing a task in the slaughtering line"; 45). Maia sarcastically points out this effacement when the narrator subtly notes Seu Milo's hypocrisy in closing the slaughterhouse on Sundays in order to go to church, as a good Catholic should do in his view. For Seu Milo, this is a sacred day, a day to consume, so to speak, Christ's flesh and blood, after exploiting the flesh and shedding blood of hundreds of cows—and of the men that slaughter them—during the week.

During Edgar's visit to the factory, the man with whom he talks interrupts their conversation upon learning that Edgar is one of the workers responsible for killing the cows. The explanation as to why the conversation is interrupted comes later, when the narrator remarks that the factory employee "imagina o trabalho que o homem diante dele faz e não gosta de pensar nisso. Olha para o resto do seu almoço sobre a mesa: um hambúrguer com molho de mostarda escura levemente apimentada e picles" ("imagines the work of the man standing in front of him and prefers not to think about it. He looks at his lunch on the table: a hamburger with a mildly spicy dark mustard sauce, and pickles."; *De gados* 19). Juxtaposing the image of Edgar killing the cows with the image of the hamburger on the table, the narrator links the beginning to the end of the process, reminding readers of the ethical implications of their meat consumption and, more broadly, of the atrocities that may pile up along the production process of any commodity.

De gados e homens is thus a reflection about the effacement of the exploitation involved in and the socioeconomic imbalances caused by acts as simple as consuming a hamburger in today's capitalist society. The novel questions the morality of consumption, interrogating to what extent the banal act of eating meat transforms the consumer into a murderer, albeit indirectly. The narrative seeks to undo the effacement of the connection between social and environmental atrocities and everyday consumption. It traces the line of direct and indirect participants in killing and exploitation, from the producer to the consumer. As the narrator points out when he gives us access to Wilson's thoughts: "São todos homens de sangue, os que matam e os que comem. Ninguém está impune" ("They all have blood in their hands, those who kill and those who eat. No one is innocent"; *De gados* 126).

Conclusion

In all three narratives addressed in this chapter, Maia challenges some of the practices of consumer capitalism that lie beneath activities such as the mass production of meat, the commodification of death, and the disposability of many of the articles that we consume. She highlights the slow violence of capitalism by suggesting that spaces such as the slaughterhouse, the coal mine, the landfill, and the crematory are neither static nor isolated. They are rather connected to other spaces and times that are not immediately apparent to us, "for the past of slow violence is never past, so too the post is never fully post: industrial particulates and effluents live on in the environmental elements we inhabit and in our bodies, which epidemiologically and ecologically are never our simple contemporaries" (Nixon 8). In other words, what happens in the spaces depicted by Maia flows into rivers, into the soil, runs through the body, travels through the air, and produces long-lasting consequences.[9]

It is important to note, however, that although Maia portrays a variety of characters—firefighters, coal miners, cattlemen, trash collectors, and cremators—her narratives at times make sweeping naturalistic claims regarding the characters' personalities that are as problematic as Bonassi's. These men are frequently called "homens brutos" ("rude men"), "ruminantes" ("ruminant"), and "bestiais" ("bestial"), being reduced at times to a psychological state that simply reflects the perceived nature of their occupations. In *O trabalho*, for instance, the narrator states: "Quando se quebra asfalto, se recolhe lixo ou se desentope esgotos diariamente, seu cérebro passa a ser um órgão sub-nutrido. É difícil entender um detalhe a mais. Se interessar por alguma coisa fica um pouco mais difícil" ("When you work drilling asphalt, collecting trash, or unclogging sewers daily, your brain becomes a malnourished organ. It is difficult to understand detailed information. Getting interested in something becomes a little more difficult"; 102). In turn, the narrator of *Carvão* argues that

> [é] impossível controlar a todos. É difícil tratar com peões. São homens brutos, de índole primária e arredios à obediência. Lidar com peões é como apascentar jumentos no deserto ... A imensidão das extensas proporções de terras ao redor pode esmagar a condição humana que existe até no mais bruto dos homens. Os jumentos são animais difíceis de dominar. Arredios, tentam derrubar quem neles monta; e, quando derrubam, eles pisam em cima e ainda tentam morder. São bestiais em muitos sentidos, esses homens e os jumentos. (74)
>
> [i]t's impossible to control all of them. It's hard to deal with peons. They are brute men, of primitive nature, and resistant

> to obedience. Dealing with peons is like taming donkeys in the desert ... The immensity of the vast lands around [them] is capable of smashing the human nature that even the most brute man has. Donkeys are difficult animals to dominate. Indomitable, they try to knock down those that attempt to mount them; and, when they do so, they stomp [on those trying to mount them] and try to bite. They are bestial in many ways, these men and donkeys.

As the passages above show, Maia's characters are often stereotyped into savages. Even though there seems to be an attempt to praise the men for not being submissive, or the intention to point out that human beings are not superior to animals, it seems rather problematic to limit this comparison to certain segments of society and to portray such segments as incapable of having complex thoughts and feelings. This is especially the case in stories told by a third-person narrator that clearly distances himself/herself from the universe that he/she portrays, as is the case of the novels discussed in this chapter. In this sense, the narratives become somewhat voyeuristic, offering the opportunity to peek into the "exotic" world of these men.

On one hand, Maia paints a bleak picture of our current experiences with consumption and hints at the serious challenges of breaking away from the world of commodities as we know it. For example, while Edgar Wilson tries to be as humane as possible when killing the cows and acknowledges the horrific nature of meat production, he does not, however, hesitate to eat the hamburger he is given at the factory. *Carvão*, in turn, repeatedly states that fire consumes everything one owns in a split second, leveling everyone's socioeconomic status to nothing, and that the only thing that really defines our identities when no possessions are left is our teeth. Yet, pieces of burned human bones are commodified by the coal industry. Nevertheless, Maia also indicates the possibility to confront and even transcend consumer capitalism, albeit through means that would lead to partial or total annihilation. If in *O trabalho* this confrontation is rather timid, represented by a moment in which the successful consumers are forced to see the faces of the failed ones that they insist on ignoring, in *De gados* and in *Carvão*, death and sacrifice, paradoxically, announce the possibility of change. Through death, eventually, everyone is leveled to dust, or through sacrifice—which also results in (redemptive)

Chapter Three

death—the social order can be disturbed, and exploitation can be put to an end, as evidenced by the shutting down of the farm near the slaughterhouse. More than denouncing the brutalization of consumer society, Maia gives an equally brutal response to it, in which its destruction meets the possibility of transcendence into a new state, one of equality and abundance for those who are made invisible today.

Maia's portrayal of our existence in consumer capitalism thus conveys a certain hope that is absent in Bonassi's and Sant'Anna's and that is less detached from everyday life than Lísias's and B. Carvalho's, in the sense that, within the fictional universe that she creates, the possibility of change concretely takes place and has real, albeit temporary, consequences. In the next chapter, I will analyze two novels that move the needle of hope a little further in a positive direction.

Chapter Four

A Consumer's Dreams and Nightmares

For those who grew up during the 1980s and the 1990s in Brazil, a time when the country more strongly embraced neoliberalism,[1] and commercials for all sorts of products abounded in various television shows, it is common to think of their childhood and teenage years in terms of the products that they consumed or desired. A quick search for "anos 1980" on google.com.br produces images of popular television shows for children such as *Xou da Xuxa*, cartoons, toys, comic books, Brazilian and North American actors and the most famous characters that they played during that time, pop icons such as Michael Jackson, Madonna, and Cindy Lauper, and many other references to consumer culture. Likewise, a search for "anos 1990" yields a collection of images that are relevant for children and teenagers of the decade in question, including the typical grunge "uniform" of the time: jeans and plaid wool shirts. This collective consumer memory also manifests itself on social media. On Facebook, for example, one can encounter groups such as "Revivendo os anos 80 e 90" ("Reliving the 1980s and 1990s"), which gathers, as of the writing of this book, over 600,000 followers and features posts as disparate a photo of an old toothpaste brand and a video of Tina Turner singing her 1991 hit "(Simply) The Best." Twenty-first century Brazilian literature that deals with consumer culture has also incorporated this imagery. Two examples of fiction that do so are the object of our analysis in this chapter: Daniel Galera's *Mãos de cavalo* (*Horse Hands*) and Michel Laub's *A maçã envenenada* (*The Poison Apple*).

In the previous chapter, I discussed how Maia's representation of the everyday life of workers who remain largely invisible in today's world unveils some of the collateral damage of consumer culture. As argued, unlike Bonassi and Sant'Anna—who represent consumer culture as totalizing—, and unlike Lísias and

Chapter Four

B. Carvalho—whose only possible way out of a dystopic world of consumption is to be found in the realm of arts—, Maia takes a step further and suggests the possibility of a radical change, albeit temporary, within the realm of the everyday proper. In this chapter, I propose that Galera's and Laub's novels under analysis, like Maia's, represent everyday life in consumer capitalism as open to change. This change, however, rather than punctual and radical, is depicted as an insistent oscillation between moments of surrender to the potentially alienating powers of consumer culture, and moments of self-awareness and self-criticism. Amidst their protagonists' obsession with troubling past experiences mediated by commodities that seem to define the rest of their lives, there are moments that signal possibilities to start anew. This new start is not to be understood as a complete break from everyday life, but rather as movements between alienation and disalienation in the terms proposed by Lefebvre (*Critique* 340). According to Lefebvre, neither of these two movements is absolute, that is, they are not points in a structured continuum toward which one decidedly progresses. Rather, they are in a dialectical relationship to one another. In this way, a disalienation can lead to deeper forms of alienation. Conversely, an alienation can be disalienating. These movements are always defined "within concrete, changing situations" (208). Lefebvre further notes that awareness of an alienation is already disalienation itself, pointing out that

> [n]o self-consciousness can close up upon itself. Man is a conscious being, conscious of what he is (of his being), but only in, by and through what he is not, otherness and action upon otherness, confrontation with otherness, want, privation, desire, work on external material, works (products or works in the strict sense of the term), and finally, what is possible. (214)

In this movement between alienation and disalienation, we might experience what Lefebvre calls the "moment," which can be understood as a point in the individual's history when "he recognizes himself within it, even if it is in a confused way" (344). In the analysis that follows, I will focus on moments of this nature experienced by the protagonists of the novels in question. In both cases, characters are pushed in and out of their everyday experiences of consuming cultural products. Moreover, at times it is consumer

A Consumer's Dreams and Nightmares

culture itself that triggers the protagonists' awareness of their fears and anxieties, leading to critical reflection about their behavior.

In Galera's novel, we follow the story of teenager Hermano and the impact on his life as an adult of his friend's accidental murder, for which he feels responsible after having hidden away while his friend was beaten to death by other kids. In Laub's narrative, we become acquainted with a similar case, experienced by the unnamed protagonist-narrator, who attempts to redeem himself for his guilt toward his girlfriend's suicide. In both stories, we encounter men in their thirties and forties who grew up immersed in consumer culture and whose perceptions of themselves and relationships with others are shaped by their experiences with commodities, particularly action movies and comic books in the case of *Mãos* and grunge music in the case of *A maçã*. Nonetheless, if there are moments when they seem to have become selfish individuals captivated by the alienating allure of consumer culture, their experiences are not totalizing. Consequently, instead of reading these novels as narratives of dystopia and alienation (Lehnen, "O fruto"; Cunha), I propose to read them as what I call narratives of *ambivalent awareness*. In these novels, characters are indeed confronted with situations of despair and do struggle to overcome them, but they attempt to work through these situations by reflecting on how their consumption mediates their personal relationships. In the process of attempting to work through, they construct a narrative of existence within consumer culture that, however tortured, opens itself up for change on several opportunities.

Galera's *Mãos de cavalo*: A Mass-Mediated Sensibility

Samoa sandals, Caloi bikes, Carlton cigarettes, a Mitsubishi car, the Canadian magazine *Gripped*: these are just a few examples of brands that appear throughout *Mãos de cavalo*. They surround characters and mediate relationships, connecting them in solidarity and in competition, as do Hollywood films, Brazilian television shows, and imported video games. The consumption of many of these products shapes the protagonist's and his friends' view of masculinity (Takeda 159). Growing up, Hermano learns what it means to be a man from comic books, action movies such as *Mad Max*, and cartoons such as *He-Man*, which paint a picture

Chapter Four

of physical prowess and invincibility (Galera 40). In real life, the hero that the protagonist aspires to be is Bonobo, a neighborhood kid who is known for being the toughest one around, with whom Hermano dreams of being friends.

In his quest for this masculinity embodied by Bonobo, Hermano develops a kind of mass-mediated sensibility, represented by a camera that follows him in the most banal moments of his daily life. At times this camera transforms his perception of reality, leading him to see himself as a hero when there is only a regular boy who fails, falls down, and sometimes gets seriously injured. The narrative signals the importance of this camera as a filter of Hermano's perception starting with the epigraph that opens the book. The epigraph is a quote attributed to North American actor Nicolas Cage: "I would walk to school and actually have crane shots worked out in my mind where the crane would be pulling up and looking down at me as a tiny object in the street walking to school" (Galera 7).

The reader gets a first glimpse of the power of this camera in the first chapter, titled "O ciclista urbano" ("The Urban Biker"). Here, a third person omniscient narrator juxtaposes the fantasy of Hermano's camera, which captures an invincible biker overcoming dangerous obstacles in the streets of Porto Alegre, Brazil, with the reality of a little boy falling hard from his bike and injuring himself. This first chapter sets the tone of the narrative's representation of the influence of consumer culture on the way that the protagonist experiences reality: as a movement between alienation and disalienation. Hermano experiences this push-and-pull throughout his life. There is neither absolute awareness nor absolute oblivion, but rather a series of dialectic movements between surrendering to the discourse on masculinity that the cultural products he consumes emphasize and questioning this masculinity as unattainable and this discourse as misguided.

Such questioning emerges during one of the downhill championships in which Hermano and his friends participate. Inspired by what the kids read in mountain bike magazines, the championships consist of competitions in which the boys go downhill with their bikes and judge each other's performance not on speed and technique but on the *impression* that the performance makes on the spectators. This criterion evidences a collective sensibility imbued by the aesthetic of action movies, for instance, in which

A Consumer's Dreams and Nightmares

special effects create strong sensations by amplifying the drama of a scene that would otherwise come across as rather unexciting.

When it is Hermano's turn to go downhill, the narrator leads us into his thoughts, revealing his desire to impress everyone as well as his questioning of this desire. As he pushes his bike uphill, Hermano feels lonely, and starts wondering whether being part of the championship makes sense. He thinks about leaving and joining his friend Morsa at his house instead. The mention of Morsa is important because he represents another possibility of masculinity; a private one which, albeit still problematically tied to the world of consumer culture via his like for videogames and his later consumption of imported cars as an adult, differs, however, from Bonobo's public demonstrations of power through physical strength. Likely because of his preference for not engaging in activities such as the downhill championship, Morsa is bullied by the other kids, who only seem to seek his company when wanting to play with his videogames. While climbing the hill, Hermano reflects on who he really is and pictures the comfort of not having to prove anything to anyone when he is with Morsa:

> [Hermano] pensou em voltar para a casa do Morsa e dizer que somente ele prestava naquele bairro. Somente o Morsa merecia consideração. Com ele não era necessário conversar. Podiam ficar vendo jogos de computador e tomando Coca em mamutais copos de vidro esverdeado, e os minutos iam se sucedendo e fazendo sentido. Sabido era o Morsa, que estava em casa jogando computador. (Galera 90)

> [Hermano] thought about going back to Morsa's house and saying that only he was worth a damn in the neighborhood. Only Morsa deserved his respect. With him, it wasn't necessary to talk. They could play computer games and drink Coke in huge greenish glasses all day long; the minutes following one another and everything making sense. Morsa knew better than us: he was at home playing computer games [instead of competing in the championship].

This questioning, however, does not dissuade him from going downhill. Hermano falls deep into the fantasies of the media that he consumes, purposely losing control of his bike, in the hopes that the fall will result in him cutting, breaking, scratching, fracturing, perforating, and smashing his body (91). The injuries

Chapter Four

that indeed result from this fall make him proud of himself as he imagines that he is Mad Max after a terrible accident in the desert, his perception again filtered by the presence of the camera. In this instance, Hermano imagines the kids going down the hill to check on him as either Mad Max's enemies running toward him to see if he is still alive or as the spectators running toward the movie hero to help him: "[o] seu filme. A cena ficou perfeita. A maquiagem não podia ter sido mais realista. Como o sangue é uma coisa bonita, pensou antes de desmaiar" ("his movie. The scene turned out perfect. The makeup could not have been more realistic. What a beautiful thing blood is, he thought before passing out"; 92). Fiction and reality blend in his imagination to the point that real blood is perceived as make-up.

Conversely, in an earlier instance, makeup is taken as real blood when Hermano, using red pencils and water, draws on his face to make it look like he is bleeding. When he looks at himself in the mirror, he concludes that his "makeup" reminds him of super heroes such as Veto Skreemer, from the comic book series *Skreemer* (1989), and Mad Max covered in blood after a crash in the homonymous 1979 movie. Hermano's camera is then switched on, as the image of his face appears in "slow motion" in the mirror, and the "makeup" is now described by the narrator as blood (Galera 45). As a fight between him and Bonobo proceeds in his imagination—a reenactment of a fight from which he ran away earlier during a soccer match—he is "beaten up" and "bleeds" to his defeat. Returning to reality, Hermano feels ashamed of having lost even in an imaginary fight. If on one hand, his shame indicates that he is still immersed in the ideal of masculinity that he has not been able to attain, his awareness of his defeat indicates a movement toward disalienation from his mass-mediated sensibility, as he is forced to confront the reality that he is not the superhero that he pictures in his mind.

A similar movement between disalienation and alienation leads Hermano to hesitate about joining everyone on the dance floor at a party, as he wonders about the reasons why he feels the need to do things he does not like. This reflection reveals some level of awareness of the societal expectations that weigh heavy on him, for he recognizes the influence on his actions of what he thinks others want to see him do (Galera 115). As with the downhill championship described above, Hermano's pondering is interrupted again by the fantasy of being a superhero after he takes a sip of alcohol

A Consumer's Dreams and Nightmares

from Bonobo's drink and feels that now something has changed because he is no longer "someone who has never had a drink" (121). Against the background of the world of superheroes, the sip functions as a kind of "spider bite," the banal incident that might change his life forever by giving him some kind of superpower. That same night, the imagination of the camera leads Hermano to picture himself and Bonobo as protagonists of a road movie:

> ... percorrendo planícies pardas da Patagônia, com cadeias de montanhas nevadas no horizonte, deixando marcas nos povoados e lembranças nas pessoas que encontrassem pelo caminho, rumo ao extremo sul, a algo imenso e inominável, o clímax de uma jornada. (122)

> ... roaming on the brown plains of Patagonia, with snowy mountain ranges on the horizon, leaving marks on the villages they visited and making memories with the people they met along the way, toward the far-south, toward something immense and unnamable, the climax of a journey.

The future here is depicted as a romanticized narrative of progress toward something great. However, the fantasy of this narrative will be interrupted in reality by the tragic death of Bonobo. His death represents a turning point for Hermano, symbolizing his impossible achievement of the masculinity that he pursues. Devastated by feelings of guilt and shame for having remained hidden away while a group of kids gave Bonobo a fatal beating, Hermano decides to stop watching movies and reading comic books, in order to dedicate himself to becoming a doctor. While this decision entails the elimination of contact with the cultural products that infused in him his problematic perceptions of masculinity, it is clear that the hero narrative still drives him. As the narrator points out, Hermano's goal is to dedicate himself completely to studying so that he can emerge, years later, as the superhero whose superpower is self-control (126). During this time, however, we learn that Hermano puts his camera away, so to speak, and does not imagine its presence again until he is an adult. Although the state of awareness that he manages to achieve in this phase of his life has setbacks, there is an attempt to break away from the influence of the media that he consumes, which he comes to perceive as toxic.

As an adult, Hermano seems to have, at least to some extent, followed the promise made by his young self to "put the camera away," stay focused, and become a doctor. However, he continues to be influenced by consumer culture in other ways, as his driving a sports utility vehicle, his international mountain climbing, and his choice of professional specialization (plastic surgery) indicate. The narrator leads us into this phase of the protagonist's life in chapters that capture a couple of hours of the day when Hermano is supposed to embark on a trip with a friend in order to climb an unexplored hill. Each chapter is titled after a precise time within these two hours and the main action is narrated in the present so as to convey the impression of a live coverage of him driving in the streets of Porto Alegre. This point of view foreshadows the return of Hermano's old habit of imagining that a camera follows him, thus mirroring the narration of the first chapter, in which we learn about the "Urban Biker."

The return of the camera coincides with Hermano's opportunity to redeem himself for Bonobo's death when he sees a group of teenagers attacking another kid. The language of the narrative in this passage conveys the presence of the camera. The scene in question unfolds as in an action movie, with tension and drama, expressed by adjectives such as "enormous" and "sanguinary," and in verbs such as "tear apart." This fantasy gives Hermano the courage to drive back and face the kids:

> [v]ê a cena toda do alto, como se o Pajero estivesse sendo acompanhado por uma grua, o carro se aproximando em alta velocidade do cenário do combate. A desvantagem numérica é gritante, mas dessa vez não vai se esconder. Vinte metros. Lembra do V8 propulsionado pelo nitro em *Mad Max 2*, rasgando o deserto da terra devastada enquanto é perseguido de perto pela gangue de piratas sanguinários sobre rodas. Dez metros. Não está somente imaginando cenas do filme. Agora ele é Mad Max, incorporou o guerreiro da estrada. (Galera 149)

> [h]e sees the whole scene from above, as if the [Mitsubishi] Pajero were being followed by a crane; the car speeding toward the combat scene. The numeric disadvantage is huge, but this time he will not hide. Twenty meters. He remembers the nitro-propelled V8 in *Mad Max 2*, tearing through the desolate desert while being followed by the gang of bloody pirates on wheels. Ten meters. He is no longer just imagining the movie scenes. Now he is Mad Max, he has incorporated the road warrior.

A Consumer's Dreams and Nightmares

As the passage above indicates, the imaginary camera captures the chase in an aerial shot, rendering the passage fast, dynamic, and dramatic: the street is the place of combat, and the fight is a display of the courage of one against the fury of many. Soon Hermano is not just imagining Mad Max; he believes he *is* Mad Max. He yells, batters the kids, and, when he gets hurt, the blood in his mouth does not taste like cowardice. Instead, he describes it as having the far better taste of bravery (151). The camera, thus, collapses fiction and reality, mirroring the previously mentioned moment when Hermano goes downhill on his bike. After the attackers flee, Hermano takes the injured kid to the hospital. He realizes that he has repressed his imagination about cartoons and movies for a long time. Referring to the moment of rescuing the child, Hermano concludes that it was

> [o] momento dos filmes, das histórias em quadrinhos e dos livros de aventura em que um homem descobre sua verdadeira natureza e se torna um herói. Está completamente embevecido por essa fantasia, tanto que a frase "Eu sou médico" lhe soa artificial, totalmente alheia a quem de fato é e ao que está acontecendo naquela manhã de domingo. (155)

> [t]he moment in movies, in comics and adventure narratives in which a man discovers his true nature and becomes a hero. He is completely delighted by this fantasy, so much so that the sentence "I'm a doctor" sounds artificial to him; completely foreign to who he in fact is and to what is happening that Sunday morning.

Soon, however, the fantasy fades away, and Hermano is flooded with a sense of reality that undoes his heroism, returning him to a state of disalienation from the world of goods that he consumes. He realizes that living the fantasy of his cartoons and movies was often dangerous or, at the very least, pointless. His unattainable expectations of courage and strength made him struggle with the fact that he is not an invincible superhero, but rather a human being with fears and doubts. Hermano perceives that his life has not been heroic, that it has been, instead, a rehearsal for heroism he never attained. He comes to see his condition as being in a state of limbo, between reality and fantasy, somewhere between distorted perceptions of who he in fact is, who he would like to have been, and who he, as a child, had wanted to be when he grew up. He looks in the mirror of

Chapter Four

his car and realizes that he is not "o herói na sua imaginação" ("the hero in his imagination"; 156). At this point, Hermano retracts back to being careful and controlled, as evidenced by his driving, which changes from shifting gears aggressively and screeching tires on curves (153) to being careful to drive so as to not block other vehicles that need to go by (156). In this way, the novel conveys that the camera is now gone again, in a similar way to how it indicates Hermano's movement from alienation to disalienation in the first chapter. In the chapter in question, after he falls off the bike, the narrator indicates that the camera is "switched off" by describing the protagonist's surroundings as mere banality: people come and go, hurrying up to get to work and "ele não é mais o Ciclista Urbano. Agora é apenas um guri de dez anos" ("he is no longer an Urban Biker. Now he is only a ten-year-old kid"; 16).

The novel further complicates totalizing views of consumer culture as an alienating phenomenon also by suggesting that Hermano's camera can actually even trigger his self-awareness. As a teenager, when Naiara tries to seduce him in her bedroom, the imaginary camera shows him the awkwardness of the scene, making him feel embarrassed. According to the narrator:

> Naiara estava interagindo com um autômato, ambos sendo observados pela verdadeira consciência de Hermano que flutuava como um espectro cínico pela bagunça vermelha de um quartinho, buscando os melhores ângulos e luzes para enaltecer as tristes e solitárias peripécias de um protagonista. E o que a câmera via agora era uma menina de treze anos fazendo tudo que lhe era possível, aplicando todo o seu precoce repertório de técnicas para tentar soprar vida em um boneco cenográfico. (140)

> Naiara was interacting with an automaton, both being observed by Hermano's true conscience, which fluctuated as a cynical spectrum over the red mess of a little bedroom, searching for the best angles and the best light to exalt the sad and lonely adventures of a protagonist. And what the camera saw now was a thirteen-year-old girl doing everything she could, using all of her precocious repertoire of techniques to try to breathe life into a doll prop.

In an inversion, the camera fails to depict the romanticized reality of the movie. Rather, it makes the couple's experience seem far less glamorous. This moment marks Hermano's realization that he

A Consumer's Dreams and Nightmares

and Naiara are only attempting to perform roles for which they may never be prepared. In other words, in this particular instance, the camera makes Hermano realize the fiction of his social performance. The role of the camera here, as in the moment in which it returns later on when he is an adult, suggests that, while consumer culture endlessly presents Hermano with unreasonable promises of heroism, it may also present him with opportunities for self-reflection about the performativity of his life. From this perspective, Galera's narrative shows that, as French philosopher Lefebvre points out, "[repetitive practice] never attains the definitive, automatic balance, a balance without contradiction" (*Critique* 239).

Indeed, contradiction is present in Hermano's life in various other ways. One of them is his wife, Adri, who is at the same time the seductress that matches hypersexualized views of women as commonly seen in the media and the artist who serves as (an ambiguous) counterpoint to consumer culture in the novel.

As the hypersexualized woman, she appears in the novel seducing Hermano in his car, at a moment when Pink Floyd's 1971 song "Fearless" comes on the radio (Galera 52). This song is very symbolic of consumer culture's continued influence on Hermano, for it depicts an individual who, like him, has a desire to impress others. The soundtrack of this amorous encounter with Adri echoes Hermano's desire to feel strong, visible, noted. In the song, the image of climbing—"You say you like to see me try / Climbing! / You pick the place and I'll choose the time / And I'll climb / The hill in my own way"—alludes to Hermano's later plan to climb the Bonete hill, while connecting the scene in the car to Hermano's first sexual experience with Bonobo's sister, Naiara. The latter occurs when he goes to her house to return the album *Houses of the Holy* (1973) by Led Zeppelin, that he had borrowed from Bonobo. The album cover, as the narrator notes, features a montage of naked children climbing a rocky formation in Ireland (Galera 134). Climbing and sex are thus connected, via the references to music, by the idea of masculinity that Bonete hill, whose name is curiously similar to that of Bonobo's, comes to represent in the novel: the masculinity that Hermano so wants to achieve. Nevertheless, climbing, according to the narrator, also takes on the more mundane function of providing an escape from work. As "um exercício prazeroso de resistência muscular e concentração, praticado com disciplina e regularidade" ("a pleasurable exercise

Chapter Four

of muscle endurance and concentration, practiced regularly and with discipline"), climbing contrasts with his earlier biking, in which he would deliberately lose control (24).

As the artist, Adri is particularly symbolic of the push-and-pull that Hermano experiences as he struggles with the negative effects that consumer culture has on him. The peak of her career is an exhibit in which she has a tree surgically removed from the ground and transplanted to the ceiling of a large empty shed. This specific tree, the narrator points out, grows extensively, destroying any pavement or wall that stands in its way. This project follows another one, in which Adri builds an ensemble of pieces of trees mixed with artificial objects such as the bumper of a car, pieces of tile, concrete, and glass signs (Galera 53). On one hand, Adri's work can be read as criticism to the destructive power of consumer culture, in the form of pieces of former commodities. On the other hand, her work also highlights nature's capacity to fight back.

The narrator describes her plastic installations as readymades, referring to a concept created by French artist Marcel Duchamp. The readymade is the product of the transformation of everyday objects into art by removing them from their everyday context and re-signifying them in an exhibition by associating them to a specific concept. By exploring the conditions of production of Adri's work, the novel suggests consumer capitalism's emptying of the power of art to intervene in everyday life. As reviews of her installation point out, some critics read the extraction of the tree as an environmental crime disguised as art in exchange for fame, given the secrecy of the project, which created much anticipation in the media (Galera 55). The criticism that Adri receives reflects the challenges of making art in an age where the quest for the new pursued by avant-garde artists such as Duchamp has long been absorbed by consumer culture. Adri's work and what it communicates to its audience, therefore, can be read as a parallel to Hermano's inner struggle: standing between the forces that surrender to and resist consumer culture. From this perspective, the choice of an image of interwoven roots of a tree for the book's cover, even though the mention to Adri's work appears as a relatively small detail in the narrative, is very symbolic. The cover can be seen as a symbol of the forces that resist and surrender to consumer culture within the protagonist, as several of his actions and thoughts demonstrate.

A Consumer's Dreams and Nightmares

Hermano marries Adri with the intention of making her feel as happy as she did at the moment of their first encounter, but they end up living each in their own way: he continues to be focused on his studies and work while she concentrates on her art. Thus, the initial thrill of the relationship represented by the amorous scene in the car to which I previously referred does not last very long, with Hermano again returning to his quiet, banal life; a life that is much less impressive than the one portrayed in "Fearless." If the influence of the image of fearlessness in the song has a limited effect on Hermano's life, so does art in Adri's, for she abandons it to pursue projects such as opening a clothing store or working as an art director of a film, both of which she eventually also leaves behind (Galera 55). In this way, art falls short of having the power to completely overcome the supposed degradation of consumer culture. Pop culture, in turn, also falls short of enacting its expected ability to swallow individuals' capacity for self-awareness completely. The parallel between Adri and Hermano, therefore, questions both art's freeing capability and consumer culture's alleged power to sustain illusions. The potential for change is located in neither art nor consumption, but rather in the push-and-pull between awareness and oblivion experienced in everyday life proper.

Another source of ambivalence in Hermano's life is his profession. While he makes a living primarily by "fixing" bodies that "só precisavam de concerto se opostos a padrões de beleza tão fictícios quanto onipresentes" ("only needed fixing if compared to beauty standards that were as fictitious as they were omnipotent"; Galera 128), he tries to educate his patients on the risks involved in plastic surgery. He attempts to show them that no matter how much beauty magazines try to portray these procedures as routine, they still involve serious risks. He recognizes the harmful impact of the culture of plastic surgery especially in the case of young women, who undergo the risk of breast augmentation surgery mainly to conform to an artificial standard. He sees these patients' view of plastic surgery as a kind of problematic psychological treatment, aimed at solving "de uma vez só um vasto repertório de anseios e problemas" ("once and for all a variety of problems and sources of anxiety"; 128). He acknowledges the necessity of plastic surgery in some cases and its illusory nature in others:

> [r]inoplastias e otoplastias que visavam corrigir deformidades ou formas distantes demais do padrão anatômico eram uma coisa, porém desaprovava a artificialidade de um seio suplantado por uma prótese e sabia que lipoaspirar uma barriguinha era, na maioria dos casos, tapar o sol com a peneira. (129)
>
> Rhinoplasties and otoplasties aimed at correcting deformities or forms that are too distant from the anatomic standard were one thing, but he disapproved of the artificiality of a breast supplanted by a prosthesis and he knew that to lipoaspirate someone's belly was, in the majority of cases, like putting a Band-Aid on a stab wound.

In this way, he once again demonstrates his capacity to distance himself from discourses on consumption, albeit doing so from within his contradictory position as someone who contributes to the perpetuation of said discourses by performing procedures that he knows to be only flawed solutions to his patients' problems.

The wavering nature of Hermano's position with respect to the images of masculinity that consumer culture presents to him manifests itself in a symbolic dream that he has the night before he is supposed to leave to Bonete. The memory of the dream is triggered by a song by Brazilian musician Elomar, "A meu Deus um canto novo" ("To God, a new hymn"; *Elomar em Concerto* 1989). The narrator cites the lines "*Bem de longe na grande viagem, sobrecarregado paro a descansar*" ("*Very far into the long journey, overtired I stop to rest*"; Galera 100, emphasis in the original). Elomar's song depicts a man in search for a new beginning, who feels like he has seen everything and who is tired of his journey in life. On one hand, the tiredness mentioned in the song can be read as Hermano's desire to abandon the strong control with which he has lived his life since Bonobo's death. On the other hand, it can be seen as a desire to free himself from the influence of media's models of success and masculinity once and for all.

The dream that he remembers after listening to the song has a similarly ambiguous meaning. In the dream, he is kidnapped and taken to a house where televisions emit a very bright light. While he senses that he must stay away from the televisions because they are "uma ameaça indescritível" ("an indescribable threat"), he ends up joining everyone else in the place as they, all mutilated, rappel down a cliff (Galera 104). The dream speaks of both the pressure of consumer culture values on him—the rappel down the cliff evokes his desire to climb the challenging Bonete; the threatening television sets reference his media consumption as a kid; the mutilated people mirror the self-harm that he caused when he was younger—as well as his awareness of the negative impact of such values and his attempts to break away from them. Both the song and the dream signal the possibility that Hermano either surrender to these values or, tired of the "long journey," abandon them. According to the narrator, when reflecting upon the significance of the dream, Hermano is not sure what it means, but he knows that "o seu significado já está incorporado à sua consciência, diluído em seu fluxo mental" ("its meaning is already incorporated into his conscience, diluted in his mind stream"; 104). In this way, the narrator indicates that, even though Hermano proceeds to pursue the hero narrative of his childhood, there lies in the back of his mind a critical view of this narrative, which indeed surfaces later, after he saves the kid's life and appears to find no redemption in this act.

Similarly ambiguous is Hermano's encounter with Naiara after the episode with the kid he helps as an adult. This encounter is foreshadowed by Elomar's previously mentioned song, which the protagonist continues to listen to as he drives away from the hospital. This time, the lines quoted are "*Ó lua nova, quem me dera, eu me encontrar com ela, no pispei de tudo, na quadra*" ("*Oh new moon, if only I could meet with her, in the beginning of it all, in the [neighborhood] block*"; Galera 106, emphasis in the original). The chapter in which he meets Naiara again is, chronologically, the last one. It ends with him abruptly breaking off their conversation without any indication of where he is headed or what he plans to do next: "Ela pergunta se ele queria tomar chimarrão, mas ele não responde. Apenas levanta da cadeira. Está na hora de ir" ("She asks if he wanted to have some *chimarrão*, but he doesn't reply. He just gets up. It's time to go"; 179). This particular episode precedes the last chapter of the novel, which concludes with Hermano still a teenager. As he returns home after Bonobo's funeral, he decides to change his life: "Agora ele sabia exatamente o que fazer. Não seria necessário fingir nunca mais" ("Now he knew exactly what to do. Never again would it be necessary to pretend"; 188).

By the time we reach the end of this chapter, we know that Hermano could never completely follow through with his plan of never needing to pretend again, given that he still longed for an opportunity for redemption. When presented to him, this opportunity brings back the sensibility of the camera that he had tried to repress for so many years. However, the openness of the scene at Naiara's house suggests that there is here an opportunity for a new beginning. This new beginning may entail new repetitions and alienations, but of a different kind, after the linearity of his daily life has been interrupted by the deeper alienation brought up by the camera and followed by the profound questioning of himself yet again. Foreshadowed by Elomar's song, which alludes to the non-cumulative, non-capitalist cyclic rhythms of nature (Lefevbre, *Critique* 340)—the new moon—, a new phase of Hermano's life is thus potentially inaugurated at the chronological end of the narrative.

The oscillation between alienation and awareness shown throughout the novel indicates that semi-conscious, potentially uncritical repetition, on one hand, and change motivated by conscious critical impulse, on the other hand, may continue to alternate in the protagonist's future. It is significant that a novel that depicts the banalities of everyday life to such a large extent ends with the juxtaposition of two scenes that represent returns and attempts to start anew. These scenes mark "moments" in Hermano's life in the sense Lefebvre proposes. The French philosopher defines "moment" as "a function of a history, the history of the individual" (*Critique* 344). In each of these moments, both as an adolescent and as an adult, Hermano has the opportunity to change the course of his life, though not in the sense of total disalienation from potentially harmful repetition. As Lefebvre stresses, repetition organizes and gives meaning and stability to our daily experiences. The moment is limited and partial. It reveals the everyday to be uncertain and transitory, but also solid and real (*Critique* 349). What Hermano can do is to start a new cycle that, within the same world of consumer culture, may inaugurate a new phase that will consist of new kinds of routinizations.

Laub's *A maçã envenenada*: Between Kurt Cobain and Imaculée Ilibagiza

The contrast between repetition and change in an everyday of uncertainty and transience mediated by commodities is key to the narrative structure of *A maçã envenenada*. Like Hermano, Laub's unnamed protagonist has an intrinsic connection with consumer culture. Specifically, the song "Drain You" by the North American band Nirvana functions as a trigger that repeatedly confronts him with his past. Also like Hermano, the protagonist of *A maçã* undergoes the push-and-pull of a dialectical movement between alienation and disalienation. He experiences alienation both toward his girlfriend, Valéria, as he becomes emotionally subordinate to her, and toward himself, in the form of a sense of guilt and failure. There is much disillusionment and crisis in both the protagonist's personal experience and that of his generation in the novel (Lehnen, "O fruto" 100). However, there is also push back, reflection, self-awareness, and above all, an important attempt at coming to terms with the past through writing. The novel, narrated by the protagonist himself, can be read as his exercise in reflecting about the past, attempting to rid himself of the blame that he feels for Valéria's death, acknowledging his self-absorbed ways, and confronting the image of his generation as disengaged from social reality and his own discomfort with having partaken in this lack of engagement. Therefore, I propose that *A maçã* be read, like *Mãos*, as a narrative of the dialectic passing between alienation and disalienation that Lefebvre postulates as essential to prevent the halt of totality that stagnating in either state would entail (*Critique* 216). In this passing, the protagonist goes back and forth between reflecting about his relationship with his girlfriend and immersing himself in everyday routines. Nirvana's music and the suicide of its lead singer, Kurt Cobain, its contrast with the Rwanda genocide, and the protagonist's survival from a car accident after Valéria's death provide him with the pull out of everyday life that leads him into reflection and, ultimately, into the very act of writing the narrative. In other words, these triggers lead the protagonist into "moments," in the sense proposed by Lefebvre described in the previous section of this chapter: recognitions of himself, however confused, within his own history.

Nirvana's music and the band's history play a central role in *A maçã*. The protagonist's age indicates that he belongs to Generation X, of which Kurt Cobain became an icon. Cobain, an idol of grunge, wrestled with the guilt of selling out to capitalism. He turned into a kind of myth—constructed by the media, critics, and fans—after taking his own life in 1994 at the age of twenty-seven. As the protagonist of *A maçã envenenada* states, after Cobain's death,

Chapter Four

> todo mundo tinha um veredito sobre Kurt Cobain, uma tese sobre como ele incorporou o espírito de uma época esmagada pelo fim das utopias, sobre como uma geração pouco educada devolvia a raiva ao emergir no fim dos anos Reagan, sobre o que era ser jovem numa América tomada por corporações, individualismo e falta de perspectivas, e como isso estava ligado à via-crúcis pessoal do cantor ... (Laub 18)

> everyone had a verdict on Kurt Cobain, a thesis about how he incorporated the spirit of a time crushed by the end of utopia; about how a generation that had little education paid back with anger at the moment it emerged at the end of the Reagan years; about what it meant to be young in an America taken over by corporations, individualism, and lack of opportunities; and how this was tied to Cobain's Via Crucis ...

The protagonist looks for answers to Valéria's death much in the same way that the media and the fans try to understand Cobain's suicide, reading everything that she wrote, said, or did, as a series of events that only after the fact seem to lead up to a tragic ending that left him with survivor's guilt (Laub 7). This perspective is also the one that the protagonist entices readers to take as they process the meaning of his own words, the actual novel, when he asks "o que a aparência, a sintaxe e o estilo de um texto diz sobre quem o escreveu?" ("what do the appearance, the syntax, and the style of a text say about the person who wrote it?"; 90). This question, meant to refer to a postcard that Valéria sent him, is also about his own writing—which is ultimately *A maçã*—and about what his narration tells us, readers, about him. As the protagonist revisits his memories in a tone that mixes journalistic account with memoir, it becomes evident that his "reality," that is, the internal reality of Laub's fictional world in *A maçã*, much like Hermano's, lies somewhere between what happened, what the protagonist assumes to have happened, and projections of his own insecurities. Expressions of doubt ("não sei se" ["I don't know if"], "como se" ["as if"], "talvez" ["maybe/perhaps"]), conjunctions that indicate other possibilities ("ou" ["or"]), and verbs in the conditional indicating hypotheses are widely used throughout the narrative, conveying this state of uncertainty.

Memory in *A maçã*, therefore, appears as process, the time of the "durante" ("during"; Gondar 23). The protagonist reconstructs his past from the questions that he poses to himself in the present,

A Consumer's Dreams and Nightmares

and the (limited) answers that he is able to provide now, years later, when he is more mature and has learned more about Valéria, about himself, and about life. In this process, his memories are constantly put into question as he admits the existence of gaps in what he says. These nebulous accounts contrast with incredibly detailed descriptions that highlight banalities—such as the clothes that Unha, a former member of the protagonist's band, wore the day he met with the protagonist after Valéria's death, or even what Unha drank and ate during that meeting (95)—conveying an impression of a supposedly objective journalistic account and at times coming across as an attempt to normalize a life that has been shaken by tragedy.

As he tells us his account of the past, linguistic mechanisms suggest the protagonist's fusion with Valéria, symbolizing his alienation toward her. This fusion is conveyed by the ambiguity of many sentences in which the protagonist appears to refer to Valéria but could be referring to himself. For example, fragment ninety-eight is a monologue directed to an interlocutor named "você" ("you"), uttered by an "eu" ("I"), who could be either Valéria addressing the protagonist or vice-versa: "De qual parte minha você mais vai sentir falta? Que parte sua faz com que eu goste de você?" ("Which part of you are you going to miss the most? What part of yours makes me like you?"; Laub 115). The protagonist also undergoes a kind of split of the self, such as in the passage below, which shows his account of when he cheated on Valéria with a girl named Tati:

> Eu não cheguei nem a completar o que deveria ter feito com ela, porque tinha bebido e o banheiro era apertado e a minha cara no espelho começou a parecer estranha na luz branca, um tanto deformada, um tanto triste, e basta reparar nisso para que a empolgação dê lugar a algo próximo ao horror, e você pede desculpas e veste a calça e quando se prepara para ir embora sem lavar as mãos ouve os gritos e batidas de Valéria na porta. (Laub 79)

> I didn't even get to finish what I should have done with her because I had been drinking alcohol; and the bathroom was tight; and my face in the mirror started to look strange in the white light: somewhat deformed, somewhat sad; and noticing this is enough to replace excitement with something close to horror; and you apologize; and put your pants on; and as you get ready to leave without washing your hands, you hear Valéria's screaming and pounding on the door.

Chapter Four

In the passage above, the narration changes from first person singular ("eu" ["I"]) to a second person singular ("você" ["you"]) used in generic terms as the protagonist's seeing his face in the mirror appears to trigger a critical awareness of what he is doing or is about to do, leading him to regret his actions. These linguistic shifts mark the separation between the "I" that does the action and an "I" that reflects about it, perhaps as the same 18-year-old of the past or as the 40-year-old of the present judging the behavior of his younger self, thus indicating a movement between alienation and disalienation throughout his life.

One of these movements concerns his belonging to Generation X. The latter is commonly viewed as apathetic and lost.[2] Nirvana's music, grunge, was considered the main cultural expression of this generation. While meant to be a critical response to neoliberalism, grunge was deemed a highly commercial version of punk, with the music video of Nirvana's song "Smells like Teen Spirit," a highly successful commercial formula that opens the album *Nevermind* (1991), becoming a kind of anthem of the Generation X and its apathy. Nevertheless, the protagonist's critical perspective toward himself as a Generation X-er can be perceived from the beginning of the narrative in his comments about several banal aspects of his youth. He acknowledges, for example, the pathetic reason why he decided to become a lawyer: because he liked movies about lawyers. Mocking his expectations of reality molded by the fantasy of Hollywood, he comments that he "achava que era possível correr atrás de criminosos sem suar ou amassar o terno" ("thought it was possible to chase criminals down without sweating or wrinkling one's suit"; Laub 45). He also confesses that the rock band in which he played with Valéria, along with his close friend Unha, had nothing original about it. Their attempt to convey the rebellion of their generation against capitalism was expressed by repetitive lyrics and the mere recycling of the basic features of *Nevermind*, thus producing music, ironically, as if in an assembly line (11). He further recognizes his illusion, as he calls it, of feeling as if he were effecting any change in the world by listening to rock and grunge bands that spoke up against capitalism, while attending a private school and having a maid who served him a grilled cheese sandwich and a milk shake every afternoon (35–36).

A Consumer's Dreams and Nightmares

But before achieving the awareness of the problematic nature of the situations in the examples above, the protagonist goes through a series of movements between alienation and disalienation regarding his individual existence, experiencing several "moments," in Lefebvre's sense. These moments disrupt the repetition of daily life, to which the protagonist alludes several times throughout the novel. These routines are tied to spaces of control and limitation: the military headquarters, the hospital, and the snack bar in England where he worked without legal permission. Albeit not necessarily pleasant, these repetitions serve to ground his existence and help him cope with his obsessions: the doubt about Valéria possibly having cheated on him with Unha, the uncertainty surrounding the reason for her death, and his wondering about his future if he had not survived a car accident without long-term complications.

The first of these moments of disruption is the arrival of a postcard two months after Valéria's death, which had been sent by her from São Paulo before she attended the 1993 Nirvana concert in the city. In the postcard, Valeria quotes lines from "Drain You," which potentially imply that the protagonist ruined her life, leading her to commit suicide. The original lines read as follows:

> One baby to another says
> I'm lucky to have met you
> I don't care what you think
> Unless it is about me
>
> With eyes so dilated
> I've become your pupil
> You've taught me everything
> Without a poison apple (Nirvana)

These lines appear translated into Portuguese in fragment 78 of the novel. In the postcard, the quote appears mistranslated, with the preposition *sem* (without) in the original translated into the preposition *ao*, so that the quote reads "[v]ocê me ensinou tudo *ao* me dar a maçã envenenada," literally, "[y]ou taught me everything *when you gave me/by giving me* the poison apple." The protagonist spends the following several years wondering whether the mistranslation was intentional and the postcard was part of Valéria's plan to take her own life by inhaling *lança-perfume*[3] during the

155

Chapter Four

Nirvana concert, as a response to his breaking up with her. A parallel the protagonist creates between his cleaning a weapon at the military headquarters where he serves and her mailing the postcard in question encapsulates his potential responsibility for her passing:

> A sexta-feira no quartel foi de sol, e eu fiz instrução de desmontagem de fuzil enquanto a oitocentos e cinquenta quilômetros de distância a minha primeira namorada entrava no correio. Eu abri a caixa da culatra enquanto ela grudava o selo no cartão-postal. Retirei o obturador enquanto ela pagava no caixa, aí separei o êmbolo, a mola, o ratinho, e até hoje não sei se os versos no postal eram apenas citações ingênuas de uma música ingênua do Nirvana ou um recado. (Laub 97)

> That Friday at the headquarters was sunny. I attended the instructional section on disassembling rifles while eight hundred and fifty kilometers away, my first girlfriend entered the post office. I opened the breechblock while she stamped the postcard. I removed the shutter while she paid at the cashier, then I separated the plunger, the firing pin spring, the breechblock carrier, and to this date I don't know if the lines on the postcard were mere naïve quotes from a Nirvana song or a message.

This parallel, although likely not necessarily corresponding to what happened in reality, given that the protagonist can only imagine what actually took place, suggests the potential mutual destruction between the two characters that the lyrics of "Drain You" represents. This song becomes a metaphor for Valéria's and the protagonist's relationship. In this sense, their relationship resulted in them "draining" each other: if the protagonist's actions may have led Valéria to commit suicide, the message on the postcard haunts him as he lives the uncertainty regarding his degree of responsibility for his girlfriend's demise.

The lyrics on the postcard act as a disalienating force in the sense that they pull the protagonist out of the automaticity at the headquarters in which he immersed himself after the funeral: "… a corneta, o hino, a bandeira, o desfile, o vestiário, …" ("… the horn, the anthem, the flag, the parade, the locker room, …"; Laub 107). The impact of receiving the postcard pushes him into a spiral of guilt that culminates with him nearly dying in a car accident. The accident, the protagonist suggests, could have been

A Consumer's Dreams and Nightmares

a suicide attempt, a decision about which he is not sure because it would have been made while he was intoxicated. Nevertheless, he survives the accident, having the time at the hospital, in the middle of his new routine of care as he recovers, to reflect about what happened (his accident, Valéria's death) and to devise a plan for the future. This plan entailed leaving Brazil and living under the radar in London, where he immerses himself again in a numbing routine, as if in a kind of self-punishment. There, he lives frugally, abandoning, albeit temporarily, the comforts of his middle-class life in Brazil. He recalls wearing the same jacket, pants, and boots for months, sharing an Underground pass with his roommate while living in a pension, working twelve hours a day at a snack bar, and earning enough per hour to buy a bagel and a soda (23–24).

The narrative calls into question his time of "sacrifice" in London, by representing Valéria's voice echoing in the protagonist's head as he writes his account (the book that we hold in our hands, *A maçã envenenada* itself) and imagines what questions she would ask if she could interview him now. In fragment 88, her voice, represented in italics, criticizes his self-centered behavior in what is ultimately a criticism of Generation X's experiences, as we can see in the following passage, which is worth citing, albeit long:

> *Você adora pensar que saiu desta história como outra pessoa. O sobrevivente que aprendeu uma lição. E ficou marcado pelo tanto que esta vida dura apronta com a gente, não é mesmo? Você quer que alguém se impressione com uns meses no quartel, é isso? Uns meses acordando cedo. Passar uniforme, veja só. Fazer a barba. Uns meses brincando de ter uma banda. A única pessoa no mundo que teve um acidente de carro. Dois meses de cama, e depois o sultão no exílio. Você sabe o nome das ruas de Londres, é isso? Foi a museus e parques? Usou o metrô pra trabalhar, veja que aventura. E depois voltou pra casa da mamãe. E terminou a faculdade. E foi ser jornalista em São Paulo. E pelo resto da vida achou que tinha tido, como se diz, uma juventude e tanto.*
>
> *Você já viu tudo aos quarenta anos. O desencantado. O sábio que dispensa a piedade das outras pessoas mas não deixa de aproveitar essa piedade que aparece em tantas formas de recompensa ... O que importa é isso, não é mesmo? Se você sofreu ou não ... Você que teve a vida cheia de aventuras e a experiência mais importante. Alguma vez você se envolveu de verdade com alguma coisa?... Abriu mão de alguma coisa valiosa? Deu alguma prova? Aceitou perder uma*

Chapter Four

> *única vez? Digo, perder de verdade, sem a recompensa de ser vítima. Só você e a sua derrota. Só você e o fim. Mais nada e ninguém. Apenas o fim.* (Laub 106–07)

> *You love to think that you came out of this situation a whole new person. The survivor who learned a lesson. And was scarred by this hard life that catches us all by surprise, isn't it? You want others to be impressed by a few months in the military, is that it? A few months waking up early. Ironing uniforms, look at that! Shaving your beard. A few months pretending to have a band. The only person in the world who had a car accident. Two months in bed, and after that a sultan in exile. You know the names of London streets, is that it? You went to parks and museums? Took the Underground to go to work, what an adventure! And after that came back to mama's house. And finished college. And became a journalist in São Paulo. And for the rest of your life thought that you'd had, how do you call it, quite a youth.*

> *You've seen everything at the age of forty. The disenchanted. The wise man who dismisses the piety of others, but who doesn't pass on the opportunity to take advantage of this piety that manifests itself in so many types of rewards ... That's what matters, isn't it? Whether you suffered or not ... You had a life full of adventure and had the most important experience. Did you ever get involved in something for real? ... Did you ever give up on something that had real value? Proved anything? Accepted losing just one time? I mean, losing for real, without the reward of being a victim. Only you and your defeat. Only you and the end. Nothing and nobody else. Just the end.*

This passage questions several facts the reader has learned about the protagonist up until this point. First, it criticizes the conformism to which his band subscribed, reproducing Nirvana's commercial formula, as we have seen. As the protagonist notes in another passage, the lyrics that he wrote were nothing more than what any unimportant songwriter of his age would write about at the time. He further conveys a sense of his generation's conformism when he points out that all the ninety thousand people attending the Nirvana concert in São Paulo would be wearing plaid shirts, in grunge fashion.

Second, Valéria's voice criticizes the protagonist's forced, meaningless, and monotonous time in the military, which stands in stark contrast with the rebellious attitude of the generation with which he identifies. The numb routine of discipline and repetition, in which the larger political life of the country does not matter (Laub 8), is conveyed by the protagonist's remark that "ninguém era capaz de entender como o brilho de uma fivela e um alfinete de gola e a extensão exata de um cadarço passaram a ser tão importantes" ("nobody was able to understand how the shine on a buckle and a pin on a collar and the exact length of a shoelace had become so important"; 38).

Third, she questions his self-exile in London, and his isolation from everyone else in a life as an undocumented worker in precarious conditions. Finally, she condemns his incidental start of a career as a journalist, due to the mere fact that he had the right connections. Collectively, these events deemed dramatic by the protagonist are rendered mere expressions of an individualism that is condensed in the title of the third part of the novel, in which the quote above illustrating Valéria's questioning appears and which is borrowed from "Drain You": "a não ser que seja sobre mim" ("unless it is about me"; Laub 83). In this way, Valéria's voice functions as the protagonist's present conscience, questioning his selfish attitudes, interrupting the cycle of alienation, driving him into a state of awareness of his limits and flaws.

The process of self-questioning—and therefore, another movement toward disalienation, that is, another "moment"—that results in the protagonist's account of his past to us, readers, takes place when he interviews Immaculée Ilibagiza, a real survivor of the Rwanda genocide. A task he takes up as a freelancer for a magazine, this interview affects him like none of the ones he had done before, as he acknowledges (Laub 45). This encounter is described in the first part of the novel, titled "Que sorte ter encontrado você" ("How lucky am I to have found you"). The title is highly ambiguous, for it could refer to several encounters in the book between the protagonist and others (Ilibagiza, Valéria, Lieutenant Pires, the music of Cobain, Unha, Alexandre—Valéria's previous boyfriend) that deeply affect him and that at times shift, and at times strengthen his perception of the past.

Although he does not describe it explicitly, several comparisons between the circumstances involving Cobain's suicide and Ilibagiza's fight to survive, along with instances in which the protagonist questions his response to Valéria's death, indicate that the encounter with his interviewee made him reflect about the ethics of his individualistic and apathetic attitude. In one of the comparisons in question, he states:

Chapter Four

> Uma forma de explicar o que aconteceu em abril de 1994: Kurt Cobain tinha esposa, uma filha de um ano e sete meses, dinheiro e fama por fazer de modo bem-sucedido aquilo que sempre gostou de fazer, além da possibilidade de abrir mão disso a qualquer momento e viver como quisesse, longe da imprensa, do público, na cidade que escolhesse, na casa que mandasse construir, cercado de pessoas de quem gostasse, e com décadas de conforto material pela frente, e mesmo assim apertou o gatilho. Já Imaculée Ilibagiza entrou num banheiro de um metro e vinte e passou noventa e um dias comendo os restos trazidos pelo pastor, dormindo e usando a privada na frente de outras sete mulheres, e vendo as outras sete fazendo o mesmo, os ruídos e o metabolismo de cada uma, um rodízio de quem ficava de pé e quem dormia e quem chorava e quem ficava doente, e durante o período ela sabia ou imaginava que ia perder a casa, a cidade, o país, a língua, a família e todas as referências que fazem uma pessoa ser quem é, mas em nenhum momento pensou em outra coisa que não sobreviver. (Laub 51–52)

> One way to explain what happened in April 1994: Kurt Cobain had a wife, a one-year-and-seven-month-old daughter, money and fame for being successful in what he always liked to do; in addition to the possibility of abandoning this any time and living however he wanted, away from the press, the fans, in whatever city he chose, in whatever house he had custom-built, surrounded by the people he liked and with decades of material comfort ahead of him and, in spite of this, pulled the trigger. Imaculée Ilibagiza, in turn, got into a less-than-four-foot bathroom and spent ninety-eight days eating leftovers brought by the pastor; sleeping and using the toilet in front of seven other women; seeing the other seven do the same, the noises and the metabolism of each one of them; taking turns standing up, sleeping, crying, getting sick; and during this time knowing or imagining that she would lose her home, her city, her country, her language, her family and everything that makes someone who they are; but not even for a moment did she think about anything other than surviving.

In this comment, the protagonist wonders about what makes someone commit suicide, when this person has everything a consumer society considers necessary to be happy: fame, success, and especially the money that grants freedom to be or to do whatever one desires. He also wonders, conversely, what gives someone the desire to live even when facing the most precarious material conditions.

A Consumer's Dreams and Nightmares

Ilibagiza thus functions in the narrative as a public figure who stands as a counterpoint to Cobain: she is life in the face of suicide, hope in the face of despair, possibility in the face of totality. Where Cobain says no, she says yes, as the following passage, one of several that compare their attitudes toward life and death, shows:

> O bilhete que Kurt Cobain deixou ... terminava com uma citação de Neil Young: é melhor queimar do que apagar aos poucos. [N]a edição brasileira das memórias de Immaculée Ilibagiza ... a penúltima frase de suas mais de trezentas páginas é: acredito que podemos curar Ruanda—e o nosso mundo—curando os nossos corações um a um. (Laub 89)

> The [suicide] note that Kurt Cobain left ... ended with a quote by Neil Young: it is better to burn than to fade away. ... the second to last sentence of the more than three hundred pages of the Brazilian edition of Immaculée Ilibagiza's book is: I believe that we can cure Rwanda—and our world—by curing our hearts one by one.

The protagonist's comparisons between Cobain and Ilibagiza represent the push-and-pull that he experiences between being drained by his past and attempting to overcome it. Ilibagiza brings to the narrative a spiritual layer of reflection about not only Valéria's death but also about the protagonist's own apparent attempt to commit suicide.

Although he expresses disdain for people with strong religious beliefs, the narrative has multiple references to the Bible that inform his view of his relationship with Valéria and his responsibility for her demise. In addition, the protagonist notes that Cobain was more religious than he appeared, possibly indicating that this might also be true of himself. An important character that serves to introduce this religious facet of the protagonist's reflection is Lieutenant Pires, whom the protagonist meets while serving in the military. Pires is described as someone who takes the Bible literally. The protagonist joins Pires's Bible study group in order to avoid having to do rough chores that Pires assigns to those who are free during that time of the day. The passages of the Bible that they read or that Pires mentions when he visits the protagonist at the hospital all refer directly or indirectly to sin, betrayal, punishment, and knowledge as punishment:

a. Deuteronomy 28:30—"And thou shalt betroth a wife, and another man shall lie with her: thou shalt build a house, and thou shalt not dwell therein: thou shall plant a vineyard, and shalt not gather the grapes thereof";

b. Ecclesiastes 1:15–18—"That which is crooked cannot be made straight: and that which is wanting cannot be numbered. I communed with mine own heart, saying, Lo, I am come to great estate, and have gotten more wisdom than all they that have been before me in Jerusalem: yea, my heart had great experience of wisdom and knowledge. And I gave my heart to know wisdom, and to know madness and folly: I perceived that this also is vexation of spirit. For in much wisdom is much grief: and he that increaseth knowledge increaseth sorrow";

c. Leviticus 4:27–28—"And if any one of the common people sin through ignorance, while he doeth somewhat against any of the commandments of the LORD concerning things which ought not to be done, and be guilty; Or if his sin, which he hath sinned, come to his knowledge: then he shall bring his offering, a kid of the goats, a female without blemish, for his sin which he hath sinned."

These passages from the Bible reference several aspects of the novel. Deuteronomy alludes to Valéria's and Unha's possible affair as a betrayal of the protagonist. Ecclesiastes points to the protagonist's knowledge about Valéria's past (her mother's potential suicide, her own attempt to commit suicide years earlier), about Ilibagiza (a strive to survive in spite of the world around her wanting her dead), about Cobain (the details of the suicide note and of everything in his life that seemed to lead up to his tragic end). This knowledge, in turn, is referenced in the very title of the novel, *A maçã envenenada*, an allusion to Adam's and Eve's consumption of the forbidden fruit from the knowledge tree, which leads to their condemnation to mortality and pain. In this parallel, Valéria's postcard stands for this forbidden fruit, for the suggestion that the protagonist's breaking up with her potentially led to her suicide is knowledge that sets him off on a quest for answers in the hopes for absolution. The mention of Leviticus, in turn, frames Valéria's death as sacrifice for having possibly betrayed the protagonist, who attempts to defend himself and justify his choice of not showing up at the Nirvana concert and, indirectly, potentially having caused her death.

Pires also provides a counternarrative to the protagonist's implied (and rather sexist) argument that Valéria, repeating Eve and the many other mythical women that would have led men into temptation, is responsible for his condemnation. The protagonist points out that, according to Pires, his wife saved him from a life of vice and indolence by introducing him to her church (Laub 86). As in the case of Ilibagiza, spirituality becomes a way out of situations of despair, allowing for survival. Although the protagonist mocks Pires's and Ilibagiza's connections with the divine—and says that after leaving the military he abandoned religion altogether—the contact with them clearly creates some discomfort within him and plays a role in his reflection. If Cobain's and Valéria's suicides push the protagonist toward doom and despair, Pires's and Ilibagiza's survival, albeit problematically tied to the potential alienation of religion, pull him back to hope and life. The contrasts between Cobain and Ilibagiza, on one hand, and Valéria and Pires, on the other hand, represent totality in opposition to possibilities to start anew in both the collective and the individual spheres, respectively. Similarly, Cobain and Valéria represent repetition, totality, and linearity, whereas Ilibagiza and Pires signify change and cycle, to put it in Lefebvre's terms.

Standing among these stories, the protagonist's trajectory is, in a way, a synthesis of them all: the (ambiguous) wish to die as a way to punish oneself, to take revenge on others, or even to appear heroic, like many of the biblical suicides to which he refers,[4] and the will to live. Here, guilt, economic debt, and Christianity intersect in the sense proposed by Friedrich Nietzsche in *On the Genealogy of Morals*. For the German philosopher in question, the sense of Christian guilt originates in a shift in the economic concept of debt. In Christianity, God, our ultimate creditor, sacrifices his son for humankind, in an act of self-punishment meant to impinge on humankind the "uttermost sense of guilt" (71), for we are the debtors who should, in an economic sense, take the punishment for our failing to pay our dues, that is, for our sins. There is a sense of Christian guilt in *A maçã*, tied to consumption as sin, which echoes this correlation between the pre-capitalist relations to which Nietzsche refers. As we have seen, Cobain's suicide is attributed, at least in part, to his difficulties in dealing with accusations that Nirvana had sold out to consumer capitalism, whereas the protagonist's struggle is, in turn, indirectly tied to his

Chapter Four

consumption of Cobain's music, the product of the singer's selling out. Moreover, there is speculation, as we have seen, about the morality of Cobain's suicide in the face of a much more materially and socially comfortable life than that of Ilibagiza's, who chose survival in spite of her drastic circumstances. The protagonist, in turn, torn between these two examples, Cobain and Ilibagiza, questions his own morals with respect to his suggested desire to commit suicide. In this sense, both Cobain and the protagonist incur into a debt to society and to God that is at once economic and moral.

Nevertheless, Laub's protagonist is given a second chance when he survives the car accident, a chance that signifies the very possibility of a new beginning. This new beginning, however, much like Hermano's, is likely not one without contradictions and uncertainty. It is rather filled with what-ifs, as the language of the novel demonstrates. To answer the previously cited question that the protagonist poses about his own text ("o que a aparência, a sintaxe e o estilo de um texto diz sobre quem o escreveu?" ["what does the appearance, the syntax, and the style of a text say about the person who wrote it?"]), we can say that the language of his text says much, for the novel has many layers and many possible readings. With respect to consumer culture, it says that, as a subject who belongs to a generation that has been defined as selfish, the protagonist may well be individualistic, but he is not unaware of his condition. He wrestles with this internal conflict, this push-and-pull between oblivion and awareness of his role in his personal relationships (his responsibility for Valéria's death, from which he attempts to absolve himself) and of his place in society (his privileged condition, the emptiness of the music that he produces—a mere copy of music that is considered commercial—, the insignificance of his little world and his little drama in the face of collective tragedies such as the Rwanda genocide).

One of the possibilities of the protagonist's new beginning is a kind of redemptive death, considering that the novel ends with the question that the protagonist poses to an interlocutor who is likely Valéria, as he narrates the night of the accident: "meu amor, é então que pergunto a você se devo ou não acelerar o carro" ("my love, that is when I ask you whether I should press on the accelerator"; Laub 119).

As the protagonist states in the very first line of the novel, "um suicídio muda tudo o que o seu autor disse, cantou ou escreveu" ("a suicide changes everything its author said, sang or wrote"; Laub 7). The word *autor* in Portuguese can be used to refer to a writer/composer or authorial figure in general, as well as to the person who commits a crime, although it implies less of a judgment than the word "perpetrator," which conveys the idea of guilt. Laub plays here with the idea of writing and killing, in reference to Cobain as both author of songs and "author" of his own death. In the context of a narrative that interprets other deaths based on what their authors said or wrote, it is possible to read *A maçã* as the protagonist's own metaphorical suicide note, in the sense that, by writing, he is attempting to "kill" his struggling self.

Conclusion

In both novels, the future is uncertain. In *Mãos*, the protagonist leaves a conversation with an old friend and we do not know what comes next. Nor do we know what the result of the writing process is for the protagonist of *A maçã*. However, instead of the indication of a surrender to the dissolution of time promoted by consumer culture and the sense of being lost in a dystopic world of an eternal present, the characters' trajectories indicate an impulse to work through, in the sense proposed by Dominick LaCapra in *Writing History, Writing Trauma* (2014):

> ... working through is not a linear, teleological, or straightforward developmental (or stereotypically dialectal) process either for the individual or for the collectivity. It requires going back to problems, working them over, and perhaps transforming the understanding of them. Even when they are worked through, this does not mean that they may not recur and require renewed and perhaps changed ways of working through them again. (148)

Therefore, if on one hand, the narratives may signal the permanence of the protagonists' tie to the past, on the other hand, they also suggest gestures toward undoing that tie, another step in the non-linear process of working through; of disalienation. In this process, consumer culture, in the form of toys, films, cartoons, and songs, emerges in both novels as both gloom and hope for the protagonists. It is gloom because it is at the core of their struggles, in the form of a perverse discourse on masculinity for Hermano and as a symbol of the individualism of a generation for the protagonist

Chapter Four

of *A maçã*. Nevertheless, consumer culture also appears as their hope, for it is primarily by way of being triggered by them—the imagination of a camera in an action movie in the case of Hermano and the song "Drain You," in the case of Laub's main characters—that the protagonists of both novels are pushed toward reflection.

From a broader societal perspective, these characters' reflections, the obsession with memory that the novels express as they pile references to several commodities that have marked the imaginary of the decades they cover—recall the Google search referenced in the opening of this chapter—operate in the twilight, to use Huyssen's metaphor in *Twilight Memories* (1995). The protagonists' reflections are in a sense, however confused and murky, an attempt to

> … slow down information processing, to resist the dissolution of time in the synchronicity of the archive, to recover a mode of contemplation outside the universe of simulation and fast-speed information and cable networks, to claim some anchoring space in a world of puzzling and often threatening heterogeneity, non-synchronicity, and information overload. (7)

The novels under analysis in this chapter can thus be read as narratives of *ambivalent awareness*, in the sense that both characters experience several shifts in their perception of reality, oscillating between surrendering to the forces that alienate them, on one hand, and resisting these forces, on the other hand. Rather than locating agents of change in another realm, as do Lísias and B. Carvalho, Laub and Galera suggest that change exists in the ambivalent experiences of everyday life proper. These experiences, exactly for being repetitive in nature, offer several opportunities for change, as opposed to one radical opening for transcendence, as proposed by Maia's narratives analyzed in the previous chapter. Laub's and Galera's novels suggest that, somewhere in the movement between alienation and disalienation that the characters experience, between the repetitiveness of everyday life and the potential for difference that comes with each repetition, lies the change that can ultimately lead to transitions in historical processes.

In the next chapter, I will focus on Faustini's representation of consumption and how it provides what I consider the most hopeful narrative of existence in consumer culture of all the fiction addressed in this book.

Chapter Five

Working-Class Consumption

"Just think about their priorities: they may even go without food, but they have money to buy CDs and DVDs," "They're alienated, easy to manipulate," "They don't have culture," "Now we have to put up with these people in airplanes too. And look at how they dress!" If you have spent enough time around certain middle-class Brazilians in recent decades, or even poked around social media, you probably heard—or read—comments such as these about the working class. They express the profound social hierarchy that exists in Brazilian society, which becomes painfully obvious when it comes to consumption. In the literary field, when writers from the *periferia* (economically impoverished areas in large urban centers) attempt to gain some ground, this social hierarchy materializes into something along the lines of "they don't know how to write properly. They make a lot of grammar mistakes." As critic Regina Dalcastagnè contends, Brazilian literature, in general, can be characterized as "a classe média olhando para a classe média" "the middle class looking at the middle class" ("Uma voz" 35). Much less often than ideal has the working class been represented in canonical works. As Dalcastagnè shows, when this class does make it to the pages of the canon, its members are often represented as exotic, violent, criminal, animalistic, of bad taste, clearly marked as separate, different, distanced from the middle-class narrators—and writers—that tell their story (49). Even scarcer is their (legitimized) presence in the literary field as producers of literature. Arguing for the need for a more inclusive definition of literature, Dalcastagnè notes:

> Aqueles que estão objetivamente excluídos do universo do fazer literário, pelo domínio precário de determinadas formas de expressão, acreditam que seriam também incapazes de produzir

> literatura. No entanto, eles são incapazes de produzir literatura exatamente porque não a produzem: isto é, a definição de 'literatura' exclui suas formas de expressão. ("Uma voz" 37)
>
> Those who are concretely excluded from the literary realm in general, due to their precarious command of certain forms of expression, believe that they would be incapable of producing literature as well. However, they are incapable of doing so exactly because they do not do it; that is, the definition of the concept of "literature" excludes their forms of expression.

All the writers addressed in previous chapters belong to the middle class. Three of them—Bonassi, Sant'Anna, and Maia—portray working-class characters in the stories analyzed here. As we have seen, all three writers approach these characters with a middle-class gaze that frames them as either brutes or easily duped consumers whose irresponsible spending with "superfluous" goods contributes to Brazil's economic crisis. In this chapter, I turn to working-class writer Faustini's representation of working-class consumption in *Guia afetivo da periferia* (*Affective Guide of the Periferia*). I contend that Faustini's portrayal of consumption is the most dynamic and complex of the ones in the corpus selected for this study. To put it in Miller's words, rather than representing consumers as "too close to the still life or portrait," Faustini "strive[s] to follow relationships through their expression in everyday worlds" (*Theory* 141). He represents consumption primarily as an act of love (155). In other words, by acquiring and consuming commodities, Faustini's characters cultivate interpersonal relationships, highlighting that, as Douglas and Isherwood have argued, consumption is a social activity (xxiii) and, as such, it is affected by malleable social codes that do not necessarily reduce it to manipulation and irrationality. As an urban ethnography (Soares 15), Faustini's work under study represents consumption as everyday practice: a dynamic, contradictory, and fluid activity. It implies that "shopping is not about possessions *per se*, nor is it to be about identity *per se*. It is about obtaining goods or imagining the possession and use of goods" (Miller, *Theory* 141). In this imagination, Faustini identifies the "crises," that is, the little interruptions of everyday life (Gumbrecht 302) that aesthetic experiences with commodities can yield. From this perspective, out of all the texts analyzed here, *Guia afetivo* constructs the most hopeful critique of everyday life in consumer capitalism in the sense that, where there is fluidity, there is also the potential for change and reinvention. For this reason, I call *Guia afetivo* a narrative of *transformative hope* with respect to its depiction of life in consumer culture.

Faustini's text, indeed, carries the idea of hope and transformation in many ways, as critics of his work have pointed out. In her study of citizenship in contemporary Brazilian literature, Leila Lehnen argues that Faustini establishes concrete and metaphorical bridges between disparate terrains of the city that are commonly viewed as socially severed from each other. In doing so, he creates spaces of agency and presents himself as a citizen of the entire city rather than as an individual relegated to economically impoverished areas (*Citizenship* 160). In her reading of *Guia afetivo*, owning commodities implies strengthening the characters' sense of citizenship, especially through home ownership, home improvement, and the improvement of public spaces (179). For Dalcastagnè, the city in *Guia afetivo* is a space of possibilities, inscribed in the protagonist's free exploration of the *urbe* ("Deslocamentos urbanos" 35). Like Lehnen and Dalcastagnè, Vinicius Mariano de Carvalho proposes to read the protagonist's wandering as an incarnation of the Afro-Brazilian *orixá* Exu's transformative power and his impetus for movement (42). My reading of *Guia afetivo* proposes that this transformative force and this agency are also encoded in Faustini's representation consumption as everyday practice.

Guia afetivo takes place in the city of Rio de Janeiro and tells us the memories of an unnamed protagonist, who is confounded with the author. Like Faustini, the main character also has a working-class origin. He grew up in Baixada Fluminense and Santa Cruz, areas inhabited predominantly by the lower-middle class, that is, by those who are able to hold a precarious middle-class status (Lehnen, *Citizenship* 178). Rio de Janeiro is often represented in various cultural productions as a fragmented city, divided between the rich and "legal" Zona Sul (South Zone) and the low-income and "illegal" Zona Norte (North Zone), a division that Faustini's narrative contests (171). In reality, these borders are much more fluid, for many from the *periferia* work low-paying jobs in the Zona Sul and many dwellers of the middle- and upper-class zone cross into the *periferia* as drug consumers (K. Bezerra 6). Like other cultural productions originating in the *periferia* today (9),[1] Faustini's narrative questions

Chapter Five

stereotyped representations of low-income inhabitants of Rio de Janeiro as criminals, uneducated, and violent (Lehnen, *Citizenship* 167). This contestation includes the acknowledgment of the contradictions of a socioeconomic reality that makes the protagonist, for instance, feel a certain sense of superiority while watching, from his grandparents' window when he was a child, slum dwellers suffer the consequences of flooding (Faustini 177).

Understanding the socioeconomic context in which *Guia afetivo* was published is important for grasping its representation of consumption. The book was released in a moment of Brazilian history when an estimated 20 million consumers ascended from class D (the second to last social class in the Brazilian social pyramid) to class C (the next higher one) in six years, thus creating a new market to which different sectors of the Brazilian economy began to cater (Oliven and Pinheiro-Machado 53) This shift, as mentioned in Chapter 1, was the result of the prioritization of social policies during President Lula's administration, which were continued by his successor, President Rousseff. For the sociologist Emir Sader, these administrations were constructing a post-neoliberal hegemony, in the sense that they also avoided fiscal austerity, prioritized South-South integration over free trade with the United States, and enhanced the role of the state in economic growth via income distribution, as opposed to emphasizing the idea of small government and the invisible hand of the market ("A construção" 138). According to Sader,

> Os governos Lula e Dilma representam uma ruptura com essas décadas [1980 e 1990], promovendo uma inflexão marcante na evolução da formação social brasileira. Por mais que o modelo neoliberal siga dominante em escala mundial e nosso próprio país ainda sofra os reflexos das transformações regressivas realizadas pelos governos neoliberais, os governos do Lula e da Dilma nos colocaram na contramão das tendências mundiais. ("A construção" 141)

> The Lula and Dilma administrations represent a rupture with these decades [the 1980s and the 1990s], promoting a marked change in the evolution of the Brazilian social formation. Although the neoliberal model continues to dominate at a global scale and our own country still suffers the consequences of the regressive transformations implemented by neoliberal governments, the Lula and Dilma administrations have placed us in the opposite direction of these global trends.

Working-Class Consumption

These socioeconomic shifts gave more visibility to the sectors of Brazilian society that most directly benefited from the Workers' Party social policies, as evidenced, for instance, by the success of Funk Ostentação (ostentation funk), which originated in the slums of São Paulo. This music exults conspicuous consumption within a narrative of personal success out of poverty, as funk artist Bio G-3's words illustrate: "Com essa ascensão econômica e tal ... eu acho que a periferia quis mostrar isso, quis mostrar que pode, entendeu? ... nem que de repente seja um esforço pra ter ... hoje em dia é mais fácil de ter condição de ter um carrinho maneiro, que antigamente era mais difícil" ("With this economic ascension and all ... I think that the *periferia* wanted to shows this, wanted to show that it can [consume/be visible], you know? ... even if [acquiring goods] is difficult ... today it is easier to be able to afford a cool car, which used to be more difficult"; Bio G-3, *Funk Ostentação: O filme* 00:29:12–00:29:31).

In music videos produced outside the circuit of big production companies, artists such as MC Guimê sing about luxury goods, which appear in the videos:

> Contando os plaquê de 100, dentro de um Citroën
> Aí nóis convida, porque sabe que elas vêm.
> De transporte nóis tá bem, de Hornet ou 1100
> Kawasaki, tem Bandit, RR tem também ("Plaquê de 100")
> Counting 100 [*reais*] bills, inside a Citroën car
>
> We invite [the girls] 'cause we know they'll come.
> We've got good wheels, riding a Hornet or a 1100
> Kawasaki, we have Bandit, we have RR too
>
> Quando dá uma hora da manhã é que o bonde se prepara pra vibe
> Abotoa sua pólo listrada dá um nó no cadarço do tênis da Nike
> Joga o cabelo pra cima ou põe um boné que combina com a roupa ("Tá patrão")
>
> When it's one o'clock in the morning it's when the *bonde* gets ready for the party
> Button up your striped polo shirt, tie your Nike shoes
> Flip your hair up or put on a cap that matches your clothes

Chapter Five

Ostentation Funk artists, mostly from São Paulo, commonly describe their music as providing a positive perspective on life in the favelas, contrasting it with Rio de Janeiro's funk's celebration of violence and drugs. They see it as the realization of the dream of a better life, where goods provide pleasure, happiness, and self-esteem amidst daily hardships (*Funk Ostentação: O filme* 2012). As Pinheiro-Machado and Scalco point out, ostentation funk "celebrates the right to happiness, luxury consumption, positive individual feelings, *favela* pride, and class boldness" ("The Right"). In this way, while many aspects of funk *ostentação* can be questioned, not the least of which the highly problematic ways in which women are often portrayed in songs and music videos by some of the male artists,[4] the genre expresses a certain happiness that comes with the comfort of being able to afford (nice) things, and to gain some form of visibility in a highly excluding society.

Similarly, rap lyrics claim the right to own commodities while denouncing the violence and social injustice of those who live in the favelas. The rap group Racionais MC's, for instance, recognizes that happiness in capitalism equals consuming, an association that is imprinted in one's mind:

> Não é questão de luxo
> Não é questão de cor
> É questão que fartura
> Alegra o sofredor
> Não é questão de preza, nêgo
> A ideia é essa
> Miséria traz tristeza e vice-versa
> Inconscientemente vem na minha mente inteira
> Na loja de tênis o olhar do parceiro feliz
> De poder comprar o azul, o vermelho
> O balcão, o espelho
> O estoque, a modelo, não importa
> Dinheiro é puta e abre as portas
> Dos castelos de areia que quiser. ("Vida loka II")

> It is not a matter of luxury
> It is not a matter of color
> It's a matter of abundance
> It makes the one suffering happy
> It is not a matter of looking good, dawg
> This is the idea
> Poverty only brings unhappiness and vice-versa

> Unconsciously my mind thinks
> About my buddy's look of happiness in the shoe story
> For being able to buy the blue, the red one
> The counter, the mirror
> The stock, the model, it doesn't matter
> Money is a whore and it opens the doors
> Of any sandcastle you want.

In another song, titled "Otus 500" ("That's another story"; literally "Other 500"), Racionais MC's portrays the desires of a subject from the *periferia*, who takes matters of social justice into their own hands by entering a rich man's house and claiming his belongings, the house, the refrigerator, a DVD. This subject dreams of owning the same things that the man owns: a pool, fancy silverware, several pairs of shoes, ties, two Mercedes-Benz vehicles, jewelry, Armani and Hugo Boss clothes, among other commodities.

With considerably less visibility in the media and with a focus on several issues besides consumption, the *literatura marginal* or *literatura periférica*[5] has also been carving out its space, be it via canonical circuits of distribution, in the case of some writers, or via cultural events such as *saraus* in low-income neighborhoods in cities like São Paulo and Brasília. This literature has also gained important ground in the field of literary criticism, with numerous articles, books, reviews, academic presentations, and curricula dedicated to it, especially thanks to the work of the Grupo de Estudos de Literatura Brasileira Contemporânea (Studies in Contemporary Brazilian Literature Group), under the leadership of Dalcastagnè, professor and scholar of Brazilian literature at the Universidade de Brasília.

One of the main names of *literatura marginal*, Reginaldo Ferreira da Silva (Ferréz), has also portrayed how consumption can be a source of happiness. In the short story "O Barco Viking" (2006), two children from the *periferia* are initially barred from a ride at the chain restaurant Habib's in São Paulo. The woman controlling the access to the ride explains: "Desculpe, meninos, mas é só para quem está consumindo" ("I'm sorry, boys, but it's just for those who are consuming/eating at the restaurant"; Ferréz 54). The narrator, a working-class man who is dining at the restaurant in question, observes the scene and invites the children to eat with him and his family. It is only by being transformed into consumers via the invitation of the narrator, that the kids are allowed access to the ride. The narrator recognizes that this access, although momentary and therefore limited, is important for the children, for it makes them happy. Moreover, the access functions as a transgressive act, symbolizing a potential change in social order in which the children would be able to stay in the ride "pra sempre" ("forever"; 55).

Access to goods as symbols of potential societal transformation also appears in Ferréz's 2005 children's book, *Amanhecer Esmeralda* (*Emerald Dawn*). In this story, the life of a little Afro-Brazilian girl named Manhã (Morning/Dawn) starts to change when she receives an emerald dress from her schoolteacher, Marcão. The gift symbolically transforms the life of the little girl, who becomes happier. Her happiness spreads through her house and her neighborhood, which begins to change into happier places. The dress, thus, acquires meaning well beyond that of mere commodity. Its biography (Kopytoff 68) includes the power to transform not just the life of the little girl, but an entire community, through a change in self-esteem.

Another prominent Afro-Brazilian writer, Conceição Evaristo, emphasizes everyday hardships when goods are absent or scarce in some of the stories in *Olhos d'água* (*Teary Eyes;* 2014), thus looking at consumption from the perspective of human rights. For example, she points out the happiness of the protagonist of "Maria" when she gets leftover fruit from her boss to take home to her kids; Kimbá's hatred for the lack of comfort of a life of poverty in "Os amores de Kimbá" ("Kimbá's loves"); and Dona Esterlinda's love for soap operas in "A gente combinamos de não morrer" ("We agreed not to die"). Nevertheless, Evaristo also cautions against the hectic routine of capitalistic accumulation in "O cooper de Cida" ("Cida's Run"). In this story, the sight of a homeless person and the waves of the ocean distract Cida, the protagonist, from her daily run, forcing her to slow down in a frantic world of promises such as "*Aprenda inglês em seis meses. Garantimos a sua aprendizagem em cento e oitenta dias*" ("*Learn English in six months. We guarantee your learning in one hundred and eighty days*"; 67, emphasis in the original). Her life is a constant race against the clock, beyond her daily physical exercise. Cida runs around the house fixing things, doing things, getting ready for work, "flying down the stairs" because the elevator is too slow. Even her reading of the headlines on the newsstands is fast-paced, thanks to "dynamic reading" classes that she took (65–66). As she slows down, she begins to ponder about the cyclic repetition of nature, "century after century," and little by little, she surrenders to this contemplation, feeling her bare feet in the sand; observing someone who enjoyed the ocean "em plena terça-feira, às seis e cinquenta e cinco da manhã" ("on a Tuesday, at six fifty-five in the morning"; 68). Emerging out of this state of wonder, Cida realizes that she needs to head back home and get back to her routine. Only not that day, for she decides not to go to work and instead, simply do nothing. Cida's decision goes against the clock of capitalist life, thus imposing a break on its rhythm, introducing a subversive change, even if only a temporary one.

Besides Ferréz and Evaristo, Faustini has achieved considerable recognition among literary scholars with his book *Guia afetivo da periferia*, published as part of the project Tramas Urbanas (Urban Plots/Stories), sponsored by Petrobrás, a semi-public oil company in Brazil. As pointed out by Lehnen, this project is part of "the circuit of cultural commodities that both attempts to generate agency for disenfranchised social segments and capitalizes on such groups" (*Citizenship* 167). Lehnen's comment points to the ambiguities surrounding cultural production in the twenty-first century, standing between activism and commercial interests. These ambiguities, as well as tensions among different positions taken by cultural producers of the *periferia*, express themselves in the audiences and spaces in which this cultural production circulates. Funk, for example, is both seen as "música de preto, pobre e favelado" ("music by/for poor, black people from the slums") and enjoyed by the Brazilian elite in lavish wedding parties and middle-class festive gatherings (Trotta 91). Funk Ostentação, in particular, functions as protest against a desire to keep the poor invisible (93), while also portraying a world of consumption with which the middle and upper classes identify, therefore facilitating its acceptance in wealthy social circles (Dias, qtd. in Gombata). *Literatura de periferia* also operates between two worlds. In São Paulo, for instance, *saraus*, or poetry evenings, have opened spaces of production and consumption of this literature in bars of the *periferia*, where small community libraries also operate and out of which several publications and independent publishers have started. These initiatives provide people from these areas access to culture in ways that would otherwise not be available. Nevertheless, this literature has also reached so–called lettered circles via mainstream publishers, social media, and partnerships

Chapter Five

with the private sector via government programs that support this cultural production (Tennina 117–44). Hence, there coexists in this literature a political activism toward giving the *periferia* a space to be both consumer and producer of culture and a desire to be consumed by mainstream readers that can be seen as controversial by some of the writers. Allan da Rosa, for example, has expressed concern about the sponsorship of corporations (Tennina 161). Indeed, private interests in the *periferia* have sought to achieve high profits and positive branding at the expense of securing true access to citizenship (K. Bezerra 89). While it is important to recognize the limitations of a project sponsored by a semi-private company that ended up involved in one of the biggest corruption scandals of Brazilian history,[6] it would be inaccurate to reduce *Guia afetivo* to mere reproduction of its conditions of production. I concur with Lehnen's argument that the novel can be seen as "a form of autoconstruction of cultural citizenship that emerges precisely at the sites where peripheral culture is devalued or negated … Culture is both a tool of insurgent citizenship and the expression of newly gained substantive political, social, and civil rights" (*Citizenship* 191). As we will see in the analysis that follows, while highlighting more positive ways in which goods mediate relationships, the novel also questions social inequalities expressed through consumption.

Consuming Together

As the title suggests, *Guia afetivo da periferia* presents an affective view of life in the *periferia*. Consumption appears as an integral part of this life and, consequently, it is seen from this affective perspective as well. This view of consumption implies that commodities can establish relationships of love (care, concern, obligation, responsibility, etc.) between individuals constituted as subjects of devotion in what Miller characterizes as a modern sacrificial ritual (*Theory* 151). According to Miller,

> … shopping may also be a ritual practice. Its foundation is a sacrificial logic whose purpose is to constitute desiring subjects. Sacrifice was based on the rites for transforming consumption into devotion. Shopping begins with a similar rite, which negates mere expenditure in obeisance to the higher purposes of thrift. It ends as the labour of constituting both the immediacy and the dynamics of specific relations of love. (155)

From this perspective, consumption can be seen as the other end of shopping in these relations of love. By portraying consumption predominantly in such terms, Faustini suggests that commodities and the act of consuming them can mean many things beyond a "materialistic dead end" (Miller, *Theory* 128).

One of the most prominent commodities portrayed in *Guia afetivo* in this sense is food, which invokes fond memories of the protagonist's relationships with friends and family members. The protagonist's mother, Dona Creuza, is often depicted as a provider of comfort in the form of food.[7] Her "prato fundo de feijão, arroz, pepino inteiro e bife de chá de dentro batido, bem passado" ("deep dish of beans, rice, whole cucumber, and a well-done steak"), which the protagonist enjoys while watching late night dubbed films on television, serves as a reward and a much needed pause in the grueling routine of riding a crowded bus after a long day of work (Faustini 31). Another family member with whom the protagonist connects via food consumption is his grandfather, who used to take him to eat fried dried meat at fairs in Maré (93). In another moment, the protagonist uses food to connect with his romantic interest by buying her a "pastel com caldo de cana" ("a pastry with sugar cane juice") in an attempt to impress her (88).

In many instances of the protagonist's life, food functions as a treat for him and his family. *Churrasquinho* (cheap kebabs sold by street vendors) at the bus station helps to alleviate his bad mood for having missed the bus. Candy and popsicles, in turn, make his daily journey on the train more pleasant. A bottle of Coca-Cola, a soda commonly viewed as one of the ultimate symbols of capitalist evil, is re-signified when purchased as a treat: a small luxury that his family reserves for special occasions, to be consumed with another small luxury, fried chicken with noodles. As a treat, the bottle of Coke appears as a small transgression in an everyday of constant pursuit of thrift out of necessity. It reaffirms the self by confirming the family members' special status (Miller, *Theory* 47). As the protagonist notes, walking to the neighborhood store to purchase the soda on Sundays was a way to partake in the communal habit of many families in the neighborhood, who also rewarded themselves with the drink after having Kool-Aid for the entire week (Faustini 106). The act of purchasing the beverage also provided him with a self-confidence that he paraded in the streets as he walked home from the store holding the bottle. On

Chapter Five

these Sundays of splurging and family reunions, the protagonist relies on his Coke as something that "organizes his senses" and provides him with a "sensorial and aesthetic discipline" that dissipates the anxiety that comes with this type of family gatherings (108). In this way, this product acquires positive uses that go beyond the commonly perceived nature of commodities as symbols of oppression.

It is important to point out, however, that the protagonist's remarks about commodities such as these do not simply romanticize them. Evidence that the protagonist is not simply "buying into" the promises of Coca-Cola commercials is that, to the comforting memory of drinking Coca-Cola, he juxtaposes the image of the television set that he watches while drinking the beverage in question. He describes the set as having "Bombril na antena para sintonizar a imagem na distante Santa Cruz" ("*Bombril*[8] on the antenna for syncing images in the distant Santa Cruz"; Faustini 108). This juxtaposition stresses the precarious technological conditions in which the product is consumed, in comparison to those of the upper-middle class during that time (consider the experience of the protagonist of *Mãos de cavalo*, for example). It displays the contradictory and complex nature of the socioeconomic context in which consumer culture emerges in Brazil, a country struggling with deep social inequalities, where television sets exist even in areas that lack the appropriate infrastructure for the technology to function.

Food portrayed as a treat is also part of the protagonist's family's grocery shopping. The protagonist remembers going to the supermarket as a child with his parents, a moment that he anxiously awaited every month. He saw these instances as opportunities to be rewarded for behaving well and for helping his parents push the cart around. His reward was eating spaghetti with ketchup at the supermarket's food court and, sometimes, managing to convince his parents to buy him gum (Faustini 151). The act of eating after shopping represents compensation not only to the protagonist, but to the parents as well, who have to exercise much discipline during the remaining time of the shopping trip, as they look for the best deals in order to save money.

As sites of consumption, supermarkets fascinated the protagonist for the large variety of new products, which he was always eager to try. According to him, supermarkets also challenged him to create new strategies to attempt to convince his parents to buy these items (Faustini 152). Therefore, for the protagonist, beyond an opportunity to acquire new commodities, going to the supermarket was a sensorial experience that stimulated creativity and provided him with opportunities to exercise relative power over his parents. Similarly, going to the neighborhood store to make last minute purchases as requested by his parents is for the protagonist more than simply purchasing goods. He notes that these moments made him feel proud, for he felt that he was contributing to the running of the household.

Besides food, many other commodities establish connections between characters in *Guia afetivo*. The protagonist remembers an ex-girlfriend for the trinkets that she used to buy in order to personalize an old vanity table her grandmother had given her (Faustini 88). In another instance, a cheap lamp is the focus of the narrative in a section titled "O Abajur da Pedro Américo" ("The Lampshade of Pedro Américo"). The object in question serves as an initial connection between the narrator and his roommate from the state of Ceará (94). Furthermore, even affective relationships between people and domestic animals are mediated by goods, such as the case of a girl's connection with her dog, who sniffs her new shoes, in what the narrator characterizes as "um gesto carinhoso" ("a gesture of affection"; 101). Lastly, television shows also facilitate bonding amongst the protagonist's friends, whose favorite pastime is to replicate narrations of soccer games that they watch on television. Rather than a numbing activity of mindless distraction, watching television until late at night is motivated by the opportunity to participate in social interactions about the content of shows broadcast the day before (171).

If goods are mediators of social relations in positive ways, many of the places of consumption that the narrator frequents appear in the story as spaces of socialization. He describes a street fair in Maré in a way that stresses the human component of trading and consumption:

> A pressa e o improviso do mundo do trabalho carioca seminal que a Maré ajuda a sustentar é substituída por bicicletas guiadas com orgulho, motos que transportam sorrisos, evangélicos engravatados seguindo a seta de sua missão, adolescentes em direção aos cursos de sonhos de sábado e sacolas de legumes e frutas em mãos firmes. Na descida da passarela, a feira da

Chapter Five

> Teixeira recebe o transeunte com sons, cores, cheiros e sabores. Os DVDs atualizam os gostos de rockeiros, funqueiros, lambadoreiros, pagodeiros e moleques fissurados em novos jogos. (Faustini 93)

> The rush and the improvisation of the Carioca work realm that Maré helps to maintain is replaced by the bicycles ridden with pride, motorcycles that transport smiles, evangelicals wearing ties following their missions, teenagers on their way to their dream courses of Saturday night, and bags filled with fruits and vegetables and carried by firm hands. Down the bridge, the Teixeira fair greets the passer-by with sounds, colors, smells, and flavors. The DVDs update the taste of fans of rock, funk, *lambada, pagode*, and kids hooked up on new videogames.

As described above, the fair is a space where a community comes together. People from a variety of groups display consumer goods more out of pride for having worked hard for it, and less out of competition with others. The fair is depicted as a democratic space, where people who have a variety of tastes come together. The commodities they buy hint at their lifestyle and their personalities. The smiles, the pride, the firm hands, the tastes, the welcoming feel: the way the protagonist describes purchasing and displaying commodities emphasizes a perception of consumption as a communal practice, quite different from the self-centered and mind-numbing postmodern behavior of which theorists of consumption such as Jameson and Baudrillard speak (Featherstone 16–17). Without necessarily denying the existence of such behavior in consumer society, Faustini's narrative shows that there are other possible ways of interacting with goods.

Aesthetic Interruptions of the Mundane

A sense that consumption has the ability to make goods personal (Miller, *Theory* 131) informs Faustini's representation of his protagonist's aesthetic experiences with a variety of commodities. These experiences can be understood as "crises" that interrupt everyday life in the sense described by Hans Ulrich Gumbrecht: "… multiple modalities of aesthetic experience [that] permeate our everyday worlds today (without becoming a part of or identical with the everyday)" (301). Faustini's protagonist's aesthetic experiences with commodities—which are quite different from Gumbrecht's example of drinking bourbon and reading a book in a high-end chair—present us with other forms of crises in everyday life that take place through commodities. In general, these crises comprise both repetition and change in that they interrupt the everyday in the same way in more than one instance, as evidenced by the use of verbs in the imperfect in the examples below. Some of the crises are fleeting, but anticipated rather than sudden moments of interruption, given the hardships of the protagonist's routine. Such is the case of ads for the protagonist's favorite popsicle, *Dragão Chinês*:

> Mas nada se comparava à sensação de tomar um picolé Dragão Chinês sabor milho verde, dentro do trem. O prazer começava pelo pregão anunciado: "O poderoso Dragão Chinês." Depois era só cuidar para não deixar de lamber nenhuma gota derretida na mão, afinal o aproveitamento tinha que ser completo— até o palito eu chupava como quem chupa osso de galinha. (Faustini 92)

> But nothing could compare to the feeling of having a Dragão Chinês corn-flavored popsicle on the train. The pleasure would start with the seller's advertising: "The powerful Dragão Chinês." After that it was just a matter of making sure to lick any drop that fell on your hand, after all, you wouldn't want to waste any of it—I would even suck on the stick as if I were sucking on chicken bones.

Advertisement becomes intertwined with the sensorial experience of tasting the popsicle, thus making secondary its primary goal, which is to convince the consumer to buy the product. Every bit of the popsicle, according to the protagonist, was to be carefully consumed, which emphasizes the affective value of said product for him.

Similarly, the banal act of carrying out a commercial transaction at the neighborhood store provides a repeated aesthetic experience for the protagonist. When purchasing eggs, the protagonist enjoys watching the storeowner wrap the items in question in old newspaper:

> De tanto comprar ovo, passei a observar o modo como o vendedor embrulhava separadamente de três em três ovos a dúzia. O barulho produzido pelo encontro das mãos com o jornal ao embrulhar os ovos em formas geométricas era hipnótico. As cores dos enlatados e ensacados que ocupavam as estantes altas próximas ao comprido balcão também ajudavam nesta sensação. (Faustini 151)

Chapter Five

> After buying eggs so many times, I began to notice the way the seller packed a dozen eggs three eggs at a time. The sound of the hands touching the newspaper while wrapping the eggs in geometric forms was hypnotic. The colors of the canned and packaged food on the tall shelves near the long counter also helped to create this sensation.

Although acknowledging the effectiveness of advertising on himself—he makes a similar comment about the Coca-Cola ad on television, stressing that the soda tasted exactly as the commercial promised—the narrator points out the different meanings that these products acquire beyond their commercial value. He does so by addressing the perspective of the consumer, that is, by looking at what consumers actually do with commodities (de Certeau 31). In these uses, he finds a sensorial experience that produces estrangement, interrupting the flow of the everyday, defamiliarizing the familiar, reframing quotidian moments. This perspective renders flexible the boundaries of the aesthetic to include the beauty of things like videogames, as described by the protagonist when he talks about his first time playing Atari:

> um estranhamento muito grande. Estava acostumado com objetos eletrônicos grandes como TVs de válvula, vitrolas que pareciam móveis. Até os botões do *Atari* eram muito diferentes dos objetos eletrônicos que até então eu conhecia. Era bom de mexer! Na tela, as formas gráficas e as cores do aviãozinho do jogo *River Raid* formavam um universo mais crível do que os monstros que lutavam contra o *Spectreman* nos episódios da TVS [sic]. Era mais impactante que o monstrinho engraçado que sai comendo tudo no jogo *Pacman*. (Faustini 156)

> a great estrangement. I was used to big electronics such as TVs with knobs, record players that looked like furniture. Even the buttons on the Atari were very different from the electronics that I was familiar with until then. It was nice to touch them! On the screen, the geometric forms and the colors of the little airplane on *River Raid* were part of a more believable universe than that of the monsters that fought against *Spectreman* on television. It had more of an impact than the funny little monster going around eating everything in *Pacman*.

Using words such as "estrangement," "credible universe," and "striking," to evaluate the sensorial experience of playing video games, the protagonist treats as an aesthetic experience what is generally considered negative addiction, highlighting sensations that tend to go unnoticed.

Another product that is a source of repeated pleasure for the protagonist is canned food. Calling attention to the mundane details of consuming canned sardines and canned corn, the narrator describes the pleasant sensations of seeing oil come out of a can of sardines as one opens it. He also takes pleasure in watching his mother open a can of Swift meat with the little key with which it came. Similar to his observations about the Coca-Cola that he used to enjoy drinking, his remarks about the mundane pleasures of consuming food end with a subtle criticism to the commercials that attempted to convince families like his that canned food was "like caviar" (Faustini 112). After narrating his childhood memories of consuming these canned goods, the narrator points out that his mother followed closely what the commercials of those products recommended and that, as a result, he sarcastically notes, now "she's no longer skinny" (113). His remark suggests the potential long-term health problems that the consumption of such products may cause, thus acknowledging that, while not to be seen statically as a negative practice, consumption may have undesired concrete side effects.

Furthermore, the protagonist also notes how consumer culture aestheticizes reality through marketing, which distorts or even effaces certain aspects of this reality. To this end, he comments on the representation of the Santa Teresa neighborhood in travel guides. Santa Teresa, as a tourist site, is described in the narrative as a space "of controlled de-control of emotions," that is, as a postmodern sites of "ordered disorder," where the middle class can enjoy emotions in a controlled way, such as parks, malls, and resorts (Featherstone 80). As one of such sites, Santa Teresa appears in the narrative as a place where social inequalities are effaced so that foreign tourists can enjoy a cable car ride, while hoping to have "end of afternoon epiphanies" in a romanticized Rio that resembles a Venice from a distant past (Faustini 79–80). From the sanitized cable cars, according to the narrator, tourists do not notice the black people who cannot afford to pay for the ride their onlookers are enjoying. He remarks sarcastically: "Fico imaginando o anúncio de Santa Teresa em outros países: venha se perder em Santa Teresa!" ("I imagine an ad about Santa Teresa in other countries: come get lost in Santa Teresa!"; 80). His statement re-signifies the verb *perder-se*: beyond the meaning of metaphorically getting lost in the tourist pleasure of a nostalgia for the past, the use of the verb by the protagonist suggests a metaphorical getting lost in the present by ignoring the surrounding social reality.

A couple of paragraphs later, the protagonist speaks from the perspective of a tourist guide to suggest, not to the foreigner, but to the "carioca[9] que um dia puder desfrutar dessa vista," ("Carioca that one day may enjoy the view") that she visit the area on a Thursday, when she will be able to see young black men and an old black lady "com peitos do tamanho de um peito de uma mulher na cena de um filme de Fellini, com o pé que, de tanto andar, cresceu para os lados" ("with breasts the size of those of a woman out of a Fellini film, with a foot that has grown sideways from so much walking"; Faustini 80). Invoking the baroque aesthetic of the Italian filmmaker, the narrator juxtaposes tourist tropical sexuality (the woman's breasts) with the rough reality of her everyday (her expanding tired feet).

Low and High

In keeping with the nuanced perspective on working-class consumption, *Guia afetivo* juxtaposes "high" and "low" culture, valuing the latter as much as the former and highlighting the commodity nature of both of them, as evidenced, for instance, by the protagonist's selling his books and records in order to be able to attend concerts (Faustini 54). Movies, pop music, popular and canonical literature appear as means to advance socially, to expand one's knowledge, to connect with others, to make money, or simply to interrupt the hardships of everyday life by providing moments of rest.

At times, these cultural products function as a sort of compass that helps the protagonist to situate himself socially, politically, and even sexually. In the case of film, he learns about sex from French cinema (he cites *La nuit américaine* [*Day for Night*], 1973), by founder of the Nouvelle Vague movement François Truffaut, as well as Leos Carax's films) as cultural capital to try to impress girls with whom he wants to be romantically involved (Faustini 82). Other films, such as *Um homem sem importância* (*A Man of No Importance*, 1971), directed by Brazilian Alberto Salvá, and Italian director Elio Petri's film *La classe operaria va in paradiso* (*Lulu the*

Tool, 1971) contribute to develop his class consciousness (79). Petri's film, in particular, functions as a kind of lens through which the protagonist sees his immediate space, in a similar way to how the main character of *Mãos de cavalo* interacts with his environment. With Petri's film in mind, Faustini's protagonist imagines his neighborhood as a "precarious futurist movie" taking place in the third world, where the aesthetic of the Italian filmmaker meets Eastern European post-punk culture (23). The development of his class consciousness leads him to engage in activities meant to symbolically take revenge on the system that forces him into low-paying jobs. One of such activities is to go to a McDonald's, one of the most iconic symbols of capitalism and capitalist alienation in the form of its Fordist approach to preparing food and its Happy Meals, simply to think (116).

In the case of literature, the protagonist values both canonical and popular Brazilian writers, pointing out the role of their work in his formative years as well as the importance of these writers' work for the experiences of others in his community. The popular teen narrative *O homem que calculava* (*The Man who Calculated*, 1938), written by Brazilian math teacher Júlio César de Mello e Souza under the pseudonym of Malba Tahan, for instance, was the first book to spark the protagonist's love of reading (Faustini 54). Similarly, he considers the highly commercially successful novels of Brazilian writer Paulo Coelho the kind of reading that working-class people who have "intellectual aspirations" enjoy (33). Popular literature appears, therefore, as a product that connotes prestige among members of the working class. Alongside these literary references, the protagonist mentions having read *A boa terra* (*The Good Earth*), a novel by North American writer Pearl S. Buck about peasant life in China. The novel became a best seller, while also awarding its author the Pulitzer Prize in 1932 and contributing to her winning the Nobel Prize in Literature in 1938. The Brazilian translation, which was part of a popular collection sold at newsstands, was crucial, according to the protagonist, for shaping his political views. He also notes that the book—along with the board game War—led him to become interested in China and, later on, to learn about communist ideas, which he continued to explore beyond that initial reading. He adds that his interest in Asian culture also stems from having watched Japanese television series when he was growing up.

Chapter Five

While popular culture leads him to high culture, the opposite movement is also true, as evidenced by his remark that it was his interest in poetry that led him to like music lyrics, particularly rock (Faustini 139). Because of his love of both forms of artistic expression, he began to tattoo parts of song lyrics onto his body, which his mother considered "coisa de marginal, coisa de gente mal-educada" ("something that criminals and bad-behaved people do"; 139). Commenting on his mother reprimanding him for his tattooes, he notes: "Ela nunca entendeu que a tatuagem era a ponte que eu criava com meus cadernos de soneto. Era a Escola Estadual Euclydes da Cunha em meu corpo. Eram os barquinhos de papel do soneto do Guilherme Almeida" ("She never understood that the tattoo was a bridge that I created with my notebook of sonnets. It was Euclydes da Cunha Public School on my body. It was the little paper boats from Guilherme Almeida's sonnet"; 139). Questioning his mother's view of rock music and tattoos as degradation, the protagonist finds less than obvious links between "high" and "low" culture that appeal to him.

Like his path from poetry to music, cinema at times sparks his curiosity for canonical literature. He mentions, for example, how Nelson Pereira dos Santos's film adaptation of Graciliano Ramos's novel *Vidas secas* (*Barren Lives*, 1938) influenced his later reading of the book. Lastly, he references Allen Ginsberg's poetry as the root of his curiosity for elements associated with science fiction, such as UFOs and aliens, as he contemplates the sky from the top of buildings and imagines that the latter float in the air (Faustini 148). These comments about high and low culture, on one hand, and visual and written texts, on the other hand, suggest the multiple possible paths of an individual's trajectory as a reader, thus validating the consumption of a variety of cultural references.

Oftentimes, the narrator juxtaposes references to "high" and "low" culture in a non-hierarchical manner as a way to contest views of working-class consumption of pop culture as a sign of inferiority or degradation. This kind of juxtaposition appears for example when, in a kind of delirium, the protagonist imagines Brazilian poet Manuel Bandeira—whose association with Romantic poetry and his proximity to working-class bohemians the protagonist identifies with—appearing together with characters from the Japanese cartoon Zodiac Knights, to the sound of the 1980s American new wave band Berlin's hit song "Take My Breathe [sic] Away" (Faustini 55). In the chapter that follows this juxtaposition, the narrator once again references Romantic poets such as Brazilian Álvares de Azevedo, whose poetry he becomes familiar with not by reading the book, but actually by listening to a record by Brazilian actor Sérgio Cardoso. He goes on to point out that he battled pneumonia—a disease he was proud to contract because it brought him closer to Romantic poets who died from it—by reading the most challenging writer he had ever heard of: Marcel Proust, whose book he had acquired at a used bookstore. These references display the protagonist's ability to navigate between high and low cultures easily. While seeking to legitimize his voice in literary discourse, he repeatedly uses his gained authority to then legitimize the consumption of popular culture, a common strategy among Brazilian working-class writers (Dalcastagnè, "Uma voz" 63).

Further legitimization comes from references to Brazilian writer Joaquim Manuel de Macedo's character Simplício from *A luneta mágica* (*The Magic Telescope*, 1869), North American F. Scott Fitzgerald's Amory Blane, and thinkers such as Leon Trotsky. The protagonist writes quotes from these writers' work on his backpack, about which he comments:

> Ter uma mochila toda rabiscada era como ter uma roupa de marca. Dentro do ônibus ou dentro do trem, colocava a mochila de modo que o passageiro ao lado conseguisse ler o que estava escrito. Eu queria ser um outdoor tanto do charmoso ceticismo burguês de Amory Blane quanto do charmoso espírito revolucionário trotskista. Se você não tem isso na sua juventude, você está morto. Apesar de tudo a minha volta propor a minha morte, eu queria estar vivo. Era como se a mochila fosse um livro de autoajuda, que eu lia para me encorajar. (Faustini 69)

> Having a backpack with doodles all over was like having designer clothes. On the bus or on the train, I would carry the backpack in such a way that the passenger next to me could read what was written on it. I wanted to be a billboard for both Amory Blane's charming skepticism and the charming revolutionary Trotskyan spirit. If you don't have this when you are young, you're dead. Despite everything around me wanting me to be dead, I wanted to be alive. It was as if the backpack were a self-help book, which I read to get encouragement.

Appropriating consumer culture's branding strategies, but subverting their commercial purpose, the protagonist attempts to "wear" high culture as a fashionable commodity, claiming to become a

Chapter Five

billboard for the writers and thinkers in question. While advocating for "high" culture in this way, he also values "low" culture by comparing the readings he mentions to self-help. Fitzgerald and Trotsky, along with the humble food prepared by his mother, give him the strength to keep trying to succeed in an environment where everything is designed to make him fail: "Ao comer o angu de milho doce, as incertezas davam lugar à coragem trotskista e à perspicácia fitzgeraldiana" ("Upon eating the corn porridge, all the uncertainties gave way to the Trotskyan courage and a Fitzgeraldian perspicacity"; Faustini 69).

If on one hand the narrator attempts to use marketing strategies to brand literature, on the other hand, he recognizes strategies used by characters in literary books in a candy seller's tactics to convince people to buy his product. Comparing the candy seller's style of announcing his product to that of a character from a story by renowned nineteenth-century Brazilian writer Machado de Assis, he points out that this man is aware of the power of fiction even without having read Machado:

> Trata-se de fruir, de buscar ao longo do dia o direito a esse instante. Ele é possível até mesmo sob o sol a pino, quando você é um camelô e arruma fileiras amarelas e vermelhas de bombons Serenata de Amor sobre a lona de plástico azul na calçada, imitando a vitrine da loja de roupa de grife atrás.
>
> Nesse momento, você deve negar-se a qualquer entendimento sociológico da vida deste rapaz que produza compaixão, pois logo em seguida ele vai oferecer três bombons por um real com uma voz anasalada, num pregão que lembra o negro que vendia cocada em *Dom Casmurro*. Ele sabe que a forma de executar o pregão é decisiva para que você compre ou não o bombom. Mesmo sem ter lido Machado, ele já se apropriou das estratégias de ficção. (Faustini 74)

> It's about fruition, about searching for the right to this moment along the day. This moment is possible even under the blazing sun, when you are a street vendor and organize the yellow and red lines of *Serenata de Amor* bonbons on a plastic cover laid on the sidewalk, imitating the window of the designer clothing store behind you.
>
> At this moment, you have to let go of any sociological understanding of this young man's life that may produce compassion, for right after that he will offer you three bonbons for one *real*

> in his nasal-like voice, advertising like the black man that used to sell coconut candy bars in *Dom Casmurro*. He knows that the way he advertises is crucial to convince you to buy the bonbon. Even without ever having read Machado, he's appropriated fictional strategies.

The protagonist's observation emphasizes the wit and creativity of the working class, thus suggesting that one does not have to be a reader of canonical fiction in order to develop what would be considered sophisticated thinking. Noting street vendors' manipulation tactics to get people to buy their product, he advocates for a non-romanticized view of the working class and for their right for their own aesthetic sense to be acknowledged.

Tactical Consumption

Faustini's nuanced depiction of working-class consumption also highlights workers' tactical behavior in order to cope with economic hardships and find creative ways of accessing products other than necessities. *Guia afetivo* depicts several moments in which characters, as consumers, take advantage of opportunities of the type described by Michel de Certeau in *The Practice of Everyday Life*. De Certeau defines tactics as actions performed by those who do not hold the power. These actions, which take place in the territory of those who are in control, are isolated operations that outwit the system when opportunities to do so present themselves (37). Tactics are, therefore, circumstantial and do not deeply modify the system that they attempt to subvert. However, they allow the subject to contest the system, thus disturbing its stability.

Describing a fair in the Madureira neighborhood that he used to frequent, the protagonist emphasizes tactics utilized by working class consumers like him. He characterizes the fair as

> um lugar de negócios, de transação, de pregão, de vendedor de balas, de lucro no centavo. Se o cartão de crédito internacional está para o Sheraton, a moeda de um centavo está para Madureira. Ainda hoje há uma babel de vozes nos calçadões, mercadões, e shoppinhos, onde o capitalismo precário carioca experimenta as delícias de todas as possibilidades de Control C e Control V no século XXI. É ali, nas coloridas capas impressas em baixa resolução dos DVDs piratas, que pegamos da mão do camelô o sentido de negociação das ruas do bairro. (Faustini 92)

Chapter Five

> A place of business transactions, of advertising, of the candy seller, of profit by the cent. The one *centavo* coin in Madureira is equivalent to an international credit card at the Sheraton. Until today there is a Babel of voices on the sidewalks, big markets, little shopping centers, where the precarious Carioca capitalism experiences the perks of all the possibilities of Control C and Control V in the twenty-first century. It's there, on the colorful covers of the pirate DVDs, printed in low resolution, that we get from the street vendor the sense of bargaining from the streets of the neighborhood.

Pointing out the importance of small business transactions among low-income consumers and salespeople, in which cents count as much as credit cards do in fancy hotels, the narrator highlights piracy as a tactic that allows low-income workers to participate in consumption. In other words, the Madureira fair represents a space where low-income consumers learn the negotiation tactics that they need to make consumption more viable for themselves and to access commodities that provide pleasure. Faustini's emphasis on working-class tactics to enjoy the pleasures of consumption acknowledges that, "[o] consumo é parte do processo civilizador capitalista, porém, ressalta-se o fato de que 'onde há consumo, há prazer; e onde há prazer, há agência'" ("consumption is part of the capitalist civilizing process, however, it is important to note that 'where there is consumption, there is pleasure; and where there is pleasure, there is agency'"; Scalco and Pinheiro-Machado "Os sentidos" 325).

Faustini's protagonist further emphasizes working-class consumers' right to pleasure when he talks about his dream of buying a set of drums. He describes returning to the music store religiously and repeatedly asking questions: "quanto custa, em quantas vezes parcela?" ("how much does it cost? In how many installments?"; Faustini 89). Speaking somewhat emotionally about this experience, he mentions the joy of witnessing others from his community finally being able to buy the instruments that they, like the protagonist, have wanted for so long. Consumption in these instances is thus represented very differently from the frantic, quick-discarding voraciousness promoted by advertising. It is rather the slow, carefully planned, patiently awaited accomplishment of a goal. Goods acquired this way, much like the savings on electricity that the protagonist's father yielded every month from using a lamp bulb he had found in a junkyard (95), are likely to bring long-term rather than fleeting pleasure, for they represent the result of patience and efforts to circumvent economic limitations. This is not to romanticize poverty, but rather to show a different side of consumption.

Characters also use certain commodities tactically as objects that allow for self-expression and self-affirmation in the face of homogenization and social exclusion. The protagonist admires female supermarket cashiers who have to wear uniforms to work every day, for affirming their individuality by wearing earrings that stand out (Faustini 78). He sees the earrings as these women's response to the daily uniformity imposed on them by their work environment. Wearing earrings provides them with the possibility of standing out in the face of the invisibility that their job forces onto them and of intervening in the repetitive boredom of their work routine. The protagonist expresses admiration for working women again when he comments on his mother's "Tupperware and Avon parties" at his house when he was a child. Suggesting once again women's defiance against the monotony and uniformity of the work environment, the protagonist notes that his mother and her friends, whose negotiations he enjoyed watching, "só usavam roupas com estampa de flores. Bem diferentes dos uniformes que eu era obrigado a vestir" ("Only wore flower-patterned clothes. [Which were] very different from the uniforms that I was forced to wear"; 162).

The protagonist affirms the power of commodities as objects of tactical action yet again when he recounts his strategies to enter spaces controlled by the upper and middle classes. By sewing tags of famous brands onto his clothes in order to look like he belongs to a higher social class, he gains access to buildings where circulation is highly controlled and monitored. As Lehnen notes, "the narrator, conscious of the power expenditure holds in the imaginary of social exclusion, manipulates the signs associated with consumption to his advantage" (Lehnen, *Citizenship* 186). The protagonist's desire to become visible via the display of certain commodities signals his understanding that acquiring goods, in many instances, is not the final goal of consumption, but a means to cultivate social relations and, in his particular case, also to undermine existing social boundaries.

Likewise, cultural capital allows the protagonist to claim membership in certain groups. Calling his favorite used bookstore his "private socialist Disneyland" (Faustini 122), he evokes the ultimate North American symbol of consumption and simulacra to refer to a space where he acquires cultural products that allows him to engage in critical political thought. Noting that he sought Russian lessons at this bookstore as a way to "sell" himself as a more devoted militant, the protagonist suggests a parallel between the social value of building cultural capital and that of visiting Disneyland as ways of attaining or maintaining status within a group.[10] From this perspective, the narrator's interest in politics translates, at least in part, into the expression of a desire to impress others. The books that he acquires at the bookstore and the Russian classes are the commodities that allow him to cultivate these social relations.

Tactics of consumption in the face of limited or no income appear throughout the text as the narrator talks about his and others' experiences as consumers: stockpiling; stretching better quality milk by mixing it with lower quality milk; using clothespins as toy war tanks and matches as soldiers; drinking a cold beverage to cool down when taking turns with relatives in front of the only fan in the household; buying books from used bookstores; getting records from street vendors, to name a few. *Guia afetivo* is, in a sense, a guide to understanding working-class consumption, which is also highlighted by several of the photos reproduced throughout the narrative. These photos display the protagonist's family's old fan (Faustini 24–25), the cover of a Stevie B. LP juxtaposed with an image of a Japanese cartoon character (52–53), movie tickets (97), bottles of Coca-Cola products on a table at a birthday party (110, 114), an Atari video game console (158–59), and candy the protagonist used to like as a child (172–73). Collectively, these photos place an emphasis on the details of his and his family's everyday life as consumers. They tell through images the story of mundane consumption portrayed in the narrative. By emphasizing the everydayness of consumer behavior, Faustini makes the *practice* of consumption visible, doing what de Certeau calls for, which is going beyond the "elucidation of the repression apparatus" seeking to see the "the practices which are heterogeneous to it [the apparatus] and which it represses or thinks it represses" (de Certeau 41). Faustini's narrative highlights, to use de Certeau's term, some of our ruses as consumers.

Conclusion

While these ruses, as tactics, are limited in scope and do not produce deep changes in the system, they challenge the reader to think about the politics of consumption as a "direct mechanism of self-inclusion in a structure that is unequal and thereby class awareness is enabled" (Pinheiro-Machado and Scalco, "The Right"). When Faustini's protagonist sees pride rather than alienation in being able to purchase commodities in a neoliberal society, when he sees food as relief from the hardships of daily life, when he sees clothes and accessories as a way to express his identity, when he sees popular books as a way to enter the lettered city, he sees politics in consumption. In these politics, there is potential for change in the daily repetition of getting up, enduring long hours of a low-paying job, and heading back home late at night to get some rest and start all over again the next day. The autobiographical tone of *Guia afetivo* suggests that its very publication confirms this possibility of change, assuming that its author shares many of his protagonist's experiences.

Guia afetivo opens up the opportunity to see consumption under a different light. Faustini questions portrayals of working-class consumption such as Bonassi's in *Luxúria*, suggesting that, as Scalco and Pinheiro-Machado contend, we are not

> diante de sujeitos cegos e amarrados à sociedade de consumo, movidos por impulsos materialistas, mas antes frente a pessoas que compram porque se relacionam e se relacionam porque compram—expressando a relação dialética que existe entre pessoas e mercadorias. ("Os sentidos" 325)

> looking at blind subjects strapped down to consumer society, moved by materialistic impulses, but rather at people who buy because they relate to one another and who relate to one another because they buy—thus expressing the dialectic relation that exists between people and commodities.

Faustini's narrative drives Scalco and Pinheiro-Machado's point home by suggesting that we should understand the act of consuming as crisscrossed by a variety of factors that include both private interests and social solidarities ("Os sentidos" 353). Moreover, the narrative under study suggests that, as Miller notes,

Chapter Five

> Consumption, far from being the continuation of the projects of production and distribution, whether in capitalist or socialist systems, is actually the point of negation, where the particularity of goods is used to create fluid relationships in direct opposition to the vastness of markets and states. So the intricacies of our relationships expressed through consumption reassure us that we are not merely the creatures and categories of capitalism or the state—this is the very opposite of the effect of commodities upon us that we usually assume, when we take goods to be merely symbols of capitalism or the state. (*Theory* 147)

In this way, voices like Faustini's are essential to open up the debate in Brazilian literature regarding consumer culture. This debate of course has brought invaluable and necessary contributions to understanding the violence of consumer capitalism and its threats to democracy. However, this debate's failure to recognize the diversity of consumption has the unintended consequence of closing itself up, making it difficult to move toward envisioning other possibilities of collective existence mediated by the things that we consume. Portrayals of consumption such as the one provided by Faustini, while not offering direct solutions to the shortcomings of today's capitalist reality, remind us that not everything about the goods that we consume stems from or results in destruction and that not all consumer behavior is about individualism and alienation. His reading of consumption offers hope—not blind and passive, but rather critical and active hope—for the potential to unite festival and everyday life (Lefebvre, *Critique* 356). Furthermore, it undoes stereotypical images of working-class consumers that narratives such as Bonassi's, Sant'Anna's, and even Maia's reproduce. The complexity of Faustini's portrayal of working-class consumption is essential in this sense because it breaks the cycle of prejudice that artistic discourses in Brazil (Dalcastagnè, "Entre silêncios" 228) contribute to perpetuate. For Winnie Bueno, Joanna Burigo, and Pinheiro-Machado, in the inclusion of those who have had little to no space in the political debate in Brazilian society, lies the vision for a truly democratic project for Brazil ("Introdução" 12). Similarly, Faustini's portrayal of consumption suggests that, in the debate about consumer culture in Brazilian letters, there are other voices that also need to be heard.

Conclusion

In January 2012, the Brazilian television network Band premiered the reality show *Mulheres Ricas* (*Rich Women*). The show, similar to the North American franchise *The Real Housewives of [Atlanta, Beverly Hills, D.C., Miami, Orange County, Potomac, New Jersey, New York]* broadcast by Bravo, and British channel E4 reality show *Made in Chelsea*, featured, as the title indicates, rich women from the cities of São Paulo and Rio de Janeiro. One of the women is Val Marchiori, a businesswoman, former model, and socialite of working-class origin, whose comments on the show in question made her famous nationwide. On episode four of the second season, which aired on January 28, 2013, Val, whose obsession with luxury brands is clearly evidenced throughout the show, made the following comment about one of the other women in *Mulheres Ricas*: "Bom, se a Cozete vai conseguir ter filho ou não vai, eu num sei. Tem tanto motorista, garçom, segurança lá na casa dela. Pode ser que consiga. [Val ri]. É bem o nível." ("Well, whether or not Cozete will be able to have a child, I don't know. There are so many drivers, waiters, security guys at her house. Maybe that will work. [Val laughs]. That's kinda her level"; 00:45:24).

Val's comment was meant to insult Cozete, whom she opposed the entire second season. The insult is an example of the common classist view that exists in Brazil, which equates belonging to the working class with being inferior; a view that Val—and the other women—express in the show frequently, in more or less subtle ways. In episode one of the second season, Val insults Cozete also by suggesting that her dress must have been purchased at the popular shopping zone of São Paulo, along the 25 de Março Street, a place where, according to her, she wouldn't shop at "até quando [ela] era pobrinha" ("even when [she] was poor"; 00:02:49). *Mulheres Ricas* spoke of its socioeconomic context: a time when, according to a study, the country was creating about 19 new millionaires per day since 2007 (Phillips). Many saw the show as a debauchery of Brazilian long-standing social inequality, which, although ameliorated by the Workers' Party's social policies, was still significantly pronounced.

Just about three months after the second—and last—season was over, June 2013 happened in Brazil, inaugurating a cycle of protests, initially against a R$0.20 raise in the bus fare, but soon aggregating a variety of groups from several segments of society, including the many who were unhappy with the government's investment in the 2014 World Cup. The protests, which echoed international movements such as the Arab Spring and Occupy, gathered the energy of a country that, according to Pinheiro-Machado, lived a moment of abundance that favored the emergence of new political subjectivities that demanded more rights (qtd. in Canofre). From this perspective, consumption was good for thinking, to use Nestor García-Canclini's expression (37).

Nevertheless, consumption as a path to social inclusion without a broader political project of society also opened the door to the rise of conservatism in Brazil, which co-opted the original agenda of June 2013, and rapidly gained visibility thanks to its strategic use of social media to organize (Gomes). After all, the crisis that led to President Dilma Rousseff's ousting was in part energized by a conservative and classist discontent with the ascension of low-income consumers made possible by the social policies implemented by the Workers' Party administration. Since Rousseff's controversial impeachment, the increasing prominence of conservative forces has been evidenced by the aggressive push of a conservative agenda by the Temer administration, the controversial imprisonment of Lula, and the dangerous rise of ultra-conservative Jair Bolsonaro, who presented himself as the anti-establishment candidate—and eventually won the election—following in Donald Trump's footsteps.

The fiction analyzed in this book is a product of and a comment on the years that led up to this context of political turmoil in the aftermath of the growth of consumption in Brazil during the Lula and Rousseff years. As such, this fiction represents consumer culture in various ways, highlighting both the constraints that consumption poses to and the possibilities that it opens up for change in capitalism. While some of the novels stress apocalyptic views of the future, at times reproducing some of the problematic perspectives of the very system that they set out to criticize, others point to the complex subjectivities that emerge in consumer capitalism, including those that are made political via consumption itself.

All the narratives point out serious constraints, many of which threaten the existence of democratic societies today—such as increased polarization—or even our very existence on this planet. Underlying these narratives' critique of everyday consumption in Brazil today, which is not unlike consumption elsewhere that consumer capitalism is the norm, is an urge for the construction of a collective project for a solidary society. And what would that project look like, according to the reading of this fiction proposed here? For Bonassi and Sant'Anna, we can infer that tamed consumption—perhaps for the working class only?—albeit not envisioned as possible in their narratives, could lead to a more civilized society and more livable cities, ending a culture of consumption that suffocates and oppresses, as streets are filled with cars and people are only interested in defending their own interests.

For B. Carvalho and Lísias, this project would entail the end of a neoliberal subjectivity that makes individuals responsible for their own success or failure, a myth that perpetuates social inequality and generates pathological individualism. It would also require breaking free from information bubbles that lead to the breakdown in communication and, ultimately, threaten democracy, given the disappearance of a common ground. Indeed, polarization leads to a decline in institutional forbearance, thus resulting in the destabilizing of democratic societies (Levitsky and Ziblatt 115). As depicted by B. Carvalho, Brazilian society is watching this very process unfold within itself.

In Maia's work, the project of a democratic society would be tied to the visibility of societal segments that carry the weight of consumerism on their shoulders as they do the daily work of collecting trash, producing coal, burying the dead, and killing animals for the sake of producing food. This project would also entail far more sustainable consumption, in an effort to stop the destruction of the environment. The representation of an abrupt temporary halt to production in Maia's novels, which in turns affects consumption, suggests a timid, but possible change for a potentially catastrophic future.

Conclusion

For Laub and Galera, change is already inherently possible in everyday life in consumer capitalism. In the repetitions of the characters' routines, there are cracks through which self-awareness and self-reflection sprout, thus potentially leading to the inauguration of new phases in one's life and, potentially, in society more broadly. Subjectivity, thus, is not completely numbed by consumption in these novels. It is rather prompted by a movement between alienation and disalienation that reveals contradictions in our experiences as consumers.

Finally, for Faustini, this project is already somewhat realized in our relationship to commodities. Without romanticizing poverty, his narrative suggests the possibility of a more balanced consumption, in which joy, patience, and solidarity can take place. This view echoes, to some extent, concepts such as minimalism, the tiny house, fair trade, and slow fashion, practices that, however, are still largely restricted to a middle class that can currently afford them. Nevertheless, the joy of consuming less, consuming slowly, consuming fairly, consuming together is already underway and narratives such as Faustini's are crucial to help us think in more hopeful ways about a more democratic and just future of consumption.

This future is also already here in the indigenous South American philosophy of *Buen Vivir*, according to which quality of life can be achieved via "co-habitation with others and Nature" (Gudynas 441). The concept, which has been incorporated into Ecuador's and Bolivia's constitutions, is born out of critiques to Western development and indigenous ideas of development. It can be conceived as "a useful concept that can support and enhance critical traditions looking for alternatives to development" (445). As Eduardo Gudynas points out, the concept is both post-capitalist and post-socialist, but should not be confused with a call for returning to pre-Columbian life in the Americas (443). For Avelin Buniacá Kambiwá, this is also an alternative for Brazil as a way to rethink production and consumption in a truly democratic future (247). In fact, twenty-first century Brazilian *literatura indígena* signals this possibility, particularly in the work of Daniel Munduruku, who addresses consumerism, among other issues, in his 2001 narrative *Meu avô Apolinário* (Graúna 134). Also in *Todas as coisas são pequenas* (2008), Munduruku touches on the limits of consumer capitalism by telling the story of Carlos, an

Conclusion

ambitious and selfish businessman who, after his plane crashes in the middle of the jungle, has an opportunity to learn another way of life from a native Brazilian he encounters (Figueiredo 297–99). In other words, in twenty-first century Brazilian literature, to use Williams's categories (122), there is both a residual view of consumption as degraded and alienating, and an emerging view of consumption as a practice of possible sustainable co-existence.

Consumption deeply marks life in capitalist societies in the twenty-first century. As realms of everyday life such as education, healthcare, information distribution, and electoral systems become increasingly commodified, understanding our relationship with consumption and imagining possibilities of facing the challenges that this commodification brings is imperative. In this process, it is essential to listen to a variety of voices in twenty-first century Brazilian fiction, thus capturing the varying narratives of consumption and their contributions to imagining possible ways of existing in a consumer society.

Notes

Introduction

1. All translations are the author's, except otherwise noted in the bibliography.

2. The path toward this goal had been paved by the "indian" literature of the nineteenth century, which had identified in the figure of the native-Brazilian a national representative (Philippou 247). José de Alencar, for instance, who sets out to build a national Brazilian identity in a series of novels that are intended to offer a detailed account of the various landscapes of the country, creates indigenous characters in his novels *Iracema* (1865), *O guarani* (1857), and *Ubirajara* (1874). For Maria Cândida Ferreira de Almeida, Alencar went beyond the apparent copy of the European medieval knight, especially in *Ubirajara*, by making specific ethnographic references to indigenous culture, which have been overlooked by literary critics. Traces of cannibalism can be identified in the novel in question, both in veiled references in the narrative and in the paratexts that accompanied the narrative. Later on, modernist poet Oswald de Andrade will, according to Almeida, "[retirar] a antropofagia das entrelinhas e das notas, colocando-a em primeiro plano e propiciando um discurso de exaltação de uma atitude brasileira diante das relações de alteridade" ("remove anthropophagy from in between the lines and from notes, bringing it to the foreground and providing a discourse of praise for a Brazilian attitude toward otherness"; 207).

3. For Julio Ramos, as Latin American countries attempted to become modern integrated nations, *modernismo*—whose Brazilian contemporary is *Simbolismo* and *Parnasianismo*—sought to free literature and art from commercial interests, as a rejection of the North American way of life, which *modernistas* perceived as undesirable chaotic heterogeneity and discontinuity. They viewed modern literature as a means to re-establish totality and continuity in the fragmented world of the unruly urban masses. They conceived of the intellectual as a leader capable of speaking from outside and above commodification, thus occupying a position that allowed him to be critical and to lead the masses toward modernity, while circumventing the dangers of commodification. The intellectual was thus a mediator between high and low cultural expressions and an agent of protection against foreign culture (235). Literature sought to represent the marginalized in a "safe" way, subjugating the voices of the masses to a will to control heterogeneity in the name of nation-building (209).

4. For Andreas Huyssen, the avant-garde was revived again by pop artists in the 1950s in Europe and died in the United States when the works of artists such as Andy Warhol seemed to confirm that art had indeed become an uncritical affirmation of capitalism (*After the Great Divide* 168).

5. Other writers who have dealt with consumption in their work, to varying degrees, include Patrícia Melo, Luiz Ruffato, Lourenço Mutarelli, Carol Bensimon, Santiago Nazarian, Cecília Giannetti, Regina Rheda, and Victor

Heringer. In other works of mine, I examine the representation of consumption in Luiz Ruffato's *Eles eram muitos cavalos* (2001), in André Sant'Anna's *Sexo e Amizade* (2007), and in two of Regina Rheda's narratives (L. Bezerra, "A representação," "Cenas cotidianas," and "Citizens of nowhere").

Chapter One

1. The idea that the middle class expanded during the Lula years is a contested one. For Marilena Chaui, for instance, it is rather the *working* class that expanded, not only due to the inclusion of many via consumption, but also because what used to be considered the middle class has largely become the working class, as a consequence of the privatization of the service sector and the decrease in job security (130).

2. According to the Caixa Econômica Federal's website, the program, which was created in 2009, establishes groups that receive subsidies according to their income. For houses in urban areas, there are four groups, whose incomes vary from R$1,800.00 to R$7,000.00 monthly. For houses in rural areas, subsidies vary according to annual income of up to R$78,000.00, divided into three different groups ("Minha casa").

3. Throughout the novel, the protagonist aspires to exert power over others while abandoning his condition of exploited low-income worker. The use of the word "senhor" links the social condition of the protagonist to slavery's lasting effects upon low-income sectors of Brazilian society. Moreover, it suggests that the protagonist stands for the desire of the oppressed to be transformed into the oppressor.

4. All quoted dialogue from *Luxúria* in italics appears as such in the original, unless otherwise noted.

5. The lack of subject expression in the sentence makes it possible to read the verb *to belong* as referring either to the woman or to her genitalia, since the verb forms for both subjects take the third person singular in Portuguese.

6. This kind of interaction has been represented in Muylaert's previously mentioned film *Que horas ela volta?* (*The Second Mother*). They are also reported regularly by domestic workers who anonymously tell their stories on the Facebook group "Eu, empregada doméstica" ("I, domestic worker"), which has over 164,000 followers as of the writing of this book.

7. "Quando precisar abrir um armário ou uma gaveta, fala comigo ... Mas, não me leve a mal: eu preferia que você não tomasse mais o seu banho aqui, com água do nosso banheiro, dentro da nossa casa, entende?" ("When you need to open a cabinet or a drawer, talk to me first ... But don't get me wrong: I'd prefer that you didn't take a shower here, using the water in our bathroom, in my house, you see?"; Bonassi, *Luxúria* 76).

8. In the 2002 election campaign, Lula's appearance was much different from in previous times when he was a presidential candidate. His tailored suits, trimmed beard, and contained demeanor were part of marketer Duda Mendonça's crafting of an image aimed at conveying a renewed and more sober version of the candidate, one that would be more appealing to those who rejected his ties to leftist ideals perceived as radical (Silva and Boni 108).

9. It is important to note that there is disagreement on whether Brazil implemented counter-cyclical measures during the time in question. Jorge Mattoso, for instance, argues quite the opposite, noting that it was the innovative nature of the administration's counter-cyclical measures that shielded Brazil from the 2008 global economic crisis (113).

10. Congresswoman Luiza Erundina declares in an interview by Rodrigo Martins in *Carta Capital* in 2016: "Só chegamos a este estágio [da crise política] por causa da nossa omissão com a reforma política, e não me refiro aqui apenas a regras eleitorais. É preciso repensar o sistema político, o Estado e o pacto federativo como um todo." ("We have only gotten to this point [in the political crisis] because of our omission in the matter of political reform, and I am not referring here only to electoral rules. It is necessary to rethink the political system, the State, and the federal pact as a whole"; "Os modelos").

11. This part of the translation—as well as any other passages from the Bible henceforth—is quoted from *The Bible.* King James Version, *Bible Hub*, biblehub.com/kjv/proverbs/6.htm. Accessed 20 March 2019.

12. While the Bible does not mention directly the seven deadly sins, the quoted passage is considered an antecedent to it (Tucker 63).

13. Pinheiro-Machado cites "o alinhamento neoliberal com o capital financeiro" ("the neoliberal alignment with financial capital") as one of the causes for a crisis of PT's ideals ("A era pós PT").

14. Vargas acted as interim president from 1930–34, then as constitutional president from 1934–37, and finally as a dictator from 1937–45. He was then democratically elected in 1951 and served until 1954, when he committed suicide in the face of his imminent ousting.

15. Juscelino Kubitscheck (1956–61) promoted great optimism about Brazil's future through his motto "50 years in 5," promising that his administration would achieve the equivalent to fifty years of development in five years. The construction of Brasília to be the capital of Brazil, with its modern architecture, was part of this developmentalist enthusiasm.

16. The idea that it was necessary to make the "cake" rise first so that it could then be divided was a metaphor used by then-Finance Minister Delfim Neto to explain the gap (and convey confidence in closing it later) between the accelerated growth of the Brazilian economy at the beginning of the 1970s, when Brazil experience the so-called "milagre econômico" ("economic miracle"), and the disparities in income distribution at the time (Habert 13).

17. See Chapter 2 for details on Cardoso's presidency.

18. From the 2014 protests on, support for a military intervention grew in Brazil among ultra-conservative groups, with members of the military speaking directly about said possibility (Sousa and Peron; R. Valente).

19. The topic has become so prominent in Brazilian culture that it is dealt with in the Netflix series *3%*, in which, every year, individuals living in absolute poverty have a chance to compete for a spot at "the Offshore," which is richer and better. The title of the series refers to the percentage of candidates who are able to pass the so-called "Process," through which they are screened. The several phases of the "Process" are designed to test the candidates' endurance of what closely resembles neoliberal expectations and ideas of success.

20. The Bullet Coalition is against gun control and human rights for convicts.

21. Along with the "Bancada da Bala" and the "Bancada do Boi" (Cattle Coalition, which includes rich landowners against agrarian reform), the "Bancada da Bíblia" (Bible Coalition, made up mainly of evangelical conservatives) is part of what Workers' Party affiliate Erika Kokai calls the "Bancada BBB." She uses the term, which was adopted by the Left thereafter to refer to conservatives in the congress of Brazil (R. Martins, "A bancada BBB").

22. Sant'Anna's use of ellipsis in the last line alludes to both meanings of the word "só" in Portuguese.

Chapter Two

1. Mao's government, like many others throughout Chinese history, manipulated Confucian thought to legitimize itself. The Cultural Revolution, which sought to destroy the so-called four olds—culture, thinking, habits, and customs—preached that Confucian thought was at the root of Mao's enemies' attempts to make China move toward exploitative capitalism. In order to prevent that from happening, Mao argued, it was necessary to eliminate Confucianism from Chinese society, even if that meant, as it did, to arrest, torture, and kill the population, and to destroy Confucius temples across the country (Rainey 180).

2. In an interview with Bernardo Sorj and Sérgio Fausto, Fernando Henrique Cardoso states, when asked about the labeling of his policies as neoliberal:

> É curioso porque as políticas de meu governo tiveram muito pouco de liberal. Estávamos preocupados em fortalecer os serviços públicos, ampliar o acesso a eles, reorganizar os gastos. O gasto social aumentou e aumentou muito. Infelizmente o grosso da comunidade acadêmica não entendeu isso. Para a maioria da comunidade acadêmica—em especial a das ciências humanas, por causa da forte penetração ideológica nas universidades—nós éramos neoliberais. Quando na verdade nós estávamos reorganizando o Estado, inovando, inclusive na área social. (56)

> It is interesting because my administration's policies had very little liberalness. We were concerned about strengthening public services, expanding access to them, reorganizing expenses. Social spending increased, and it increased a lot. Unfortunately, the majority of the academic community did not understand this. For the majority of the academic community—especially those in the social sciences, due to the strong ideological penetration in universities—we were neoliberal. When the truth is that we were reorganizing the state, innovating, including in the social area.

3. About the impact of the crises on different sectors of the Chinese population, Teiwes writes: "the degree of enthusiasm varied, with rural youths and peasants in some relatively well-off villages believing the Socialist Education Movement's propaganda on the power of Mao's Thought on the eve of the Cultural Revolution, whereas peasants in poor regions complained about the Great Leap losses and reportedly showed minimal affection toward Mao. Meanwhile, various urban groups continued to follow Mao, often rationalizing that others must be responsible for recent disasters" (143).

4. In the Iran-Contra affair, the Reagan administration secretly provided arms indirectly to Iran while the latter was subject to an arms embargo. They did so via Israel, who sent the arms and then received payment from the U.S. The scheme was carried out in exchange for seven American citizens who were being held by the Iranian paramilitary group Hezbollah. It was also arranged for part of the proceeds from the sales of the arms to fund the Contras, a right-wing rebel group in Nicaragua that, backed by the United States, opposed the socialist Sandinista government. At the time, U.S. military backing of the Contras had been prohibited by the Boland Amendment passed by Congress.

5. Krista Brune points out in the article "Mediating Language, Translating Experience: Negotiating Postdictatorial Metropolis in *Duas praças*" that Lísias uses fragmented language in his novel *Duas praças* to represent a disconnect between experience and communication, engaging the reader in acts of translation of the protagonist's thoughts into words (19).

6. The protests started in São Paulo due to an increase of R$0.20 in the bus fare. Soon the protests grew into a much wider movement, with the focus shifting to the escalating spending on infrastructure in preparation for the 2014 World Cup and to a fight against corruption ("Brazil Unrest").

7. The particle was discovered in 2013 and was called the God particle because it was believed to have caused the "Big Bang." For more information, see: www.cbsnews.com/news/god-particle-why-the-higgs-boson-matters/

8. Brazilian country music.

9. See more details about this phrase in Chapter 1.

10. It is in the New Testament, that is, in the Christian Greek Scriptures, that the reference to the word "being God" can be found. The most well-known reference appears in John 1:1: "In the beginning was the Word, the Word was with God and the Word was God."

11. Paradoxically because the very existence of different languages reflects the diversity of cultures and ways of living/seeing the world. Language death, from a social perspective, is the death of diversity, knowledge, and history (Crystal 66) in so far as it limits our abilities to communicate with others, ultimately decreasing our chances to survive.

Chapter Three

1. Just four years later, another dam disaster brought catastrophic consequences to another city: Brumadinho, in the state of Minas Gerais. The mining company Vale, which co-owns Samarco with the BHP group, was again involved. As of the writing of this book, 186 people were killed and more than 100 remain missing ("Brumadinho Dam Collapse").

2. The film explores the limits between reality and fiction by parodying the language of documentaries in order to talk about the social injustices of capitalism. The film caused controversy when some viewers, taking it literally, expressed repulsion against the population of Ilha Grande dos Marinheiros, where the film was shot ("Ilha das Flores: depois que a sessão acabou"). In the film, the population appears competing with pigs for food that is dumped into a pigsty.

3. Maria Fernanda Garbero highlights this connection in her review of Maia's work ("Sujos" 2018), which Maia herself explains in an interview by Olívia Fraga (Maia, "Dificilmente").

4. For example, the narrator describes the cremation process as follows:
   Caso a mercadoria sofra danos, basta preencher a urna funerária com sobras de cinzas que são guardadas pelo funcionário da manutenção do forno. Este sempre apanha uns punhados de cinzas provenientes de muitas cremações e guarda-as num galão de plástico. Depois são moídas de modo uniforme e repõem a falta dos grãos perdidos dos outros. (Maia, *Carvão* 27)

   > In case the merchandise becomes damaged, all that is necessary is to fill the urn with the rest of the ashes that are kept away by the employee who does the maintenance of the furnace. He always picks up a handful of ashes from many cremations and puts them away in a plastic container. Afterward, the ashes are ground uniformly, and are used to replenish the particles that were lost from other bodies.

5. The following passage about Palmiro exemplifies their poor health: "De tanto aspirar fuligem dos muitos anos em que trabalhou numa carvoaria e dos anos seguintes em que cremou corpos, seu pulmão ficou debilitado. Sua respiração tornou-se barulhenta, e constantemente, num ruidoso escarro elimina pela boca uma secreção gosmenta em pedaços de papel higiênico que costuma carregar nos bolsos das calças" ("Due to all the soot that he inhaled during the many years that he worked in a coal mine and the years after that when he cremated bodies, his lungs became debilitated. His breathing became noisy, and, in constant and loud expectoration, he spits gooey sputum in pieces of toilet paper"; *Carvão* 29).

6. Others characters in Maia's novel also behave very similarly to Steinbeck's, particularly J. G., from *Carvão animal*, who echoes Lennie, the big guy who talks and behaves like a child in *Of Mice and Men*.

7. A search for the sentence on a search engine yields quotes in websites on veganism that attribute the quote to Adorno, including a reference on

goodreads.com. In a discussion board on Michigan State University's website (msu.edu), participants note that they have tried to confirm the source of the quote, but that the quote does not seem to appear in any of Adorno's work. I myself was not able to confirm it either, having thus to rely on this discussion board as the best source of information that I was able to find.

8. Edgar Wilson is a recurrent character in Maia's novels. In *O trabalho sujo dos outros*, his ambiguous nature also becomes evident, for example, when he helps his friend "retrieve" his kidney from his sister's body, while showing solidarity and compassion for his friend's suffering due to his health issues.

9. Maia revisits this issue in *Enterre seus mortos*, when she describes the damage caused by a quarry to a nearby city: dead animals, injured people, lung diseases, and polluted waters (26).

Chapter Four

1. According to Amann and Baer, in their article "Neoliberalism and Its Consequences in Brazil," most of Latin America had adopted the Washington Consensus by the end of the 1980s. Brazil increasingly moved in that direction, with the process accelerating at the very beginning of the 1990s with Fernando Collor de Melo (1990–92) and later on with Fernando Henrique Cardoso, as I discuss in Chapter 2 (Amann and Baer 946–47).

2. The term Generation X is used, with some variation, to refer to the age group that was born between the early 1960s and the late 1970s. As Catherine Strong notes in her book *Grunge: Music and Memory*, this generation is usually described as a group of young individuals who feel disconnected from society. They are constructed as "tolerant, but cynical, [living] lives centered on consumption and mass media and overwhelmingly downtrodden by the more successful Baby Boom generation" (135). Furthermore, this generation is commonly characterized by a lack of interest in politics and current affairs, as well as by a lack of commitment to promoting social change. In sum, Generation X-ers are in general perceived as apathetic, disillusioned individuals.

3. *Lança-perfume* was a deodorizing spray that became popular in Brazilian Carnaval at the beginning of the twentieth century. The product became illegal in the 1960s due to deaths following the inhaling of the substance.

4. The protagonist mentions several biblical characters who committed suicide:
    i. Abimelech, "who opts for suicide out of pride, shame at his conidition, and concern for his image" (Shemesh 158)
    ii. Samson, who, out of revenge, would have carefully planned his suicide and kept the plan concealed (159)
    iii. Saul, whose motive is similar to Abimelech's (161)
    iv. Ahithophel, whose suicide is unclear, but appears to have been motivated by his anticipation of future events and results from

calculated consideration (165)

v. Zimri, whose suicide is also motivated by revenge, similar to Samson's (167)

vi. Judas, whose suicide is accounted for in Matthew 27:3–10, which is not, however, the only version of his death.

Chapter Five

1. In *Postcards from Rio: Favelas and the Contested Geographies of Citizenship* (2017), Kátia Bezerra demonstrates how various cultural products by favela-based groups promote other perspectives on *favelas* (slums) and their inhabitants, claiming their right to the city and contesting neoliberal discourses on urban development that mask capitalist exploitation as social inclusion and the promotion of citizenship (9).

2. The project published several titles that deal with life in the *periferia*, including accounts on social projects in addition to narratives such as Faustini's (Lehnen, *Citizenship* 166).

3. By 2017, Kondzilla, a production company owned by Konrad Dantas, had produced more than 60 music videos, which together had surpassed 100 million views on YouTube (A. Pereira).

4. Women often appear in these videos as another object that the singer is able to consume along with the cars, houses, and brand clothing and accessories that he displays. In "O cara do momento" ("The Dude of the Hour"), for instance, Menor da Chapa appears in the video with women surrounding him in a Jacuzzi and around his car. In "Olha como nós tá" ("Check Out How We're Doing") by MC Buru, women appear dancing, in a typical funk fashion that reproduces moves that evoke sexual intercourse, around the cars that the protagonist of the music video flaunts. Most of the time, all the viewer sees of the women dancing is close-up shots of their buttocks or shots that focus on their bodies from the waist down, thus portraying them as just another object to be consumed. The lyrics of "Baile de favela" ("Favela Party") by MC João in turn, are particularly aggressive toward women, suggesting gang rape in lines such as "os menor preparado pra foder com as checa dela" ("the under-aged kids ready to fuck up her pussy"). Nevertheless, it is important to also point out that women have carved out their space in funk. *Funkeiras* such as Ludmilla provide a woman's perspective of women's sexuality in songs like "Hoje," for example, which portray women as agents of their own sexuality. An even more empowering example of funk made by women is MC Soffia, a *funkeira* from São Paulo who started her career at 12 years old, whose "Menina Pretinha" ("Little Black Girl") celebrates Afro-Brazilian young girls: "Menina pretinha / Exótica não é linda / Você não é bonitinha / Você é uma rainha" ("Little black girl / Exotic is not beautiful / You are not cute / You are a queen"). The song touches on consumption by valuing toys that represent Afro-Brazilian girls, such as black dolls, as opposed to Barbies.

5. According to Érica Peçanha do Nascimento, "a expressão 'literatura marginal' serviu para classificar as obras literárias produzidas e veiculadas à margem do corredor editorial; que não pertencem ou que se opõem aos cânones estabelecidos; que são de autoria de escritores originários de grupos sociais marginalizados; ou ainda, que tematizam o que é peculiar aos sujeitos e espaços tidos como marginais" ("the expression *literatura marginal* served to classify literary works that are produced and distributed by alternative channels, outside of the editorial market; that do not belong or that oppose established canons; whose writers come from socially marginalized groups; or yet that broach what is peculiar to subjects and spaces considered marginal[ized]"; 22). For Lucía Tennina, the term *literatura periférica* was the second one to have most impact in the characterization of this group of writers. Cautioning that there are authors who do not identify with the term *literatura marginal*, Tennina notes that "a literatura marginal da periferia não é um conjunto homogêneo do qual se pode derivar uma representação unitária, mas sim algo que se define a partir de sua mobilidade como um processo performativo de posicionamento do sujeito que escreve em relação a certa ideia de 'marginalidade' a partir da qual toma a palavra em determinado espaço, momento, serie literária ou circunstância" ("*literatura marginal* from the *periferia* is not a homogenous collection that can be said to represent everyone, but rather something that defines itself based on its mobility as a performative process of positioning the subject that writes in relation to a certain idea of 'marginality', from which he/she speaks in a certain space, moment, literary series, or circumstance"; 33).

6. The Operação Lava-Jato (Operation Car Wash) was launched in 2014 to investigate black market money dealers involved in the use of small businesses such as car washes to launder illegal profits. The operation expanded after it was discovered that the dealers were working for a Petrobrás executive and grew exponentially as it reached the upper echelons of Brazilian political class, implicating companies with business all over the world (Watts).

7. Tennina notes that the "sacralization" of the mother figure is a common trope in the *literatura de periferia* written by male authors, which reinforces the view that women belong in the domestic sphere (181).

8. *Bombril* is both a famous Brazilian brand of cleaning products and the generic term for steel wool. It is being used in the latter sense here.

9. The word *carioca* refers to someone from the city of Rio de Janeiro.

10. Trips to Disneyland became an important status symbol in the 1980s and 1990s among Brazilian middle-class families, who increasingly opted for these trips instead of debutante balls for their daughters. According to Maureen O'Dougherty, going to Disneyland became not just a practical way to save money for a middle class in crisis, but also a way for parents to escape the unpredictability of everyday life in Brazil as the country went through several economic plans that repeatedly failed to save the economy. Disney provided them with the safe, predictable, anonymous environment for which they longed amidst the difficulty keeping up appearances during the economic turmoil of the time (105).

Works Cited

3%. Created by Pedro Aguilera. Netflix, 2016–.

Alencar, José de. *O guarani*. Domínio Público, www.dominiopublico.gov.br/pesquisa/DetalheObraForm.do?select_action=&co_obra=1843. Accessed 4 Dec. 2019.

———. *Senhora*. Ministério da Cultura. Domínio Público. www.dominiopublico.gov.br/pesquisa/DetalheObraForm.do?select_action=&co_obra=2026. Accessed 4 Dec. 2019.

———. *Ubirajara*. Domínio Público, www.dominiopublico.gov.br/pesquisa/DetalheObraForm.do?select_action=&co_obra=16679. Accessed 4 Dec. 2019.

Almeida, Maria Cândida Ferreira de. *Tornar-se outro. O topos canibal na literatura brasileira*. Annablume, 2002.

Amann, Edmund, and Werner Baer. "A ilusão da estabilidade: A economia brasileira no governo FHC." *Democracia, crise e reforma*, edited by Angela D'Incao and Hermínio Martins, Paz e Terra, 2010, pp. 139–69.

———. "Neoliberalism and Its Consequences in Brazil." *Journal of Latin American Studies*, vol. 34, 2002, pp. 945–59.

"Após Cunha manobrar, Câmara aprova redução da maioridade penal em 1º turno." *Notícias Uol*, 2 July 2015, noticias.uol.com.br/cotidiano/ultimas-noticias/2015/07/02/com-pedalada-regimental-reducao-da-maioridade-penal-e-aprovada-na-camara.htm. Accessed 15 July 2017.

Assis, Machado de. *Memórias póstumas de Brás Cubas*. Expressão Cultura, 2001.

———. "O sermão do Diabo." Biblio, biblio.com.br/defaultz.asp?link=biblio.com.br/conteudo/MachadodeAssis/osermaododiabo.htm. Accessed 4 Mar. 2019.

Astrolábio, Laura. "A crise, a violência no Rio de Janeiro e a grande mídia." *Tem saída? Ensaios críticos sobre o Brasil*, edited by Winnie Bueno et. al., Editora Zouk, 2017, pp. 185–89.

Barbarena, Ricardo Araújo. "A hipercontemporaneidade ensanguentada em Ana Paula Maia." *Letras de hoje*, vol. 51, no. 4, Oct.–Dec. 2016, pp. 458-65.

Barbieri, Therezinha. *Ficção Impura. Prosa brasileira nos anos 70, 80 e 90*. Editora UERJ, 2003.

Barbosa, Livia. *Cultura e empresas*. Kindle ed., Zahar, 2002.

Barbosa, Nelson. "Dez anos de política econômica." Sader, pp. 135–44.

Works Cited

Baudrillard, Jean. *Simulacra and Simulation*. Translated by Sheila Faria Glaser, U of Michigan P, 1994.

Bauman, Zygmunt. *Consuming Life*. Polity, 2007.

———. *Liquid Modernity*. Polity, 2012.

———. *Liquid Times. Living in an Age of Uncertainty*. Polity, 2007.

Benjamin, Walter. "The Work of Art in the Age of Mechanical Reproduction." Translated by Harry Zohn. *The Norton Anthology Theory and Criticism*, edited by Vincent B. Leitch, et al., W. W. Norton & Company, 2001, pp. 1166–86.

Berlet, Chip, and Carol Mason. "Swastikas in Cyberspace." *Digital Media Strategies of the Far-Right in Europe and the United States*, edited by Patricia Anne Simpson and Helga Druxes, Lexington Books, 2015, pp. 21–36.

Bettencourt, Lúcia. "Vik Muniz: a problematização da imagem: Subversões e perversões do consumo artístico." Twelfth International Congress of the Brazilian Studies Association, 21 Aug. 2014, King's College, London. Panel Presentation.

Bezerra, Kátia da Costa. *Postcards from Rio. Favelas and the Contested Geographies of Citizenship*. Fordham UP, 2017.

Bezerra, Ligia. "Cenas cotidianas: Cultura de consumo e mídia em contos de André Sant'Anna." *Estudos de literatura brasileira contemporânea*, vol. 45, 2015, pp. 261–79.

———. "Citizens of Nowhere: Undocumented Migrants in Regina Rheda's Narratives." *Veredas: Revista da Associação de Lusitanistas,* vol. 28, 2017, pp. 19–33.

———. "A representação da cultura de consumo em *Eles eram muitos cavalos.*" *Estudos de literatura brasileira contemporânea,* vol. 48, 2016, pp. 177–90.

Biroli, Flávia. "O fim da Nova República e o casamento infeliz entre neoliberalismo e conservadorismo moral." *Tem saída? Ensaios críticos sobre o Brasil,* edited by Winnie Bueno et. al., Editora Zouk, 2017, pp. 17–26.

Bonassi, Fernando. *Luxúria*. Record, 2015.

———. "Luxúria, de Fernando Bonassi." Interview by Simone Magno. *Blog da Editora Record*, 7 Oct. 2015, www.blogdaeditorarecord.com.br/2015/10/07/luxuria-de-fernando-bonassi/. Accessed 6 July 2016.

Boucher, Geoff. *Understanding Marxism*. Acumen, 2012.

"Brazil Unrest: 'Million' join protests in 100 cities." *BBC News*, 21 June 2013, www.bbc.com/news/world-latin-america-22992410. Accessed 27 Apr. 2017.

Brown, Wendy. *Undoing the Demos: Neoliberalism's Stealth Revolution*. MIT P, 2015.

"Brumadinho Dam Collapse in Brazil: Vale Mine Chief Resigns." *BBC*, 3 Mar. 2019, www.bbc.com/news/business-47432134. Acessed 7 Mar. 2019.

Brune, Krista. "Mediating Language, Translating Experience: Negotiating Postdictatorial Metropolis in *Duas praças*." *The Proceedings of the UCLA Department of Spanish and Portuguese Graduate Conference*, vol. 1, no.1, 2012, pp. 15–32.

Bueno, Winnie, et al., editors. *Tem saída? Ensaios críticos sobre o Brasil*. Editora Zouk, 2017.

Bueno, Winnie, Joanna Burigo, and Rosana Pinheiro-Machado. "Introdução." *Tem saída? Ensaios críticos sobre o Brasil*, edited by Winnie Bueno et. al., Editora Zouk, 2017, pp. 12–14.

Byrne, Rhonda. *The Secret*. Kindle ed., Atria Books, 2006.

Cândido, Antônio. "Literature and Underdevelopment." *The Latin American Cultural Studies Reader*, edited by Ana Del Sarto, Alicia Ríos, and Abril Trigo, Duke UP, 2004, pp. 35–57.

Canofre, Fernanda. "Sob o signo de 2013: Como o ano que ferveu em protestos continua afetando o Brasil." *Sul 21*, junho2013.sul21.com.br/sob-o-signo-de-2013-como-o-ano-que-ferveu-em-protestos-continua-afetando-o-brasil/?ModPagespeed=off. Accessed 26 Jul. 2018.

Carneiro, Flávio. *No país do presente: Ficção brasileira no início do século XXI*. Rocco, 2005.

Carvalho, Bernardo. *Reprodução*. Companhia das Letras, 2013.

———. "'Você acha que usa a Internet, mas está sendo usado por ela,' diz Bernardo Carvalho." Interview by Raquel Cozer. *Folha de São Paulo*, 21 Sep. 2013, www1.folha.uol.com.br/ilustrada/2013/09/1344976-voce-acha-que-usa-a-internet-mas-esta-sendo-usado-por-ela-diz-bernardo-de-carvalho.shtml. Accessed 21 July 2017.

Carvalho, Jailton. "Bancada da bala faz nova investida contra Estatuto do Desarmamento." *O Globo*, 10 Mar. 2017, oglobo.globo.com/brasil/bancada-da-bala-faz-nova-investida-contra-estatuto-do-desarmamento-21040383. Accessed 15 July 2017.

Carvalho, Vinicius Mariano de. "Escrevendo-se na cidade: Exu e o *Guia afetivo da periferia*, de Marcus Vinicius Faustini." *Estudos de Literatura Brasileira Contemporânea*, no. 45, 2015, pp. 37-48.

The Century of the Self. Directed by Adam Curtis, BBC Two, 2002.

Certeau, Michel de. *The Practice of Everyday Life*. Translated by Steven Rendall, U of California P, 1984.

Works Cited

Chaui, Marilena. "Uma nova classe trabalhadora." Sader, pp. 123–34.

"Comissão rejeita revogação do estatuto." *Senado notícias*, 6 June 2017, www12.senado.leg.br/noticias/materias/2017/06/06/comissao-rejeita-revogacao-do-estatuto-do-desarmamento. Accessed 4 Mar. 2018.

Crystal, David. *Language Death*. Cambrige UP, 2000.

Cruz, Sonia M. Chacaliaza. "Realismo brutal. Aproximaciones a la narrativa de Ana Paula Maia." *Actas VI Congreso Internacional Cuestiones Críticas*, 2015, www.celarg.org/int/arch_publi/chacaliazacruzcc2015.pdf. Accessed 4 Apr. 2018.

Cunha, João Manuel dos Santos. "Mãos de cavalo e a permanência da literatura em tempos de midiatização digital." *Novas leituras da ficção brasileira no século* XXI, edited by Helena Bonito Pereira, Mackenzie, 2011, pp. 197–224.

Dalcastagnè, Regina. "Deslocamentos urbanos na literatura brasileira contemporânea." *Brasiliana—Journal for Brazilian Studies*, vol. 3, no. 1, July 2014, pp. 31–47.

———. "Entre silêncios e estereótipos: relações raciais na literatura brasileira contemporânea." *Literatura e exclusão*, organized by Laeticia Jensen Eble and Regina Dalcastagnè, Editora Zouk, 2017, pp. 217–38.

———. "Uma voz ao sol: Representação e legitimidade na narrativa brasileira contemporânea." *Estudos de literatura brasileira contemporânea*, vol. 20, July–Aug., 2002, pp. 33-87.

Davis, Shoshana. "God particle: Why the Higgs boson matters." *CBS News*, 19 Mar. 2013, www.cbsnews.com/news/god-particle-why-the-higgs-boson-matters/. Accessed 8 September 2016.

Dealtry, Giovanna. "Cidade em ruínas: a história a contrapelo em *Inferno Provisório*, de Luiz Ruffato." *Estudos de literatura brasileira contemporânea*, vol. 34, July–Dec. 2009, pp. 209–21.

Delgado, Gabriel Estides. "A classe feito corpo: pertencimento e discriminação." *Estudos de literatura brasileira contemporânea*, vol. 45, 2015, pp. 183–99.

D'Incao, Angela, and Hermínio Martins, editors. *Democracia, crise e reforma. Estudos sobre Fernando Henrique Cardoso*. Paz e Terra, 2010.

Douglas, Mary, and Baron Isherwood. *The World of Goods*. Routledge, 2004.

Elomar. "A meu Deus um canto novo." *Elomar em Concerto*. Kuaru, 1989.

Evaristo, Conceição. *Olhos d'água*. Pallas, 2014.

Ewen, Stuart. *Captains of Consciousness. Advertising and the Social Roots of the Consumer Culture*. McGraw-Hill, 2001.

Faustini, Marcus Vinícius. *Guia afetivo da periferia*. Aeroplano Editora, 2009.

Featherstone, Mike. *Consumer Culture ad Postmodernity*. Sage, 2007.

Felski, Rita. "The Invention of Everyday Life." *New Formations*, vol. 39, 1999–2000, pp. 15–31.

Ferréz. *Amanhecer Esmeralda*. Objetiva, 2005.

———. "O barco Viking." *Ninguém é inocente em São Paulo*. Objetiva, 2006, pp. 53–55.

Figueiredo, Eurídice. "Eliane Potiguara e Daniel Munduruku: Por uma cosmovisão ameríndia." *Estudos de literatura brasileira contemporânea*, vol. 53, Jan.–Apr., 2018, pp. 291–304.

Freixo, Adriano, and Thiago Rodrigues, editors. *2016, o ano do golpe*. Oficina, 2016.

Fuguet, Alberto, and Sergio Gómez, editors. *McOndo*. Mondadori, 1996.

Funk ostentação: O filme. Directed by Konrad Dantas and Renato Barreiros, 2012.

Galera, Daniel. *Mãos de cavalo*. Companhia das Letras, 2006.

Garbero, Maria Fernanda. "A brutalidade como lugar: os bastardos de Ana Paula Maia." *LL Journal*, vol. 10, no. 2, 2015, pp. 1–11.

———. "Sujos, brutos, invisíveis: os trabalhadores de Ana Paula Maia." *Cult*, 1 Mar. 2018, revistacult.uol.com.br/home/os-trabalhadores-de-ana-paula-maia/. Accessed 4 Apr. 2018.

García-Canclini, Néstor. *Consumers as Citizens: Globalization and Multicultural Conflicts*. Translated by George Yúdice, Minnesota UP, 2001.

Gardiner, Michael. *Critiques of Everyday Life*. Routledge, 2000.

Goertzel, Ted G. *Fernando Henrique Cardoso: Reinventing Democracy in Brazil*. Lunne Rienner Publishers, 1999.

Gombata, Marsílea. "Classe média adere ao funk ostentação." *Carta Capital*, 11 Sep. 2013, www.pragmatismopolitico.com.br/2013/09/classe-media-adere-ao-funk-ostentacao.html. Accessed 8 Mar. 2019.

Gomes, Luís Eduardo. Porto Alegre, junho de 2013: A fragmentação da luta contra o aumento da passagem. *Sul 21*, junho2013.sul21.com.br/porto-alegre-junho-de-2013-a-fragmentacao-da-luta-contra-o-aumento-da-passagem/?ModPagespeed=off. Accessed 26 Jul. 2018.

Gondar, Jô. "Quatro proposições sobre memória social." *O que é memória social?*, edited by Jô Gondar and Vera Dodebei, Contra Capa Livraria, 2005.

Graúna, Graça. *Contrapontos da literatura indígena contemporânea no Brasil*. Mazza Edições, 2013.

Gudynas, Eduardo. "Buen Vivir: Today's tomorrow." *Development*, vol. 54, no. 4, 2011, pp. 441–47.

Gumbrecht, Hans Ulrich. "Aesthetic Experience in Everyday Worlds: Reclaiming an Unredeemed Utopian Motif." *New Literary History*, vol. 37, no. 2, pp. 299–318.

Habert, Nadine. *A década de 70. Apogeu e crise da ditadura militar brasileira*. Editora Ática, 1992.

Hall, Stuart. "The Culture Gap." *Marxism Today*, Jan. 1984, pp. 18–22.

Harvey, David. *A Brief History of Neoliberalism*. Kindle ed., Oxford UP, 2005.

———. *A Companion to Marx's Capital*. Verso, 2010.

Hendrix, Jimmi. "Drifting." *The Cry of Love*, 1971.

Hill, Napoleon. *Think and Grow Rich*. The Ralston Society, 1937.

Huyssen, Andreas. *After the Great Divide. Modernism, Mass Culture, Postmodernism*. Indiana UP, 1986.

———. *Twilight Memories*. Routledge, 1995.

Ilha das Flores. Directed by Jorge Furtado, Casa de Cinema de Porto Alegre, 1989.

"Ilha das Flores: Depois que a sessão acabou." *Editorial J*, 16 Dec. 2011, www.editorialj.eusoufamecos.net/site/noticias/reflita/ilha-das-flores-depois-que-a-sessao-acabou/. Accessed 5 Apr. 2018.

Kambiwá, Avelin Buniacá. "Crise, democracia e a esquerda no século XXI: Um olhar da mulher indígena." *Tem saída? Ensaios críticos sobre o Brasil*, edited by Winnie Bueno et. al., Editora Zouk, 2017, pp. 241–47.

Kopytoff, Igor. "The Cultural Biography of Things: Commoditization as Process." *The Social Life of Things: Commodities in Cultural Perspective*, edited by Arjun Appadurai, Cambridge UP, 1986, pp. 64–91.

LaCapra, Dominick. *Writing History, Writing Trauma*. Johns Hopkins UP, 2014.

Laub, Michel. *A maçã envenenada*. Companhia das Letras, 2013.

Lefebvre, Henri. *Critique of Everyday Life, Volume II*. Translated by John Moore, Verso, 2002.

———. *Everyday Life in the Modern World*. Translated by Sacha Rabinovitch, Transaction Publishers, 2005.

Lehnen, Leila. *Citizenship and Crisis in Contemporary Brazilian Literature*. Palgrave Macmillan, 2013.

———. "O fruto do desencanto: suicídio e alienação em *A maçã envenenada*, de Michel Laub." *Revista da Associação Internacional de Lusitanistas*, vol. 4, July–Dec., 2015, pp. 99–119.

"Leia íntegra da carta de Lula para acalmar o mercado financeiro." *Folha Online*, 24 June 2002, www1.folha.uol.com.br/folha/brasil/ult96u33908.shtml. Accessed 12 June 2018.

Levitsky, Steven, and Daniel Ziblatt. *How Democracies Die*. Crown, 2018.

Lewis, Charlton T., and Charles Short. *A Latin Dictionary*. Perseus Digital Library, 1985–2007, www.perseus.tufts.edu/hopper/. Accessed 3 July 2017.

Lidner, Melanie. "What People Are Still Willing to Pay For." *Forbes*, 15 Jan. 2009, www.forbes.com/2009/01/15/self-help-industry-ent-sales-cx_ml_0115selfhelp.html. Accessed on March 21, 2017.

Lima, Venício A. de. *Mídia. Teoria e política*. Editora Fundação Perseu Abramo, 2004.

Lísias, Ricardo. *O livro dos mandarins*. Alfaguara, 2009.

Lowry, Malcolm. "China." *The Voyage That Never Ends. Fictions, Poems, Fragments, Letters,* edited by Michael Hofmann, New York Review Books, 2007.

Ludymilla. "Hoje." *Hoje*, Warner Music Brasil, 2014.

Lynch, Colum, and Rebecca Hamilton. "International Criminal Court Charges Sudan's Omar Hassan al-Bashir With Genocide." *The Washington Post*, 13 July 2010, www.washingtonpost.com/wp-dyn/content/article/2010/07/12/AR2010071205295.html. Accessed 22 June 2016.

Macedo, Edir. *Plano de poder: Deus, os cristãos e a política*. Thomas Nelson Brasil, 2011.

Machado, Maria Helena. "'A imagem é simbólica,' diz especialista sobre foto de babá empurrando carrinho em protesto." Interview by Letícia Duarte. *Zero Hora*, 19 Mar 2016. zh.clicrbs.com.br. Accessed 20 May. 2016.

Maia, Ana Paula. *Carvão animal*. Record, 2011.

———. *De gados e homens*. Record, 2014.

———. "Dificilmente um homem é questionado por escrever sobre mulheres." Interview by Olívia Fraga. *Nexo*, vol. 31, Mar. 2018, www.nexojornal.com.br. Accessed 4 Apr. 2018.

———. *Enterre seus mortos*. Companhia das Letras, 2018.

———. *O trabalho sujo dos outros. Entre rinhas de cachorros e porcos abatidos*. E-pub, Record, 2009.

———. "'Ir aonde ninguém quer ir': entrevista com Ana Paula Maia." Interview by Christian Grünnagel. *Estudos de literatura brasileira contemporânea*, vol. 45, Jan.–June 2015, pp. 351–71.

Works Cited

Martín-Barbero, Jesús. *Communication, Culture and Hegemony: From the Media to Mediations*. Translated by Elizabeth Fox and Robert A. White, Sage Publications, 1993.

Martinho-Ferreira, Patrícia. "Urban Space and Female Subjectivity in Contemporary Brazilian Literature." *Transmodernity: Journal of Peripheral Cultural Production in the Luso–Hispanic World*, Jan. 2016, pp. 110–30.

Martins, Heitor. "Canibais europeus e antropófagos brasileiros. Introdução ao estudo das origens da antropofagia." *Oswald de Andrade e os outros*. Editora do Conselho Estadual da Cultura, 1973, pp. 11–39.

Martins, José de Souza. "Brasil tem uma ocorrência de linchamento por dia." *Uol Notícias*, 14 July 2015, noticias.uol.com.br/cotidiano/ultimas-noticias/2015/07/14/brasil-tem-uma-ocorrencia-de-linchamento-por-dia-veja-analises-do-fenomeno.htm. Accessed 15 July 2017.

Martins, Rodrigo. "A bancada BBB domina o congresso." *Carta Capital*, 14 Apr. 2015, www.cartacapital.com.br/revista/844/bbb-no-congresso-1092.html. Accessed 15 July 2017.

———. "Os modelos que defendíamos se esgotaram." *Carta Capital*, 7 July 2016, www.cartacapital.com.br/revista/901/modelos-que-defendiamos-se-esgotaram. Accessed 15 July 2017.

Marx, Karl, and Friedrich Engels. *Capital; Manifesto of the Communist Party*. Encyclopaedia Britannica, Benton, 1952.

Mattoso, Jorge. "Dez anos depois." Sader, pp. 111–22.

MC João. "Baile de favela." *Baile de favela*, GR6 MUSIC, 2015.

MC Soffia. "Menina Pretinha." www.vagalume.com.br/mc-soffia/menina-pretinha.html. Accessed 28 Sep. 2018.

Miguel, Luis Felipe. "Quatro poderes e um golpe." Freixo and Rodrigues, pp. 96–115.

Miller, Daniel. "Consumption as the Vanguard of History." *Acknowledging Consumption: A Review of New Studies*, edited by Daniel Miller, Routledge, 1995.

———. *A Theory of Shopping*. Cornell University Press, 1998.

"Minha casa, minha vida." *Caixa Econômica Federal*, www.caixa.gov.br/voce/habitacao/minha-casa-minha-vida/paginas/default.aspx . Accessed 26 Feb. 2019.

Moretzsohn, Sylvia Debossan. "A mídia e o golpe: Uma profecia autocumprida." Freixo and Rodrigues, pp. 116–40.

Mulheres ricas. Directed by Diego Guebel. Rede Bandeirantes, 2012–13.

"Multilevel Marketing: Last Week Tonight with John Oliver." *YouTube*, uploaded by Last Week Tonight with John Oliver, 16 Aug. 2015, www.youtube.com/watch?v=s6MwGeOm8iI. Accessed 1 May 2017.

Nascimento, Érica Peçanha do. *Vozes marginais na literatura*. Aeroplano Editora, 2008.

Navarro, Lourdes García. "Brazil Enslaved." *NPR*, 12 Sep. 2015, www.npr.org/2015/09/12/439257489/brazil-enslaved. Accessed 20 May 2016.

Nibert, David Alan. *Animal Rights/Human Rights: Entanglements of Oppression and Liberation*. Rowman & Littlefield, 2002.

Nietzsche, Friedrich. *On the Genealogy of Morality*. Hackett Pub., 1998.

Nirvana. "Drain You." *Nevermind*, DGC Records, 1991.

Nixon, Rob. *Slow Violence and the Environmentalism of the Poor*. Harvard UP, 2011.

Nozaki, William. "A periferia afastada da política." Interview by Glauco Faria. *Revista do Brasil*, vol. 127, 9 Apr. 2017, www.redebrasilatual.com.br/revistas/127/a-periferia-afastada-da-politica. Accessed 2 July 2017.

"O cara do momento." Published by Melhor do Funk HD, 5 Mar. 2013, www.youtube.com/watch?v=zD-eqzoVJzw. Accessed 28 Sep. 2018.

O'Dougherty, Maureen. *Consumption Intensified: The Politics of Middle-Class Daily Life in Brazil*. Duke UP, 2002.

"Olha como nós tá." Published by Pdrão Vídeo Clips, 28 Feb. 2012, www.youtube.com/watch?v=9T44W-QMe4s. Accessed 28 Sep. 2018.

Oliveira, Nelson de. *Geração de 90: Manuscritos de computador: Os melhores contistas brasileiros surgidos no final do século XXI*. Boitempo Editorial, 2001.

Oliven, Ruben George, and Rosana Pinheiro-Machado. "From 'Country of the Future' to Emergent Country: Popular Consumption in Brazil." *Consumer Culture in Latin America*, edited by John Sinclair and Anna Cristina Pertierra, Palgrave Macmillan, 2012, pp. 53–65.

Palaversich, Diana. "Rebeldes sin causa: realismo mágico vs. realismo virtual." *Hispamérica*, no. 86, 2000, pp. 55–70.

Pariser, Eli. *The Filter Bubble. How the New Personalized Web is Changing What We Read and How We Think*. Penguin Press, 2012.

Paz-Soldán, Edmundo, and Debra A. Castillo. "Introduction: Beyond the Lettered City." *Latin American Literature and Mass Media*, edited by Debra A. Castillo and Edmundo Paz-Soldán. *Hispanic Issues*, vol. 22, Garland, 2001, pp. 1–20.

Works Cited

Pellegrini, Tânia. *A imagem e a letra*. Fapesp, 1999.

Pereira, Alexandre. "Funk ostentação em São Paulo: Imaginação, consumo e novas tecnologias." *Revista de Estudos Culturais*, vol. 1, 2014.

Pereira, Victor Hugo Adler. "Documentos da pobreza, desigualdade ou exclusão social." *Estudos de Literatura Brasileira Contemporânea*, vol. 30, Jul.–Dec. 2007, pp. 11–26.

Pezzullo, Phaedra, and Stephen P. Depoe. "Everyday Life and Death in a Nuclear World. Stories from Fernald." *Public Modalities: Rhetoric, Culture, Media, and the Shape of Public Life*, edited by Daniel C. Brouwer and Robert Asen, University of Alabama Press, 2010, pp. 85–108.

Philippou, Styliane. "Modernism and National Identity in Brazil, or How to Brew a Brazilian Stew." *National Identities*, vol. 7, no. 3, Sep. 2005, pp. 245–65.

Phillips, Dom, and Davilson Brasileiro. "Brazil Dam Disaster: Firm Knew of Potential Impact Months in Advance." *The Guardian*, 1 March 2018, www.theguardian.com/world/2018/feb/28/brazil-dam-collapse-samarco-fundao-mining. Accessed 3 Apr. 2018.

Phillips, Tom. "Mulheres Ricas: Brazil's Rich Women Brings Lives of Super-Rich to TV." *The Gardian*, 3 Jan. 2012, www.theguardian.com/world/2012/jan/03/mulheres-ricas-brazil-rich-women?INTCMP=SRCH. Accessed 23 June 2018.

Pietrani, Anélia Montechiari. "Um espaço (ainda) para o afeto, a utopia, a literatura." *Miscelânea*, vol. 9, Jan.–Jun. 2011, pp. 116–28.

Pinheiro-Machado, Rosana. "A era pós PT." *Carta Capital*, 25 May 2016, www.cartacapital.com.br/politica/a-era-pos-pt. Accessed 9 July, 2017.

———. "A falência do PT, a ascensão da direita e a esquerda órfã." *Carta Capital*, 25 May 2015, www.cartacapital.com.br/politica/a-falencia-do-pt-a-ascensao-da-direita-e-a-esquerda-orfa-7538.html. Accessed 9 August 2018.

———. "Fazendo *guanxi*: Dádivas, etiquetas e emoções na economia da China pós-Mao." *Mana*, vol. 17, no. 1, 2011, pp. 99–130.

———. "From Hope to Hate." 7 Feb. 2019, Arizona State University. Invited Talk.

———. "Imaginar novas saídas." Bueno et al., pp. 235–39.

———. "O Reich tropical: a onda fascista no Brasil." *Carta Capital*, 15 Oct. 2014, www.cartacapital.com.br/sociedade/o-reich-tropical-a-onda-fascista-no-brasil-2883.html. Accessed 16 Nov. 2016.

———. "The Right to Pleasure: Poverty, Politics, and Consumption in an Emerging Brazil." Brazilian Studies Association Conference, 1 Apr. 2016, Brown University, Providence. Panel Presentation.

Pinheiro-Machado, Rosana, and Lúcia Mury Scalco. "Da esperança ao ódio: Juventude, política e pobreza do lulismo ao bolsonarismo." *Instituto Humanitas Usininos*, 4 Oct. 2018, www.ihu.unisinos.br. Accessed 3 Mar. 2019.

———. "The Right to Pleasure: Politics, Poverty and Consumption in Neoliberal Brazil." 2017.

Pink Floyd. "Fearless." *One of These Days*, Odeon, 1971.

"Plaquê de 100." *YouTube*, uploaded by MC Guimê, 2 July 2012, www.youtube.com/watch?v=gyXkaO0DxB8. Accessed 8 July 2018.

Postman, Neil. *Amusing Ourselves to Death: Public Discourse in the Age of Show Business*. Viking, 1985.

Prendergast, John. "Blood Money for Sudan: World Bank and IMF to the 'Rescue.'" *Africa Today*, vol. 36, no. 3, 1989, pp. 43–53.

"Pronunciamento de final de ano do Presidente da República." *YouTube*, uploaded by Planalto, 22 Dec. 2009, www.youtube.com/watch?v=OCbIxxVffi4. Accessed 6 June 2018.

Quandt, Christiane. "Efeitos do medial em A guerra dos bastardos (2007) de Ana Paula Maia." *Brasiliana—Journal for Brazilian Studies*, vol. 3, no. 2, Mar. 2015, pp. 297–320.

Que horas ela volta? Directed by Ana Muylaert. África Filmes/Globo Filmes/Gullane Filmes, 2015.

Racionais MC's. "Otus 500." *Nada como um dia após outro dia*, Zimbabwe Records, 2002.

———. "Vida Loka II." *Nada como um dia após outro dia*, Zimbabwe Records, 2002.

Rainey, Lee Dian. *Confucius & Confucianism: The Essentials*. Wiley-Blackwell, 2010.

Ramos, Julio. *Divergent Modernities: Culture and Politics in Nineteenth Century Latin America*. Translated by John D. Blanco, Kindle ed., Duke UP, 2001.

Resende, Beatriz. *Contemporâneos: expressões da literatura brasileira no século XXI*. Casa da Palavra: Biblioteca Nacional, 2008.

Rossi, Amanda. "Congresso aprova decreto de intervenção federal no Rio de Janeiro; entenda o que a medida significa." *BBC News Brasil*, 21 Feb. 2018, www.bbc.com/portuguese/brasil-43079114. Accessed 15 June 2018.

Sader, Emir, organizer. *10 anos de governos pós-neoliberais no Brasil: Lula and Dilma*. Boitempo Editorial, 2013.

———. "A construção da hegemonia pós-neoliberal." *10 anos de governos pós-neoliberais no Brasil: Lula and Dilma*, edited by Emir Sader, Boitempo Editorial, 2013. pp. 135–43.

Works Cited

Sant'Anna, André. *O Brasil é bom*. Companhia das Letras, 2014.

Santiago, Silviano. "Literatura e cultura de massas." *O cosmopolitismo do pobre*. Editora UFMG, 2004, pp. 106–22.

Santos, Lidia. *Tropical Kitsch: Media in Latin American Literature and Art*. Translated by Elisabeth Enenbach, Markus Weiner, 2006.

Scalco, Lucia Mury, and Rosana Pinheiro-Machado. "Os sentidos do real e do falso: O consumo popular em perspectiva etnográfica." *Revista de Antropologia*, vol. 53, no. 1, Jan.–June 2010, pp. 321–59.

Schøllhammer, Karl. *Ficção brasileira contemporânea*. Civilização Brasileira, 2009.

Silva, Adriana Brita da, et al. "A extrema-direita na atualidade." *Serv. Soc. Soc.* São Paulo, vol. 119, July–Sep., 2014, pp. 407–45.

Silva, Cristiane Sabino, and Paulo César Boni. "A trajetória imagética de Lula: de líder sindical a presidente da República." *Discursos fotográficos*, vol. 1, 2005, pp. 89–113.

Silverman, Malcom. *Protesto e o novo romance brasileiro*. Translated by Carlos Araújo, Civilização Brasileira, 2000.

Shemesh, Yael. "Suicide in the Bible." *Jewish Bible Quarterly*, vol. 37, no. 3, 2009, pp. 157–68.

Soares, Luiz Eduardo. "Prefácio." *Guia afetivo da periferia*, by Marcus Vinícius Faustini, 2009, pp. 15–18.

Soper, Kate. "Neither the 'Simple Backward Look' nor the 'Simple Progressive Thrust': Ecocriticism and the Politics of Prosperity." *Handbook of Ecocriticism and Cultural Ecology*, edited by Hubert Zapf de Gruyter, 2016, pp. 157–73.

Sorj, Bernardo, and Sérgio Fausto. "O sociólogo e o político. Entrevista com Fernando Henrique Cardoso." *Democracia, crise e reforma*, edited by Angela D'Incao and Hermínio Martins, Paz e Terra, 2010, pp. 29–60.

Sousa, Bertone de Oliveira. "A teologia da prosperidade e a redefinição do protestantismo brasileiro: uma abordagem à luz da análise do discurso." *Revista Brasileira de História das Religiões*, vol. 4, no. 11, Sep. 2011, pp. 221–45.

Sousa, Nivaldo, and Isadora Peron. "Manifestantes pedem intervenção militar com base em regra que não existe na Constituição." *Estadão*, 12 Apr. 2015, politica.estadao.com.br/noticias/geral,manifestantes-pedem-intervencao-militar-com-base-em-regra-que-nao-existe-na-constituicao,1668381. Accessed 12 July 2017.

Speranza, Graciela. *Fuera de campo: literatura y arte argentines después de Duchamp*. Anagrama, 2006.

Steinbeck, John. *Of Mice and Men*. Covici Friede, 1937.

Strong, Catherine. *Grunge: Music and Memory*. Ashgate Publishing, 2011.

Süssekind, Flora. *Cinematograph of Words. Literature, Technique, and Modernization in Brazil*. Translated by Paulo Henriques Britto, Stanford UP, 1997.

———. "Ficção 80: Dobradiças e vitrines." *Papéis colados*. Editora UFRJ, 1993, pp. 239-52.

Takeda, Anna Carolina Botelho. "A obssessão pela virilidade em *Mãos de cavalo*: Poder e ruína." *Revista Estação Literária*, vol. 16, June 2016, pp. 153–64.

"Tá patrão." *YouTube*, uploaded by MC Guimê, 10 Nov. 2011. www.youtube.com/watch?v=QToec6FkpzY. Accessed 8 July 2018.

Taylor, Talbot J. *Mutual Misunderstanding: Scepticism and the Theorizing of Language and Interpretation*. Duke UP, 1992.

Teiwes, Frederik C. "Mao and His Followers." *A Critical Introduction to Mao*, edited by Timothy Cheek, Cambridge UP, 2010, pp. 129–57.

Tennina, Lucía. *Cuidado com os poetas! Literatura e periferia na cidade de São Paulo*. Editora Zouk, 2017.

The Gang Is All Here. Directed by Busby Berkeley, Twentieth Century Fox, 1943.

"Trecho do pronunciamento em cadeia nacional do Presidente Lula 22/12/2008." *YouTube*, uploaded by *Memorial da Democracia*, 28 July 2016, www.youtube.com/watch?v=BLH9AV5_WTE. Accessed 6 June 2018.

Trotta, Felipe da Costa. "O funk no Brasil contemporâneo—Uma música que incomoda." *Latin American Research Review*, vol. 51, no. 4, 2016, pp. 86–101.

Tucker, Shwan R. *The Virtues and Vices in the Arts: A Sourcebook*. The Lutterworth Press, 2015.

Tyner, James A. *Violence in Capitalism: Devaluing Life in na Age of Responsibility*. U of Nebraska P, 2015.

Valente, Rubens. "General fala em intervenção se Justiça não agir contra corrupção." *Folha de São Paulo*, 17 Sep. 2017, www1.folha.uol.com.br/poder/2017/09/1919322-general-do-exercito-ameaca-impor-solucao-para-crise-politica-no-pais.shtml. Accessed 10 Oct. 2017.

Valente Jr., Valdemar. "Narrativa e Escatologia." *Macabéa*, vol. 3, no. 2, July–Dec., 2014, pp. 131–33.

Veloso, Caetano. "Um índio." *Bicho*, 1977.

Works Cited

Watts, Jonathan. "Operation Car Wash: Is This the Biggest Corruption Scandal in History?" *The Guardian*, 1 June 2017, www.theguardian.com/world/2017/jun/01/brazil-operation-car-wash-is-this-the-biggest-corruption-scandal-in-history. Accessed 8 Apr. 2019.

Williams, Raymond. *Marxism and Literature*. Oxford UP, 1977.

"What went wrong with Brazil?" *The Documentary*. BBC World Service, 14 June 2016, www.bbc.co.uk/programmes/p0555kjv. Accesed 7 July 2017.

Wong, Edward. "Trump Has Called Climate Change a Chinese Hoax. Beijing Says It Is Anything But." *The New York Times*, 18 November 2016, www.nytimes.com/2016/11/19/world/asia/china-trump-climate-change.html?_r=0. Accessed 21 July 2017.

Zweig, Stefan. *Brazil Land of the Future*. Translated by Andrew St. James, Viking Press, New York, 1941.

Index

Abalurdes (fictional city), 118–19, 121–22
Adorno, Theodor, 4–5, 6, 125, 206n7
Adri (*Mãos de cavalo* character), 145–47
advertisements/advertising, 6, 9, 28, 57, 137, 181–82, 190
Affective Guide of the Periphery. See Guia afetivo da periferia
affective memories, 14–15
Afro-Brazilians, 10, 33–34, 169, 174–75, 208n4
agency, 169, 175, 190
"A ilusão da estabilidade" (Amann, Baer), 78
alcohol, 140–41, 180–81
Alencar, José de, 9, 201n2
alienation, 3, 4–5, 15, 17, 94, 110, 197; consumption as, 17, 69–70; disalienation and, 16, 18, 136, 140, 143, 150, 153–54; in *Luxúria*, 35–38; time and, 103–4
Almeida, Maria Cândida Ferreira de, 201n2
"Alone" ("Só"), *O Brasil é bom*, 56–58, 208n22
"Always wear a condom" ("Use sempre camisinha"), *O Brasil é bom*, 60
"Amando uns aos outros" ("Loving one another"), *O Brasil é bom*, 54
Amanhecer Esmeralda (*Emerald Dawn*) (Ferréz), 174
Amann, Edmund, 78, 207n1
ambiguity, 94, 98, 153, 175
ambivalent awareness narratives, 3, 18, 137, 166–68
"Os amores de Kimbá" ("Kimbá's loves"), *Olhos d'água*, 174
Amusing Ourselves to Death (Postman), 89
Analects (Confucius), 74

Andrade, Oswald de, 10, 201n2
Animal Charcoal (*Carvão animal*) (Maia), 14, 17–18, 114, 119–23
animalization, 62–63, 124–25
antidepressants, 35, 37
Argentina, 12
art/artists, 5–6, 145–46
Assis, Machado de, 9–10, 188–89
Atari (video game console), 182
Aurélia (*Senhora* character), 9
authoritarianism, underlying neo-liberalism, 49, 54, 80
automatons, characters compared to, 35, 38–39
avant-garde, European, 12, 201n4
Azevedo, Álvares de, 187

Baer, Werner, 78, 207n1
"Baile de favela" (song), 212n4
Bairro Novo (New Neighborhood, fictional), 24–25
Banana Republic (pejorative phrase), 46
bananas, symbolism of, 46–47
"Bancada da Bala" (political faction), 53, 204n21
Band (television network), 195
Bandeira, Manuel, 186
banking crisis, 78–79
banks, 57, 78, 81; in *Luxúria*, 25–26; Paulo working at, 68–69, 70–72, 82–84
Barbieri, Therezinha, 4
"O Barco Viking" (Ferréz), 173
Barren Lives (*Vidas secas*) (Ramos, G.), 186
al-Bashir, Omar Hassan Ahmad, 81–82
Baudrillard, Jean, 5, 85, 180
Bauman, Zygmunt, 17–18, 70, 88, 108–9, 112, 117; on commodification of the self, 67–68, 119
Benjamin, Walter, 6, 7

225

Index

Berkeley, Busby, 46
Berlin (band), 186
Bernays, Edward, 28
Bettencourt, Lúcia, 116–17
Between Dogfights and Slaughtered Hogs (*Entre rinhas de cachorros e porcos abatidos*) (Maia), 114
Bezerra, Kátia, 208n1
Bible, 43–46, 53, 104, 116, 203n12, 205n10; in *De gados e homens*, 125, 127–29; in *A maçã envenenada*, 161–63, 207n4
biking, in *Mãos de cavalo*, 138–40, 142–44, 146
von Bingen, Hildegard, 100–101
Bio G-3 (funk artist), 173
black women, working-class, 33–34
blogs, 89, 92
A boa terra (*The Good Earth*) (Buck), 185
Bolsa Família (income distribution programs), 1, 64
Bolsonaro, Jair, 54, 91, 196
Bombril (cleaning brand), 178m 209n8
Bonassi, Fernando, 14, 16–17, 34, 39, 54, 135–36, 197; social inclusion policies criticized by, 21–23; working-class portrayal by, 62–66. *See also Luxúria* (*Lust*)
Bonobo (*Mãos de cavalo* character), 137–41
The Book of Mandarins. *See O livro dos mandarins*
bosses, 40, 43, 123, 174
Bourdieu, Pierre, 6
Brás Cubas (character), 9–10
O Brasil é bom (*Brazil Is Good*) (Sant'Anna), 14, 17, 46–49, 60–66; neoconservatism in, 49–54; social inclusion policies criticized in, 21–22; socioeconomic relations in, 54–60

Brasília, Brazil, 173, 204n15
Brasilien (Zweig), 40
"O Brasil não é ruim" ("Brazil is not bad"), *O Brasil é bom*, 60–61
Bravo (television network), 195
Brazil. *See specific topics*
Brazilian Center for Analysis and Planning. *See* Centro Brasileiro de Análise e Planejamento
Brazilian fiction. *See specific topics*
Brazilian funk (*funk ostentação*), 3
Brazilian identity, 10, 201n2
Brazil Is Good. *See O Brasil é bom*
"Brazil is not bad" ("O Brasil não é ruim"), *O Brasil é bom*, 60–61
Brexit, 90–91
Brown, Wendy, 8, 17, 22, 65
Buck, Pearl S., 185
Bueno, Winnie, 194
Buen Vivir (indigenous philosophy), 198
Bufo & Spallanzani (Fonseca), 12
Bullet Coalition (organization), 204n20
Burigo, Joanna, 194
Byrne, Rhonda, 67, 82

Cage, Nicolas, 138
cake metaphor, 46, 203n16
camera motif, 23, 138, 140–45, 149–50, 166
Cândido, Antônio, 6–7
capital, 9–10; cultural, 184, 191–92
Capital (Marx), 41–42
capitalism, consumer, 6, 16, 60, 61, 83, 102, 109, 122; art commenting on, 146–47; collateral damages of, 18, 112, 123, 135; communism and, 51–52; liquid modernity in, 68; meritocracy myth in, 50, 204n19; religion and, 43–45;

Index

solitude and, 56; time in, 41–42, 178–79; violence of, 17–18, 58, 123, 194
car accidents, 120, 151, 155–57, 158, 164
"O cara do momento" (song), 212n4
Cardoso, Fernando Henrique (FHC), 1, 36, 48, 80, 207n1; neoliberalism under, 8, 46, 76–78, 204n2; Paulo admiring, 68, 75–78
Cardoso, Sérgio, 187
cariocas (people from Rio de Janeiro), 184, 190, 209n9
Carta Capital (magazine), 91, 204n10
Carvalho, Bernardo, 14, 101–2, 105, 135–36, 197; on consumption, 16, 17, 68–69. *See also Reprodução (Reproduction)*
Carvalho, Vinicius Mariano de, 169
Carvão animal (Animal Charcoal) (Maia), 14, 17–18, 112, 118–22
Catholicism, 132–33
Centro Brasileiro de Análise e Planejamento (CEBRAP, Brazilian Center for Analysis and Planning), 78
Centro de Estudos de Sociologia Industrial e do Trabalho (CESIT, Center for the Studies on the Sociology of Industry and Work), 78
The Century of the Self (documentary), 28
Certeau, Michel de, 189, 192
CESIT. *See* Centro de Estudos de Sociologia Industrial e do Trabalho
characters, 14, 35, 38–39, 62, 201n2; stereotypical, 132–33. *See also specific characters*

characters, nameless, 69, 169; in *Luxúria*, 23, 28; in *A maçã envenenada*, 138
Chaui, Marilena, 202n1
childhood, memories, 14, 84, 135, 183; of Hermano, 137–38, 149
children, 21, 37–38, 58, 135; working-class, 173–74
China, 40, 95, 101–2, 185, 204n3; in *O livro dos mandarins*, 71–72, 79–80, 84, 109; in *Reprodução*, 69, 73–75; Sudan conflated with, 86–88
"China" (Lowry), 101–2
Chiquinho ("Lodaçal" character), 58–60
Chorume (fictional lake), 116, 121
Christianity, 45, 61, 162–64
"Cida's Run" ("O cooper de Cida"), *Olhos d'água*, 174–75
Cien años de soledad (García Márquez), 13
cinema, 7, 8, 11, 184–85
citizenship, 169, 176, 208n1
class, 4–5, 33, 51–52, 117, 169–70, 183–84; death and, 118–22; discerned by language, 55–56. *See also specific classes*
"classe baixa-alta" ("upper-lower class"), 48–49, 51
La classe operaria va in paradiso (Lulu the Tool) (film), 184–85
classism, 51–52
climbing, in *Mãos de cavalo*, 141–42, 145–46
coalminers, 14, 18, 118, 206n5
Cobain, Kurt, 151–53, 159–62, 164
Coca-Cola, 139, 177–78, 182, 183, 192
Coelho, Paulo, 185
collateral damages of consumer capitalism, 18, 112, 123, 135

227

Index

Collor de Mello, Fernando (Mello), 1, 36, 76, 207n1
colonization, 28, 104
"Comentário na rede sobre tudo o que está acontecendo por aí" ("Online Comment on All That Is Happening Out There"), *O Brasil é bom*, 49, 52–53
comic books, 137, 140
commercials. *See* advertisements/advertising
commodification, 9–10, 25, 28, 109; of information, 90, 92; self, 67–69, 119
communication technologies, 88–92
communism, 50, 51–52, 75, 80, 185
competition, 60, 65, 74–75
Confucius (fictional consulting firm), 75, 82–83
Confucius/Confucian philosophy, 73–75 204n1
consumer power, 15, 22, 29–30, 50–51, 121
consumer society, Brazil as, 14–15
consumption, 1–8, 16–19, 18–19, 31, 72, 118; as alienating, 16, 69–70; in *O Brasil é bom*, 46–49; emotional pleasures of, 4, 5–6, 176–84, 189–92; love as, 168, 176–80; by low-income workers, 113–15, 122–23; tactical, 14, 189–92; violence of, 29, 115. *See also* narratives; working-class, consumption
contradictions, 22–23, 145
"O cooper de Cida" ("Cida's Run"), *Olhos d'água*, 174–75
corporations, 175–79, 209n6; monopolies by, 36–37; in *O livro dos mandarins*, 68–69, 74–75, 82
corruption, 36, 40, 60, 64, 80–81, 176, 208n6; protests against, 91, 205n6
O cosmopolitismo do pobre (*The Cosmopolitanism of the Poor*) (Santiago), 7
countercyclical policies, 40, 203n9
covers, book: for *O Brasil é bom*, 46–47; for *Mãos de cavalo*, 146–147
cows, in *De gados e homens*, 123–26, 126–28, 129
Cozer, Raquel, 105
cremators, 118–22, 206n4
crime, 52–53, 129
crises, 168–69, 180–81; banking, 78–79; economic, 1–2, 25–26; environmental, 111; time and, 101–4, 109
Critiques of Everyday Life (Gardiner), 15
Crivella, Marcelo, 91
cultural capital, 184, 191–92
Cultural Revolution, Chinese, 75, 204n1, 204n3
Cultural Studies, 6–8
"The Culture Gap" (Hall), 6
"The Culture Industry" (Adorno, Horkheimer), 4–5
Curtis, Adam, 28

Dalcastagnè, Regina, 167–68, 169
Darfur, Sudan, 81
dead bodies, as commodities, 118–24, 133
death, 128–22, 131–33; in *De gados e homens*, 123, 126–28; in *A maçã envenen*ada, 137, 151–53, 155–56, 159–64; in *Mãos de cavalo*, 137, 141–42, 148
death penalty, 52–53, 58
debts, 34, 76, 78, 163; in *Luxúria*, 23, 26–27, 34
De gados e homens (*Of Cattle and Men*) (Maia), 14, 17–18, 113, 118, 121, 122–31, 133

democracy, 80–81, 90, 105–6
dentist (*Luxúria* character), 29–30, 43
Depoe, Stephen P., 122
desires, consumer, 27–28
Deuteronomy, Bible, 162
dialectical relationships, 138, 146–50; between alienation and disalienation, 16, 18, 136, 140, 144, 151, 154–55
dialogues, 54–55; in *Reprodução*, 93–97, 106
dictatorships, military, 45, 50, 53
The Dirty Work of Others (*O trabalho sujo dos outros*) (Maia), 14, 17–18, 112–14, 121, 133
disalienation, 156–57, 159, 166; alienation and, 16, 18, 136, 140, 144, 151, 154–55; in *Mãos de cavalo*, 140, 143
Disarmament Statute (Estatuto do Desarmamento), 53
diseases, 120–21
Disneyland, 191–92, 209n10
Doce River, 111
dogs, 31–32, 179
domestic abuse, 34, 38
Dona Creuza (*Guia afetivo da periferia* character), 177, 209n7
Dona Zema (*Carvão animal* character), 120
Douglas, Mary, 6, 168
Dragão Chinês (popsicle), 181
"Drain You" (song), 151, 155–56, 159, 166
dreams, 148–49
"Drifting" (song), 42
drugs, 58–60
Duas praças (Lísias), 205n5
Duchamp, Marcel, 146
"O duelo" (Sant'Anna), 12
dystopias, 3–4, 17, 22, 24, 47, 64, 108

E4 (television network), 195
Ecclesiastes, Bible, 162
economic crisis, in Brazil, 1–2, 25–26
Edgar Wilson (*De gados e homens* character), 128–31, 133, 207n8
education, 30, 77
eggs, 181–82
elite class/upper class, 48–49, 50–51, 63, 116, 195
Elomar (musician), 148–50
Emerald Dawn (*Amanhecer Esmeralda*) (Ferréz), 174
emotional pleasures of consumption, 4, 5–6, 176–84, 189–92
entrepreneurs/entrepreneurship, 23, 44, 59, 65–66, 72, 76, 82
Entre rinhas de cachorros e porcos abatidos (*Between Dogfights and Slaughtered Hogs*) (Maia), 114
environmental crises, 111, 112, 121–23, 205n1
envy, 29–30, 43
Erasmo Wagner (*O trabalho sujo dos outros* character), 114–18
Ermenegildo Zegna (brand), 86
Erundina, Luiza, 203n10
escrivã (registrar), 106–7
Estatuto do Desarmamento (Disarmament Statute), 53
"o estudante de chinês" ("the student of Chinese," *Reprodução* character), 14, 69, 92, 108–9; Paulo compared to, 88–90, 102, 109; police interrogating, 69, 93, 97
Europe, 4, 90–91
Evaristo, Conceição, 174
everyday life, 15–21, 54, 117, 122; commodification of the self in, 68; numbness in, 35–38;

Index

violence in, 29–35, 37–38.
See also consumption
exploitation, of low-income workers, 121–25; in *De gados e homens*, 123; in *Luxúria*, 33–34, 202n3, 206n6; in *O livro dos mandarins*, 82–83; in *O trabalho sujo dos outros*, 113, 116

Facebook, 135
factory workers, 30, 38–46
failure, narratives of, 3, 24–25, 69; in *O livro dos mandarins*, 79, 83–88
fairs, 177, 179–80, 189–90
families, working-class, 23–28, 63–64, 177–80
fantasy narratives, 140–44, 142–43
fascism, 80, 90
Faustini, Marcus Vinícius, 14, 16, 18, 168–69, 177, 193–94, 198
favelas (slums), 172, 208n1
"Fearless" (song), 145
Featherstone, Mike, 15
female officer (*Reprodução* character), 93, 97, 98–100, 104, 107
Ferreira da Silva, Reginaldo (Ferréz), 173–74
Festival (Lefebvre concept), 27
FHC. *See* Cardoso, Fernando Henrique
fiction, Brazilian. *See specific topics*
film. *See* cinema
The Filter Bubble (Pariser), 90
filter bubbles, 90–92, 94–95, 105–6
fire, 118, 120–21, 133
firefighters, 14, 120–22
first-person narrators, 49–50
Fitzgerald, F. Scott, 187–88
flag, Brazilian, 46, 50
Folha de São Paulo (newspaper), 105
Fonseca, Rubem, 12

food, 177–80, 181–82, 183
Fordism, 68, 185
fragmentation, information, 93–97
Franco, Itamar, 77
Frankfurt School, 4–5
Freud, Sigmund , 28
Fuguet, Alberto, 12–13
funkeiras, 208n4
funk ostentação (ostentation funk), 3, 171–73, 175
Furtado, Jorge, 115, 206n2
future, language of the, 93, 96, 101–2

Galera, Daniel, 14, 16, 18, 135, 198
The Gang Is All Here (film), 46
García Márquez, Gabriel, 13
Gardiner, Michael E., 15
Gasparian, Fernando, 78
gaze, 129, 168
gender, 162–63, 165, 172, 191, 208n4, 207n7; in "Amando uns aos outros," 54–55; in *Luxúria*, 25, 29–32, 45–46; in *Mãos de cavalo*, 142–49; in *O livro dos mandarins*, 82–83; in *Reprodução*, 93, 97, 98–100, 104, 107
Generation 2000 (*Geração 00*, writers), 13
Generation of 1990 (*Geração de 90*) (Oliveira), 13
Generation X, 151, 154, 157–59, 207n2
genital mutilation, 83
genocide, 81, 151, 159–64
Geração 00 (Generation 2000, writers), 13
Geração de 90 (*Generation of 1990*) (Oliveira), 13
Germany, 4, 121
ghostwriter, 68, 87
Ginsberg, Allen, 186
Globo Television (television network), 77

230

God particle, 94, 205n7
gold teeth, 120
Gómez, Sergio, 12–13
The Good Earth (A boa terra) (Buck), 185
Grunge (Strong), 207n2
grunge music, 137, 151–53, 154
Grünnagel, Christian, 113
Grupo de Estudos de Literatura Brasileira Contemporânea (Studies in Contemporary Brazilian Literature Group), 173
guanxi (Chinese practice), 72
Gudynas, Eduardo, 198
Guia afetivo da periferia (Affective Guide of the Periphery) (Faustini), 14, 18, 168–70, 175; consumption in, 176–80, 189–92
guilt, 137, 141; in *A maçã envenenada*, 151, 152, 154–57, 163–65
Gumbrecht, Hans Ulrich, 180–81
gun control laws, 52–53, 204n20

Hall, Stuart, 6, 7
hamburger factory, 124–25, 130–31, 131
happiness, 56, 173–74
Harvey, David, 41, 49, 76–77, 80
hecatomb (ritual), 126
Heidegger, Martin, 15
Helmuth *(De gados e homens* character), 123, 130
He-Man (cartoons), 137
Hendrix, Jimi, 42
Hermano *(Mãos de cavalo* character), 136, 150–51; disalienation experienced by, 140, 143; masculinity sought by, 137–41, 145–46, 148, 166
hero narratives, 141, 142–44, 149
Hezbollah, 205n4
hierarchies, social, 14, 65, 167
high and low culture, 11–12, 13, 184–89

Hill, Napoleon, 59
"Hoje" (song), 208n4
Holocaust, 125, 206n7
O homem que calculava (The Man who Calculated) (de Mello e Souza), 185
Um homem sem importância (A Man of No Importance) (film), 184–85
Horkheimer, Max, 4–5, 6
Horse Hands. See *Mãos de cavalo*
housekeeper (*Luxúria* character), 30, 33–34, 206n6
Houses of the Holy (album), 145
humanization, 124–28
human rights, 52–53, 174
hunters, society of, 108–9
Huyssen, Andreas, 12, 103–4, 166, 201n4
hyperreality, 86, 109
hypersexuality, 145
hypocrisy, 130–31

ICC. *See* International Criminal Court
identity, 10, 12, 46, 201n2; in *O livro dos mandarins*, 70–74, 83–84
Igreja Bola de Neve (Snowball Church), 45
Ilha das Flores (Isle of Flowers) (film), 115, 206n2
IMF. *See* International Monetary Fund
Immaculée Ilibagiza *(A maçã envenenada* character), 159–64
impeachment: of Collor de Mello, 1, 76; of Rousseff, 36, 53–54, 91, 196
Incan comedies, 93
income distribution programs, 1, 24, 48, 170–71, 204n2
indigenous characters, 201n2
"Um índio" ("A Native") (song), 107–8
individuality/individualism, 4, 44,

64–65, 75–76, 159, 166, 194, 198
inflation, 77–78, 80
information era, 88–92, 97–101, 110
inheritance, 120
International Criminal Court (ICC), 81
international interests, 81–82, 205n4
International Monetary Fund (IMF), 78, 81–82
Internet, 89–92, 105
invisibility, of low-income workers, 113–15, 118, 122–23, 135, 189
IRA. *See* Irish Republican Army
Iran-Contra affair, 82, 205n4
Irish Republican Army (IRA), 82
Isherwood, Baron, 6, 168
Isle of Flowers (Ilha das Flores) (film), 112, 206n2
Israel, 205n4

Jameson, Fredric, 12, 180
Janjaweed (militia), 81
Jesus ("O juízo final" character), 61
Jesus Cristinho (character), 47–49
J.G (*Carvão animal* character), 120–21, 206n6
Jornal Nacional (news program), 44
Jornal Nacional das Igrejas (*National Church News*) (fictional news program), 44
Judas (*O Brasil é bom* character), 48
"Judgment Day" ("O juízo final"), *O Brasil é bom*, 61

Kambiwá, Avelin Buniacá, 198
"Kimbá's loves" ("Os amores de Kimbá"), *Olhos d'água*, 174
Kokai, Erika, 204n21
Kondzilla, 208n3
Kubitscheck, Juscelino, 46, 203n15

LaCapra, Dominick, 165
lança-perfume (deodorizing spray), 155–56, 207
language, 55–56, 100; of the future, 93, 96, 101–2; power of, 97, 104–8, 105n11
language/linguistic analysis, Portuguese, 23; in "Amando uns aos outros," 54–56; in "O Brasil não é ruim," 60–61; in *Guia afetivo da periferia*, 187–88; in *O livro dos mandarins*, 84, 88, 205n5; in *Luxúria*, 30–31, 37–38, 201n5; in *A maçã envenenada*, 152–58, 165; in *Mãos de cavalo*, 142–44; in "Nós somos bons," 49–50; in *Reprodução*, 93–97, 104–8; in *O trabalho sujo dos outros*, 116
Latin America, 7, 8–9, 10–11, 208n1
Laub, Michel, 14, 16, 18, 135, 198
lawyers, 154
Led Zepplin, 145
Lefebvre, Henri, 15, 18, 27, 28, 136, 145, 150
the Left (politics), 6, 35–36, 39–40, 42–44, 202n8
Lehnen, Leila, 169, 175–76, 191
leisure, commodification of, 25, 28
Leviticus, Bible, 162–63
lingua ignota (artificial language), 100–101
linguistic prejudices, 51–52
liquid modernity, 17, 68
Lísias, Ricardo, 14, 79, 135–36, 197; on consumption, 16, 17, 68–69
"Literatura e cultura de massas" ("Literature and Mass Culture") (Santiago), 7
"Literatura e sub-desenvolvimento" ("Literature and Underdevelopment") (Cândido), 6–7
literatura indígena, 189

Index

literatura periférica / literatura marginal, 172–74, 175–76, 208n5
literature, Brazilian, 3, 7, 104–10, 201n3; *literatura periférica/literatura marginal* as, 172–74, 175–76, 208n5; working-class representation in, 14, 16, 18, 21, 62–66, 167–68. *See also specific books*
"Literature and Mass Culture" ("Literatura e cultura de massas") (Santiago), 7
"Literature and Underdevelopment" ("Literatura e sub-desenvolvimento") (Cândido), 6–7
Liuli. *See* "the teacher of Chinese"
O livro dos mandarins (fictional text), 72–75, 87
O livro dos mandarins (*The Book of Mandarins*) (Lísias), 14, 17, 68, 108–10; failure in, 83–88; names in, 70–73; neoliberalism in, 73–83
"Lodaçal" ("Swamp"), *O Brasil é bom*, 54, 58–60
London, 157–59
love, 9–10, 168, 176–80
"Loving one another" ("Amando uns aos outros"), *O Brasil é bom*, 54
low culture, high and, 11–12, 13, 188–93
low-income workers, 18, 21, 78–79; invisibility of, 113–15, 117, 122–23, 135, 191. *See also* exploitation, of low-income workers
Lowry, Malcolm, 101–2, 103
Ludmilla (artist), 208n4
Lukác, György, 15
Lula, o filho do Brasil (*Lula, the Son of Brazil*) (film), 47–48
Lula da Silva, Luís Inácio (Lula), 36, 77, 170, 198; consumption under, 1–3, 8, 21, 202n1; Estatuto do Desarmamento under, 53; income distribution programs by, 1; Jesus Cristinho as reference to, 47–49; *Luxúria* protagonist paralleling, 39, 43–46; neoliberal conservatism of, 50–51; Sant'Anna addressing, 22; working-class betrayed by, 39, 48–49, 202n8
Lulu the Tool (*La classe operaria va in paradiso*) (film), 184–85
lust, 23, 24–25, 28, 29, 46
Luxúria (*Lust*) (Bonassi), 14, 17, 23–28, 47, 61–66, 193; everyday violence in, 29–35; factories in, 38–46; social inclusion policies criticized in, 21–22; working-class portrayals in, 62–66
luxury goods, 9, 21, 63, 171–73, 195
lynching, 53, 58
lyrics, music, 7, 42, 107–8, 145, 149, 188; "Drain You," 155–56, 159; funk ostentação, 171–73

A maçã envenenada (*The Poison Apple*) (Laub), 14, 18, 135, 150–67; *Mãos de cavalo* compared to, 151, 165–67
Macedo, Edir, 91
Machado, Maria Helena, 33
Made in Chelsea (reality show), 195
Mad Max (character), 140, 143
Mad Max (film), 137–38, 139–40
Mad Max 2 (film), 142–43
Magno, Simone, 39
Maia, Ana Paula, 14, 16–18, 112–14, 132–34, 197, 207n9
mainstream media, 36, 112, 175–79
Malba Tahan. *See* de Mello e Souza, Júlio César

233

Index

male power, 30–31
Manhã *(Amanhecer Esmeralda* character), 174
A Man of No Importance (*Um homem sem importância*) (film), 184–85
Manuel de Macedo, Joaquim, 187
Mao, Zedong, 75, 79–80, 204n1, 204n3
Mãos de cavalo (*Horse Hands*) (Galera), 14, 18, 135, 185; imaginary camera in, 23, 138, 140–45, 149–50, 166; *A maçã envenenada* compared to, 151, 165–67
Marchiori, Val, 195
Márcia (*Reprodução* character), 106–7, 110
Maré, Brazil, 177, 179–80
"Maria," *Olhos d'água*, 174
Mariana, Minas Gerais, 111
marijuana, 58
Martín-Barbero, Jesús, 11
Martins, Heitor, 10
Martins, José de Souza, 53
Marx, Karl, 5, 41–42
Marxism and Literature (Williams), 7–8
masculinity, 3, 30–32; in *Mãos de cavalo*, 137–41, 145–46, 148, 166
mass culture, 4–7, 11–12, 135
mass-mediated sensibility, 137–50
MC Buru (artist), 208
McDonald's, 185
MC Guimê (artist), 171
MC João (artist), 208n4
McLuhan, Marshal, 89
McOndo (Fuguet, Gómez), 12–13
MC Soffia (artist), 208n4
meat, production of, 112–13, 122–32
Mello. *See* Collor de Mello, Fernando
de Mello e Souza, Júlio César, 185
memories, 14–15, 135, 177–80;

childhood, 14, 84, 135, 137–38, 149, 185; in *Guia afetivo da periferia*, 169–70; in *A maçã envenenada*, 152–54
Mendonça, Duda, 204n8
"Menina Pretinha" ("Little Black Girl") (song), 208n4
Menor da Chapa (artist), 208n4
mental health, 84–85, 95–97; in *Luxúria*, 25–28, 36, 37–38
meritocracy, 50, 72, 203n19
"A meu Deus um canto novo" ("To God, a new hymn") (song), 148, 149
microaggressions, 29, 49; middle class, 32–33, 202n6, 202n7
middle class, 117, 157, 167–68, 169, 197–99, 204n1, 209n10; microaggressions, 32–33, 202n6, 202n7; perspectives, 14, 16, 25, 63–64, 167; prejudices, 22–23, 62–66; protests by, 53–54
Miguel, Luis Felipe, 36
military, 11, 158, 158–59
Miller, Daniel, 18, 125, 168, 176–77, 193–94
Minas Gerais, Brazil, 111, 205n1
Minha Casa, Minha Vida (My House, My Life) (program), 24, 202n2
mining, coal, 112, 118, 206n5
Miranda, Carmen, 46
MLMs. *See* Multilevel Marketing companies
modernismo (cultural movement), 10–11, 201n3
modes of consumption, 4
"the moment" (Lefebvre concept), 18, 135, 150, 153
money, 9, 26–27, 56–58
monologues, 105, 151
monopolies, 36–37
morality, 48, 54, 73–74, 129, 162
Morsa (*Mãos de cavalo* character), 137

234

movies, 137–38, 141, 142, 154, 166, 184
Mulheres Ricas (*Rich Women*) (reality show), 195–196
Multilevel Marketing companies (MLMs), 72–73
Munduruku, Daniel, 198–99
Muniz, Vik, 116–17
murder, 128; in *Luxúria*, 23, 28; in *Mãos de cavalo*, 137, 141
music, 94, 107; *funk ostentação*, 3, 171–73, 175; grunge, 137, 151–52. See also lyrics, music
Muylaert, Anna, 3
My House, My Life (Minha Casa, Minha Vida) (program), 24, 202n2

Naiara (*Mãos de cavalo* character), 144–45, 149
names: in *O livro dos mandarins*, 70–73, 83–84; in *O trabalho sujo dos outros*, 117–18
narratives, 4, 17, 49, 140–41; *ambivalent awareness*, 3, 18, 137, 165–67; failure, 3, 24–25, 69, 79, 83–88; hero, 141, 142–44, 149; *temporary radical suspension*, 3, 18, 114; *totalizing dystopia*, 3, 17, 22–23, 65, 135–36; *transformative hope*, 3, 18, 169; *utopic reinvention*, 3, 17, 70, 108–10. See also success, narratives of
narrators, 63, 155–56, 167–68, 173–74; in *Carvão animal*, 119–21, 121–22, 132–33; in *De gados e homens*, 123–24, 127–19, 130–31; first-person, 49–50; in *Guia afetivo da periferia*, 177–80, 182–84; in *Luxúria*, 23–24, 33, 35, 41; in *Mãos de cavalo*, 138–39, 142, 144, 148–49; in *O livro dos mandarins*, 71, 85, 87; in *O trabalho sujo dos outros*, 114–15, 132; in *Reprodução*, 93–97, 103; third person, 63, 93, 133, 138
narrators, *O Brasil é bom*, 23, 47–48; in "Comentário na rede sobre tudo o que está acontecendo por aí," 52–53; in "Lodaçal," 58–60; in "O Brasil não é ruim," 60–61; in "Só," 56–58
Nascimento, Érica Peçanha do, 208n5
national identity, 10, 12, 46
nationalism, 54, 80, 90
National Mail Service, Brazil, 21
National Public Radio (NPR), 33–34
"A Native" ("Um índio") (song), 107–8
native Brazilians, 104–5
Navarro, Lourdes García, 33–34
Nazi Germany, 4
neoconservatism, 49–54, 91
neoliberalism, 1, 13, 50–51, 65, 90, 135, 207n1; authoritarianism underlying, 49, 54, 80; Brown on, 8, 17, 22; of FHC, 8, 46, 76, 204n2; Harvey defining, 76–77; of the Left and, 39–40, 42–44; in *O livro dos mandarins*, 73–83; Paulo exemplifying, 77, 82–83; subjectivities of, 8, 197
neoliberal rationality, 17, 22
neo-Marxism, 4–5
neo-Nazis, 91–92
neo-Pentecostal churches, 45
Nervo, Amado, 8
Neto, Delfim, 203n16
networking, 68, 72, 73, 82
Nevermind (album), 154
New Confucianism, 75
"new middle class," 14, 21, 49. See also "classe baixa-alta"

Index

New Neighborhood (Bairro Novo, fictional), 24–25
Nicaragua, 205n4
Nietzsche, Friedrich, 163–64
Nirvana (band), 151, 154, 155, 158, 163
Nixon, Rob, 18, 111
Nobel Prize, 185
North America, 11, 45, 78, 201n3
"Nós somos bons" ("We Are Good"), *O Brasil é bom*, 49–50
Nozaki, William, 63–64
NPR. *See* National Public Radio
numbness, everyday, 35–38
nursing homes, 40–41

objectification, 30, 208n4
objectivity, 97–101, 153
occupations, 58–59, 107–8, 132, 154; bank employee as, 68–69; coalminers as, 14, 18, 118, 206n5; cremators as, 118–22, 206n4; factory workers as, 30, 38–46; firefighters as, 14, 120–22; military, 156, 158–59; plastic surgeon as, 141–42, 145–46; slaughtermen as, 14, 18, 113–14, 122–31; trash collectors as, 14, 18, 114–17
O'Dougherty, Maureen, 208n10
Of Cattle and Men (*De gados e homens*) (Maia), 14, 17–18, 112, 118, 121, 122–31, 133
Of Mice and Men (Steinbeck), 123–24
"Olha como nós tá" ("Check Out How We're Doing") (song), 208n4
Olhos d'água (Teary Eyes) (Evaristo), 174
de Oliveira, Nelson, 13
Olympics, 60
online behavior, 3, 69, 92
"Online Comment on All That Is Happening Out There" ("Comentário na rede sobre tudo o que está acontecendo por aí"), *O Brasil é bom*, 49, 52–53
On the Genealogy of Morals (Nietzsche), 163
Operação Lava-Jato (Operation Car Wash), 209n6
oppression, 5, 34, 65
Ortega y Gasset, José, 102–3

Pacman (videogame), 182
Palaversich, Diana, 12–13
Palmiro (*Carvão animal* character), 119–20, 208n5
"paraíbas" (pejorative term), 48
"Paraíso das piscinas" ("Pool paradise") (fictional place), 25, 62
Pariser, Eli, 90, 93, 104
Partido dos Trabalhores (PT, Workers' Party), 1, 17, 36–37, 40, 64–65, 171; *Luxúria* alluding to, 24, 203n13; social inclusion policies under, 21–23, 46
Paula (*O livro dos mandarins* character), 86
Paulo (*O livro dos mandarins* character), 68–69, 108; al-Bashir admired by, 81–82; failures of, 83–88; FHC admired by, 68, 75–78; Mao admired by, 79–80; "o estudante de chinês" compared to, 88–89, 102, 109
Paulson (*O livro dos mandarins* character), 70, 71–72
Pellegrini, Tânia, 4
Pense e fique rico (*Think and Grow Rich*) (Hill), 59
People for the Ethical Treatment of Animals (PETA), 125
Pereira dos Santos, Nelson, 186
periferia (impoverished areas in large urban centers), 167,

167–71, 175–76, 208n1, 208n2, 208n5
personalization, of filter bubbles, 90
PETA. *See* People for the Ethical Treatment of Animals
Petri, Elio, 184–85
Petrobrás (oil company), 175, 209n6
Pezzullo, Phaedra, 120
Philippou, Styliane, 11
Pinheiro-Machado, Rosana, 21, 54, 64, 91, 172, 193–94
Pink Floyd, 145
Pires, Glória, 47
Plano de poder (Macedo), 91
Plano Real (*Real* Plan), 36
plastic surgeon, 141–42, 147–49
Poe, Edgar Allan, 117–19, 128
poeta Paulo (*O livro dos mandarins* character), 68, 70, 87
poetry, 9–10, 87, 177, 188–89
The Poison Apple. See A maçã envenenada
police: "o estudante de chinês" interrogated by, 69, 93, 97; female officer, 93, 97, 98–100, 104, 107
political influence, 36
pollution, 24, 118, 121–22, 123, 126
polysemy, 99
pool, as status symbol, 24–26, 28
"Pool paradise" ("Paraíso das piscinas") (fictional place), 25, 62
pop culture, 10–12, 18, 135, 166, 184–89, 192
popsicles, 181
post-2003 Brazil, 14, 40, 61–66
postcard, in *A maçã envenenada*, 152, 155–56, 162–63
Postcards from Rio (Bezerra), 208n1
Postman, Neil, 17, 89, 94, 96
Postmodernism and Consumer Culture (Featherstone), 15
postneoliberalism, 2, 170–71
poverty, 1, 13, 45, 58, 171, 174, 191, 198
power, 16, 30–31, 49, 77, 116, 139; consumer, 15, 22, 29–30, 50–51, 125; of language, 97, 104–8, 205n11; in *Luxúria*, 25, 29–30, 39–40, 202n3; tactical consumption and, 189–92
The Practice of Everyday Life (de Certeau), 189
"Pra ser sincero" ("To Be Honest"), *O Brasil é bom*, 49, 51–52
precarity, 117–18, 119–20, 169, 188
prejudices, 47, 51–52, 58, 108, 194; middle class, 22–23, 62–66; of "o estudante de chinês," 69, 89, 94–95
Prendergast, John, 82
prison, 52–53
privatization, 1, 11, 76, 202n1
privileges, 31–32, 50
production, 4, 6; of meat, 114, 122–31
productivity, 41–42, 58, 85
professionalization, of writers, 12
professional success, 68–69, 76, 82
professions. *See* occupations
propaganda, 35, 79, 94–95, 204n3
prosperity theology, 3, 45, 72–73
protagonist, in *A maçã envenenada*, 135, 136–40; disalienation experienced by, 156–57, 159; Hermano compared to, 150–51; memories of, 152–53
protagonist, in *Luxúria*, 24–27, 29–30; alienation experienced by, 35, 37–38; as factory worker, 38–46; Lula paralleled by, 39, 43–46
protagonists, 16, 65; in "Amando uns aos outros," 55–56; "o estudante de chinês" as, 14, 88–89, 93–97, 102; in *Guia afetivo da periferia*,

237

169–70, 176–84, 192–93; in "Lodaçal," 58–60; Paulo as, 68–69, 70, 73, 102; in "Pra ser sincero," 51–52; in *O trabalho sujo dos outros*, 114–16. See also Hermano (*Mãos de cavalo* character)
protests, 50, 53–54, 91, 196, 203n18, 205n6; funk ostentação as, 175–76
Proust, Marcel, 187
psychological states: in *Luxúria*, 27–28; of Paulo, 84–85; in *Reprodução*, 95–97
PT. See Partido dos Trabalhores
Puig, Manuel, 12
Pulitzer Prize, 189

Que horas ela volta? (*The Second Mother*) (film), 3, 202n6

race, 10, 33–34, 169, 173–74, 208n4
Racionais MC's (rap group), 172–73
radio, 11, 142
Ramos, Graciliano, 186
Ramos, Julio, 201n3
rape, 32, 53, 81
readymades (art), 144
real (Brazilian currency), 8
The Real Housewives (reality show), 195
reality, 85–89, 99–100, 105; in *A maçã envenenada*, 150–51; mass media distorting, 137–50
Real Plan (Plano Real), 36, 77–78
"Rebeldes sin causa" (Palaversich), 12–13
recessions, 77
Rede Globo (television network), 36, 44
refugees, 4
relato (report) structure, in *Luxúria*, 23–24, 26–27

religion, 43–46, 91, 130–31, 161–63; in *O Brasil é bom*, 47–48
repetition, 145, 149–50, 154–55, 174–75; in *Luxúria*, 35, 37–38; in *O livro dos mandarins*, 70, 88
report. See *relato*
representations, working-class, 14, 16, 18, 21, 62–66, 167–68
Reprodução (*Reproduction*) (Carvalho, B.), 14, 17, 68, 108–10; dialogues in, 93–97; information technology in, 88–92, 93–97; objectivity in, 97–101; power of language in, 104–8
retirement, 41
Rich Women (*Mulheres Ricas*) (reality show), 195–99
"The Right to Pleasure" (Pinheiro-Machado, Scalco), 64
Rincão (*O livro dos mandarins* character), 84
Rio de Janeiro, Brazil, 36, 91, 169–70, 208n1
rituals, 126, 176–77
River Raid (videogame), 182
romance. See love
Rosa, Allan da, 176
Rousseff, Dilma, 2–3, 50, 170; impeachment of, 36, 53–54, 91, 196
Rwanda, genocide in, 151, 159–64

sacrifice, 122–26, 155–56, 161, 176–77
Sader, Emir, 170–71
Salvá, Alberto, 184–85
Samarco (mining company), 111, 205n1
Sant'Anna, André, 12–13, 16–17, 54, 58, 135–36, 197; social inclusion policies criticized by, 21–23; working-class portrayal by, 62–66. See

also *O Brasil é bom* (*Brazil Is Good*)
Santa Teresa (neighborhood), 183–84
Santiago, Silviano, 7
São Paulo, Brazil, 175, 205n6
sarcasm, 59, 60–61, 130, 183
Scalco, Lucia Mury, 21, 54 64, 172, 193
schizophrenia, 95, 97, 106
schools, violence in, 34, 37–38
The Second Mother (*Que horas ela volta?*) (film), 3, 204n6
The Secret (Byrne), 67, 72, 74, 82
The Secret (film), 67
segregation, 33
Seixas (*Senhora* character), 9
self, commodification of, 67–69, 119
self-awareness, 136, 140, 144, 147, 151, 184–85, 198
self-help books, 67–68, 72–74
Senhora (Alencar), 9
sensibility, mass-mediated, 137–50
"O sermão do Diabo" (Assis), 10
Serra, José, 36
sertanejo (Brazilian country music), 94
Seu Milo (*De gados e homens* character), 122, 124–25, 128, 130–31
sex, 144–46, 184–85, 208n4; violence and, 29–31, 34, 53, 202n5
Silva, Adriana, 91–92
Silverman, Malcom, 4
simulacra, 85–88, 116–17, 191–92
sins, 23, 43, 205n12
Skreemer (comic book), 140
slaughtermen, 14, 18, 113–14, 122–31
slavery, in Brazil, 25, 33, 65, 202n3
slow violence, 18, 111–12, 118–24, 132
"Smells like Teen Spirit" (song), 154

Snowball Church (Igreja Bola de Neve), 45
"Só" ("Alone"), *O Brasil é bom*, 54, 56–58, 204n22
social inclusion policies, 21–23, 46
social media, 54, 72–73, 88–90, 135
social mobility, 3, 23–24, 50–51, 58–60
socioeconomics, Brazilian, 21–22, 116, 129, 180, 197–198; in *O Brasil é bom*, 54–60; death and, 118–22
solidarity, 2, 22, 65
solitude, 56
Soper, Kate, 113
Spectreman (TV show), 184
status symbols, 86, 211n19; dogs as, 31–32; pool as, 24–26, 28
Steinbeck, John, 123–24, 208n6
stereotypes, 132–33, 194
strike, labor, 114–15, 117
Strong, Catherine, 207n2
"the student of Chinese." *See* "o estudante de chinês"
Studies in Contemporary Brazilian Literature Group (Grupo de Estudos de Literatura Brasileira Contemporânea), 173
subjectivities, 17, 198; consumer culture and, 18, 70; neoconservative, 49–54; neoliberal, 8, 197
success, narratives of, 3, 59; in *O livro dos mandarins*, 71, 79, 82, 86; professional, 68–69, 76, 82
Sudan, 71, 81–84, 85, 86–88
suicide, 126–28, 203n14; in *Luxúria*, 23, 28; in *A maçã envenenada*, 137, 151–52, 155–56, 159–64, 207n4
superficiality, 95, 105
supermarkets, 178–79
survival, 119, 155–57, 158, 159–65

239

Süssekind, Flora, 12
sustainability, 112–13
"Swamp" ("Lodaçal"), *O Brasil é bom*, 54, 58–60

Tablada, José Juan, 8
tactical consumption, 14, 189–92
"Take My Breathe Away" (song), 186
Tati (*A maçã envenenada* character), 153
taxi drivers, 58, 81, 86
"the teacher of Chinese" (Liuli), 69, 93, 97, 107
technologies, 8–11, 13, 17, 58, 178; information, 88–92; in *Luxúria*, 38–39
teeth, 120
Teiwes, Frederik C., 204n3
telegraph, 89–90
telemarketing, 51
television, 11, 58, 64, 89, 96, 135, 179
Temer, Michel, 36, 91, 196
temporality, crises of, 103–4
temporary radical suspension narratives, 3, 18
Tennina, Lucía, 208n5
Think and Grow Rich (*Pense e fique rico*) (Hill), 59
third person narrators, 63, 93, 133, 138
3% (Netflix series), 203n19
time, 165, 174–75; in *Luxúria*, 41–42; in *A maçã envenenada*, 152–53; in *Reprodução*, 101–4, 109
"To Be Honest" ("Pra ser sincero"), *O Brasil é bom*, 49, 51–52
"To God, a new hymn" ("A meu Deus um canto novo") (song), 148, 149
Toninho ("Lodaçal" character), 58–60
totalizing dystopia narratives, 3, 11, 22–23, 65, 135–36
O trabalho sujo dos outros (*The Dirty Work of Others*) (Maia), 14, 17–18, 112–14, 121, 133
Tramas Urbanas (Urban Plots/Stories), Petrobrás, 175
transformative hope narratives, 3, 18, 169
translations, 99, 155–56, 185
trash collectors, 14, 18, 114–17
tropicalidade, national identity and, 46
Tropicalist movement, 11–12
Trotsky, Leon, 187–88
Trump, Donald, 90–91, 95, 196
Tucumán Arde (art movement), 12
Turner, Tina, 135
Twilight Memories (Huyssen), 166

Ubirajara (Alencar), 201n2
unconscious, theory of the, 28
unemployment, 73, 80
uniforms, 34, 135, 158, 191
United States (U.S.), 4, 49, 90–91, 95, 170, 205n4; gun control laws in, 53; MLMs in, 72–73
Universal Church of the Kingdom of God, 91
upper class. *See* elite class
"upper-lower class" ("classe baixa-alta"), 48–49, 51
Urban Plots/Stories (Tramas Urbanas), Petrobrás, 175
U.S. *See* United States
"Use sempre camisinha" ("Always wear a condom"), *O Brasil é bom*, 60
utopic reinvention narratives, 3, 17, 70, 108–10

vacations, 55
Vale (mining company), 205n1
Valéria (*A maçã envenenada* character), 151–89, 162, 165
Vargas, Getúlio, 46, 203n14

Veloso, Caetano, 107–8
Veto Skreemer (comic book character), 140
victim blaming, 53
Vidas secas (*Barren Lives*) (Ramos, G.), 188
videogames, 139, 182, 184
violence, 54, 60, 74, 81–82, 102–3, 172; of consumer capitalism, 17–18, 58, 123, 194; of consumption, 29, 115; everyday, 29–35; numbness to, 35, 37–38; sexual, 29–31, 34, 202n5; slow, 18, 111–13
voyeurism, 133

Warhol, Andy, 201n4
"We Are Good" ("Nós somos bons"), *O Brasil é bom*, 49–50
Wesley, Ernesto, 120–21
wife (*Luxúria* character), 28, 29–31, 32–35, 45–46
Williams, Raymond, 7–8, 203
"William Wilson" (Poe), 117–19, 128
women, 162–63, 191, 208n4, 209n7; in *O livro dos mandarins*, 82–83; in *Reprodução*, 93, 97, 98–100, 104, 107
Workers' Party (Partido dos Trabalhores). *See* Partido dos Trabalhores
working-class, 33–34, 122n5, 202n1; families, 23–28, 63–64, 177–80; Lula betraying, 39, 48–49, 202n8; in *Luxúria*, 23–28; narrators, 172–74; representation of, 14, 16, 18, 21, 62–66, 167–68. *See also* low-income workers
working-class, consumption, 8, 22–23, 48–49, 63–64;

Faustini representing, 168–70, 184–89; of pop culture, 184–89; tactical, 189–92
World Bank, 81
World Cup (2014), 60, 196, 205n6
World War II, 53
writers, Brazilian, 9–12, 13, 193–94, 201n5; Afro-Brazilian, 173–74; middle class, 167–68, 197–99; *O livro dos mandarins* commenting on, 87. *See also specific writers*
Writing History, Writing Trauma (LaCapra), 165

Xou da Xuxa (children's show), 135

Young, Neil, 161

Zeca (*De gados e homens* character), 128
Zero Hora (newspaper), 33
Zhou dynasty, China, 74
Zodiac Knights (cartoon), 186
Zweig, Stefan, 40

About the Book

As in other contemporary consumer societies, advertisements instruct Brazilians on what to buy in order to become who they aspire to be; companies commodify ideas, emotions, and even social causes. Twenty-first-century Brazilian fiction highlights how our interactions with commodities connect seemingly disconnected areas of everyday life, such as eating habits, the growth of prosperity theology, and ideas of success and failure. *Everyday Consumption in Twenty-First-Century Brazilian Fiction* is the first in-depth study to map out the representation of consumption in Brazilian fiction written in the twenty-first century. It is also the first to provide a pluralistic perspective on the representation of consumption in this fiction that moves beyond the concern with aesthetic judgment of culture based on binaries such as good/bad or elevated/degraded that has largely informed criticism of this body of literary work. The book contends that current Brazilian fiction provides a variety of perspectives from which to think about our daily interactions with commodities and about how consumption affects us all in subtle ways. Collectively, the narratives analyzed in the book present a wide spectrum of more or less hopeful portrayals of existence in consumer culture, from totalizing dystopia to transformative hope.

About the Author

Lígia Bezerra was born in Várzea Alegre, Brazil. She moved to the United States in 2006, where she completed a master's in Portuguese at the University of New Mexico and a doctorate in Portuguese with a minor in cultural studies at Indiana University. She also holds a master's in linguistics from the Universidade Federal do Ceará. She taught Portuguese and English language and linguistics in Brazil and has taught Portuguese and Spanish language as well as Lusophone and Latin American culture in the United States. She is an Assistant Professor of Brazilian Studies at Arizona State University, where she directs the Portuguese program. Bezerra's research interests include Lusophone and Latin American literature and culture, consumption, and everyday life. She has published articles in journals such as *Cultural Studies, Chasqui, Romance Quarterly*, and the *Luso-Brazilian Review*. She has given invited talks at institutions in Argentina, Brazil, the United Kingdom, and the United States.

In *Everyday Consumption in Twenty-First-Century Brazilian Fiction*, Lígia Bezerra makes a concerted effort to map out representations of consumption in the twenty-first century Brazilian fiction. This richly documented study identifies the ways in which a variety of narratives help us reflect on the interconnections between power dynamics in everyday consumption and spheres of exclusion. The book compares and contrasts different perspectives on consumption, unveiling how consumption mediates several spheres of everyday life in Brazil. Through a close analysis of the works produced by eight contemporary Brazilian writers, the author proposes four different categories of analysis: narratives of totalizing dystopia, narratives of utopic reinvention, narratives of temporary radical suspension and narratives of transformative hope. The author demonstrates a masterful grasp of a wide body of cross-disciplinary theoretical work.
—Katia Bezerra, Professor, University of Arizona

www.ingramcontent.com/pod-product-compliance
Lightning Source LLC
Chambersburg PA
CBHW061440300426
44114CB00014B/1763